Learng in Grou

Learning in Groups

SECOND EDITION

◇ DAVID JAQUES ◆

**KOGAN
PAGE**

To Penny, Damian, Sophie and Daniel, the rest of the Group

First published by Croom Helm in 1984.
This second edition published by Kogan Page in 1991. Reprinted 1992.
Reprinted 1992, 1994, 1995.

Kogan Page Limited
120 Pentonville Road
London N1 9JN

© 1984, 1991, 1992, 1994, 1995 David Jaques

British Library Cataloguing in Publication Data
A CIP record for this book is available from the British Library.

ISBN 0 7494 0440 X

Typeset by AsTec, Newport, Saffron Walden, Essex
Printed and bound in Great Britain by Clays Ltd, St Ives plc

Contents

Acknowledgements

To my colleagues at the Centre for Higher Education Studies (formerly University Teaching Methods Unit) for permission to reproduce various extracts from their publications and for all the ideas and experience in group teaching that I got during my five years' work with them; especially to Roy Cox and David Warren Piper.

To other colleagues who have helped with perceptive comments on the drafts, but especially Gillian Hill.

To the Nuffield Foundation for permission to reprint large extracts from their newsletters in Chapter 8.

To Malcolm Knowles for permission to include a section on group behaviour from his book *Introduction to Group Dynamics* in Chapter 2.

To Jean Rudduck and the Society for Research into Higher Education for permission to reprint the various extracts on pages 78–80, and the contract on pages 191–4, from *Learning Through Group Discussion*.

To Hutchinsons for permission to reproduce the diagram from *The Psychology of the Learning Group* by McLeish, Matheson and Park.

To Graham Gibbs for the use of the checklist on page 178.

Finally to a host of people who have contributed ideas and material to conferences and workshops I have attended. I have acknowledged the source wherever possible but in many cases I have been unable to trace the origins.

Preface

Teaching and learning in small groups has a valuable part to play in the all-round education of students. It allows them to negotiate meanings, to express themselves in the language of the subject, and to establish a more intimate contact with academic staff than more formal methods permit. It also develops the more instrumental skills of listening, presenting ideas and persuading. Yet, many tutors find the task of leading difficult to perform satisfactorily and fall back with some disappointment on their reserve position of authority, expert and prime talker. New lecturers are not always given suitable induction to group teaching: even when training in small group techniques is given, it is not easy to replicate in a training exercise the competitive tension of a seminar. And if it were possible to do so, the seminar, as a model of group interaction, would promote a rather limited view of the rich variety of experience that small groups can contribute to learning.

My aim in this book is therefore not just to promote understanding of group methods but to develop skills for tutors and students alike as well as widening the range of possible group experiences. The title 'Learning in Groups' is meant to suggest that groups are not merely a valuable vehicle for learning about the skills and concepts of a subject discipline, but are also a way of learning *about* groups: developing abilities in co-operative work for later life.

There are several possible starting points for the reader. Some may prefer to look at the chapter on techniques first before referring back to aims. Others may need to pick up ideas on questioning techniques before gaining awareness of theoretical bases for them.

What you choose to accept and use from the book will reflect your own practice and philosophy of teaching. It might therefore be a good idea if I first state my own position on learning in groups.

- I assume that students are adults and should be encouraged to learn as adults. Knowles (1979) describes this orientation as andragogy as opposed to pedagogy. At the same time I recognize that many students in their late teens are still maturing as they cope with identity crises (Erikson 1971) and an uneasy relationship with authority. Nevertheless the assumption of an adult–adult relationship is one which I believe brings about a more productive teaching and learning relationship.

- Co-operation is a key word in learning groups. Competition in groups may sharpen the critical faculty of a few, but is more likely to dull the appetite for discussion among most. Co-operation doesn't just happen. We learn to co-operate through practice and this requires a clear and co-ordinated strategy for learning about working together and improving skills in co-operation. Co-operation also means each and every member of the group taking a part and sharing responsibility for its success.

- We all learn from experiences, whether happy or bitter ones, but we often fail to extend this learning beyond the immediate event. Thus when a group discussion grinds to a halt we may record that it has done so and that it is frustrating, but do little more. However if we were to be a little more observant about what happened, reflect on, and examine, the events and our part in them, then we would be more likely to develop rules and principles to guide us in our next, similar, experience. The 'experiential' learning cycle (Figure 0.1) is based on Kolb (1984), and contains three assumptions:
  - we learn best when we are personally involved in the learning experience;
  - knowledge of any kind has more significance when we learn it through our own initiative, insight and discovery;
  - learning is best when we are committed to aims that we have been involved in setting, when our participation with others is valued and when there is a supporting framework in which to learn.

- Despite the pre-eminence of intellectual aims in learning groups it is often the emotional needs and undercurrents which are most powerful; yet these are most frequently neglected. The sense of identity and social belonging which a student can gain from a well-run group should not be underestimated. Nor should the inhibiting effect of tutor authority, a competitive atmosphere and the students'

Figure 0.1 *Experiential learning cycle*

fear that they may make fools of themselves. Four important words seem to be missing in most academic courses: support, commitment, enjoyment and imagination. The first three may be created in a group where a climate of open communication, involving trust, honesty and mutual respect, takes place. Imagination should blossom in this climate. It might also create it.

For most tutors the first two chapters will provide a base on which to build their understanding of groups. The field of group dynamics has no unifying theme. Rather than try to present one approach to the various problems and issues in groups, therefore, I have provided a rather eclectic view, drawing on various theoretical and research approaches which seem to shed light on problems, or are a source of ideas for more rewarding and imaginative group techniques.

There follow two short chapters on learning and communication, following which Chapter 5 examines the kind of aims that are suitable to learning groups, and relates the necessary aims of groups in general to specific ones in academic learning. Chapter 6 is a discussion of what tutors and groups might be expected to do and examines a variety of tasks and techniques. Many of these are examples of more challenging and stimulating approaches than one would normally find in the traditional seminar or tutorial.

Chapter 7 answers the question: what personal tasks and skills does the tutor have to learn in order to prepare for and handle group interaction? It looks particularly at the kinds of intervention a tutor could make during the progress of discussion. Chapter 8 addresses the place of learning groups in the social and educational environment of the college and several case studies of real schemes are used to illustrate it. Chapter 9 provides some practical suggestions for evaluation both the leadership role and the group as a whole, and the book finishes with a set of training activities for improving participation in groups at all levels.

I have tried to write a book that is both readable and practical; one which permits flexibility, yet covers the essential content.

David Jaques
Hatfield

The second revised edition includes many textual improvements, though it retains the same basic structure and content. The references have been updated and examples of more recent theory and practice in groups have been incorporated.

David Jaques
Oxford 1991

1 Theories about Group Behaviour

WHAT IS A GROUP?

Many writers have attempted to establish clear definitions of groups; each one betrays assumptions about what happens in groups, both in the terminology and in what is chosen for emphasis. Rather than trying to single out or invent a unitary definition, let us look at some of the characteristics most commonly described by practitioners. This will provide a more comprehensive picture of the range of dynamic qualities within each group. A group can be said to exist as more than a collection of people when it possesses the following qualities:

- Collective perception: members are collectively conscious of their existence as a group.
- Needs: members join a group because they believe it will satisfy some needs or give them some rewards.
- Shared aims: members hold common aims or ideals which to some extent bind them together. The achievement of aims is presumably one of the rewards.
- Interdependence: members are interdependent inasmuch as they are affected by and respond to any event that affects any of the group's members.
- Social organization: a group can be seen as a social unit with norms, roles, statuses, power and emotional relationships.
- Interaction: members influence and respond to each other in the process of communicating, whether they are face to face or otherwise deployed. The sense of 'group' exists even when members are not collected in the same place.
- Cohesiveness: members want to remain in the group, to contribute to its well-being and aims, and to join in its activities.
- Membership: two or more people interacting for longer than a few minutes constitute a group.

None of these characteristics by itself defines a group but each indicates important aspects. However, not all of them can be expected to relate to every group and some of the qualities may be seen as part of others. *Interaction* will not take place without some need to influence, share and be responded to – all of these give rise to attempts to communicate with others. Nevertheless, if a group is consciously to regard itself as a group it must exist long enough for a rudimentary pattern of interaction to develop. Some group-dynamics theorists argue that a group has to comprise at least three people before significant group behaviour can occur. For the purpose of this book however, I shall include the dyad or pair, even though it may lack some important characteristics, as a special type of group with valuable potentialities for learning.

A group may be considered as an entity, but it is illuminating to study the individual experience of members as well. Some writers (eg Allport 1924) argue that groups have no separate reality – only individuals are real – and that all the norms, roles, relationships, etc, exist only in the minds of individuals functioning as a collection of people. Others, Freud for instance, see the dynamics of group behaviour as a sort of collective extension of individual psychopathology. The most suitable picture for our purposes is probably one in which group phenomena are held to be real to the extent that group members respond consciously or unconsciously to such phenomena *as if they existed*. In this book we shall consider the group from both individual and collective viewpoints, working on the assumption that a better understanding of group process will develop from considering both in relation to one another.

THEORY OR RESEARCH?

Let us now consider what contribution theory and research make to an understanding of the complex processes which take place in a group.

Opinion is divided on the most fruitful approach to studying groups. On the one hand, as Shaw (1977) explains, there are those who consider that group phenomena can be validly assessed and understood only by rigorous analysis of empirical observations. On the other hand, some maintain that research evidence will almost certainly be trivial and that theoretical analysis is the only means to a comprehensive understanding of the complex phenomena evident in groups. While it is true that, without theory, most of the research findings would merely be a collection of random and unrelated facts, it is impossible to construct a theory without *some* empirical understanding: empirical 'facts' serve to underline the broader statements of theoretical insights. Theory in its turn serves to illuminate and organize research data in a way which extends their meaning beyond the situations from which they were derived.

PSYCHODYNAMIC THEORY

Freud, in his *Group Psychology and the Analysis of the Ego* (1921) claimed that people are drawn into, and remain in groups because of emotional ties between members, and that one of the principal mechanisms in the effecting of such ties is identification – the process whereby a person wants to be like his or her parent(s). To use Freud's terms, people 'introject' a preferred person (the leader), or the qualities they like in that person, into their own being, while at the same time 'projecting' some of the bad or painful qualities of themselves onto others. When each member of a group assimilates the same qualities of the leader they can identify with each other.

Introjection and projection are two processes which are common to most relationships between people and usually take place at the unconscious level (that is, the participants are not usually aware of them unless attention is drawn to them). Another Freudian concept which has relevance to groups is that of *transference*, a common phenomenon in which fears, loves and longings experienced in early childhood, usually in relation to parents and siblings, are re-awakened in later life when they are displaced on to another person. Although at this stage their power is unconscious it can be felt both in one-to-one and group relationships. It is not unusual for a student to reject, resent or conversely respect a tutor to an unrealistic extent simply because the tutor triggers the same feelings in the student (usually at an unconscious level) as did one of the students' parents. Sometimes the resentment becomes more generalized so that all people in authority and even the institution itself become the objects of hatred.

The Freudian school thus saw the basic processes in a group as outward manifestations of the inner lives of its members: the intrapersonal expressed as the interpersonal. Out of this approach has developed one of the most powerful interpretations of group interaction – that commonly known as the Tavistock model. Bion (1961), one of its key figures, proposed that a group operates simultaneously at two levels: the *work group* and the *basic assumption group*. The work group meets to perform a specific and overt task. However, this is frequently obstructed, or diverted by the powerful emotional drives of the basic assumption activity. The basic group behaves *as if* it shared the following tacit assumptions or motives:

- Obtaining security and protection from one individual on whom it can *depend*. This can be the designated leader or any member who is accepted in the role. The group unconsciously assumes that some sort of magic resides in the leader. In learning groups, students frequently direct attention to the tutor's remarks, as if he were the source of all wisdom, to the exclusion of their colleagues' contributions. Even if they lose respect for a particular tutor there is a sense in which the position is endowed with authority or at least that there is some external power which determines what should be learned whether or not the tutor is the medium.
- Preserving itself from annihilation – either attacking something (*fight*) or avoiding the task (*flight*). Commonly the group will scapegoat some other person or group in order to avoid a difficult problem. *Flight* on the other hand takes the form of withdrawal, passivity, dwelling in the past, or jesting. The group seems happy to distract itself from its task by focusing on some other harmless and irrelevant issue. 'In this mode, the group uses its energy to defend itself from its own internal fears and anxieties, and consequently neither develops nor achieves an effective output' (de Board 1978).

- Engaging in *pairing*. Two individuals form a bond in which warmth, closeness and affection are shown. Pairing has as its basic assumption that the purpose of the group is to bring two people together who will somehow save the group from its current predicament. Frequently this happens when the group is bored, lost or resentful in its discussion and is unable to express or otherwise cope with these feelings. In learning groups pairing may take three possible forms. In the first, two students provide mutual respect and support for each other to the exclusion of other members who are thus rendered inactive. Alternatively, the pair could engage in intellectual battle, each partner representing a different side of a conflict that has been preoccupying the group. Again the rest of the group are mere bystanders. Finally, the tutor may pair with the group as a whole and collude with them in their wish to avoid work.

Pairing is often characterized by a sense of unreal hope: 'Everything will be okay when we get a new room', 'It'll come all right after Christmas'. The need to face up to and work through disappointments and failures is conveniently avoided by this unreal but seductive promise of things to come. Pairing can also be likened to two cells coming together in order for the group to reproduce itself – that is to say, develop another task and direction for the group distinct from the agreed one. Though this coupling may not result from an explicit sexual attraction there may well be a quasi-sexual bonding with its 'offspring' as the idea, the brainchild, that will save the group from its failings.

Dependency, *flight/fight*, and *pairing* are described as the assumptions of the basic group whose primary task is seen as survival. It is important to recognise that the basic group which operates under these assumptions is the same one that is engaged in the work task; they are the same members operating under different models with varying degrees of intensity. Where the overt tasks of the work group and the covert tasks of the basic group meet, conflict is likely to occur.

These theoretical concepts have been developed through a wealth of experience of groups at conferences in human relations training at the Tavistock Institute and have been applied with some degree of success to industrial and organizational settings. However, they are not always easy to accept and to identify without a certain amount of training. To some extent they may be of little relevance in a well-run seminar group committed to its task of intellectual development, though it is arguable that every tutor should at least be aware of them as a latent force lest they be drawn into a collusion on any of the basic assumptions and thus frustrate the achievement of the work task.

The Tavistock approach has brought into focus other issues of value in our understanding of group dynamics. Banet and Hayden (1977) list these concepts as authority, responsibility, boundaries, projections, organization and large group phenomena.

Authority

Whenever decisions have to be made about process or the allocation of tasks, a group is likely to experience authority problems. Whose job is it to decide? Can the group give any one person that sanction? Where a designated 'authority person' exists, a group may either find itself dependent on them, or counterdependent (attacking authority). Freud (1921) regarded the small group as an analogue of the family. The leader of a group is therefore likely to have childhood feelings transferred onto her or him; such feelings as infantile dependency (which arouses as many bad feelings as good) and disobedience or rebellion. Redl (1942), quoted in McLeish et al (1973), provided classroom pupils with different kinds of teacher personalities, and discovered that within each class there were 'conflicted individuals' who had difficulty in coping with their unconscious emotions and images in respect of a particular teacher. If and when a 'conflicted individual' acts out his or her repressed feelings about authority with a teacher who happens to trigger them off, other students who may be incapable of handling such feelings give tacit approval to the conflicted student as a sort of representative of their own antipathy. In this way a pattern of beliefs and behaviours, a classroom 'culture', is established for any group of students with a particular teacher.

The teacher's role when authority conflicts occur would seem to be to aid the students' growth by refusing to join battle, and to help them understand the consequences of their action. Many students who object to the authority of the teacher are not really seeking an alternative to the status quo. They are probably fighting the tutor as a way of avoiding the need to accept that learning is their own responsibility and that they have to face the consequences of the choices they make. It is important therefore for the teacher to create the conditions in which the students can make conscious choices of alternative courses of action, supportively but firmly bringing such issues out into the open (see contract, pages 191–4)

Responsibility

There is a feeling in groups where visible authority is present that the ultimate responsibility for each person's action and its consequences resides in the figure of authority. In learning groups, students rarely take responsibility for the role they play in contributing to a successful experience. Whether they are accustomed to challenging authority overtly or to accepting it with resentment and bad grace, they may never have examined the consequences of that particular attitude. Somehow the responsibility for what happens is assumed to lie firmly on the shoulders of the tutor who may find himself unable to shrug it off.

Some tutors are prone to the 'mother-hen' syndrome: they tend their 'little chicks', protecting them from the supposed deceptions practised by others. They may try to establish this sort of relationship with any person or group they encounter. It is a pattern of behaviour they have acquired through their own upbringing and which they readily transfer to any willing 'brood'. Many of us respond to a student's sense of helplessness by offering to meet it and without questioning its nature. The problem here is that the teacher who is an incurable helper, in satisfying one of his or her basic needs, may fail to develop the student's capacity for self-growth into greater autonomy and responsibility.

Boundaries

All of us have a physical and psychological boundary in relation to others. Our own skin constitutes a physical boundary while the distinction between our private thoughts, feelings and fantasies, and the 'known' outside world constitutes another. The same can be said of the group; both in a subjective sense and a more objective and symbolic sense boundaries distinguish one group from another. The *physical space* occupied by the group and the *time span* it covers are obvious and objective boundaries. Both of these are typically under the control of the tutor. Less tangible and more subjective are the *task* boundary, which determines what the group should or should not do, and the *input* boundary which requires members to undergo certain social procedures before membership is acquired. Evidence of the strength of subjective boundaries can be readily perceived if a stranger – perhaps a new student – arrives unannounced in an established group, or if the tutor invites a colleague to sit in on a seminar.

Projection

Sometimes the negative feelings we have towards other people are too dangerous to permit of conscious expression and, as a mechanism to defend us against the anxiety that this produces, we attribute these feelings, motives or qualities to the person or persons towards whom our feelings are really directed. We thus experience the feelings as coming 'at us' rather than 'from us'. This is the mechanism known as projection. Some students may for instance see the tutor as hostile when they are in fact feeling hostility to the tutor but are unable to recognize it. They will usually hotly deny the existence of the feeling if challenged.

Just as individuals can plant their own bad feelings on others in the group, so a group can spend a lot of time and energy in projecting its own conflicts or inadequacies onto another group or the institution. This is more particularly true of staff groups and student political and union meetings than of learning groups and is what happens when a group adopts the 'fight' stance described on pages 15.

Organizational structure

The power relationships in the group, whether determined by outside factors (eg the curriculum, the tutor's position in the institutional hierarchy) or by internal concerns such as qualities or skills of individuals, can have a profound effect on the work of a group. Structural relations of this kind may manifest themselves in who sits where, who takes initiatives, who defers to whom, and in the pecking order of contributions. In general, structures which are not revealed and discussed lead to feelings of mistrust. The structure of a group does not automatically exist from the beginning but develops through a process of differentiation and sorting. It can also change according to the mood of members or the special requirements of the task in hand. The recognition of this problem had led some group leaders, for instance Hill (1977), to allocate special roles and responsibilities in a group on a rotating basis.

Large groups

As the size of a group increases, so its characteristics change (see Figure 1.1). In the view of Rice (1971), six is a critical number for groups in all sorts of situations. With six or less the degree of intimacy offered by close proximity can make it difficult for group members to register their feelings about the group. Leadership tends to be fluid and interchangeable. As the group size increases, the climate of the group changes. Individuals become less constrained by the norms of the group and become more aware of their feelings. Leadership and other roles become more established. With numbers of 12 to 25 the likelihood of full face-to-face interaction decreases and sub-groups start to emerge. When the group is over 25 in number, face-to-face interaction between everyone becomes impossible. Some people, because of the group's size, may have to sit behind others, and anyone speaking may fail to see, or be seen by, everyone in the group. When leadership occurs it takes on a clear cut, 'external' role.

Whereas in the small group it is easy to think but difficult to feel, in the large one the opposite is likely to be the case. It becomes difficult to mobilize the intellect, issues become polarized, splitting ('I all right/you all wrong') takes over as a defence against anxiety about chaos, and, in order to manage this, people are likely to stereotype each other. The leader or teacher, as someone who is evidently different, is likely to be subject to these perceptions more than most and the authority/dependency problem will almost certainly be sharper and more acute.

Leaders become invested with all sorts of power and expertise. But as soon as they come up with something the group regards as 'inferior' their credibility will sag and they may be attacked for their inadequacy! Power is more sharply polarized; too sudden or big a change in the power relationship is likely to produce

	Number of members	Changing characteristics	
↑ M o r e c o h e s i o n	2–6	Little structure or organization required; leadership fluid.	M o r e t e n s i o n ↓
	7–12	Structure and differentiation of roles begins. Face-to-face interaction less frequent.	
	12–25	Structure and role differentiation vital. Sub-groups emerge. Face-to-face interaction difficult.	
	25–?	Positive leadership vital to success. sub-groups form; greater anonymity. Stereotyping, projections and flight/fight occur.	

Figure 1.1 *Changing characteristics of groups with increase in membership*

a flight/fight situation. If the group challenges the leader, and if in turn it is challenged back, it might retreat or withdraw. An example of this would be when a lecturer, after playing a formal and omniscient role, invites the class informally to come up with some of its own ideas.

Another experience of people in large groups is that their identity becomes more fragile and their sense of reality is distorted. The mechanism of projection (see page 18) is likely to operate: unwanted parts of the self are pushed onto others, and fantasies about other people's motives, attitudes and intentions abound.

So much for the undercurrents. At the behavioural level, it becomes evident that the larger the group, the more formal and oratorical the spoken contributions become. In the educational context we can see that students have two kinds of relationship open to them: one is with small discussion or learning groups with which they already have some identity, and the other with the wider group membership, many of whom they know from social or sporting contacts, or even in another learning group. In training 'workshops' there is a constant alternation between small groups of different sizes and the large plenary group. In some ways this mixture can provide participants with a sense of a home base (their sub-group) amid the feeling of identity loss that the large group may create. The tutor in workshops however is able to circulate round the sub-groups and is thus less likely to be on the receiving end of displaced or projected bad feeling through becoming more 'real' to participants. Yet, challenges of the authority/dependency kind might still exist and they can be all the more powerful for having the support of a sub-group rather than just an individual.

The complex play of relationships in a large group and the emotional swirl that is likely to go with it is thus, at least potentially, fraught with confusion, inaction and frustration. Strong leadership is both needed and gratefully accepted. As Rice points out, 'In this condition an individual who can define some positive goal can exercise powerful leadership.' How the tutor takes that role, or dodges it, is sometimes of critical importance in large groups. It is of consequence in smaller groups too.

'Habeas emotum'

Many of the above issues may seem far-fetched to academic tutors, especially those in the physical sciences and engineering whose central concern is not with personal feelings and group process but with the imparting of a body of knowledge. Yet, with these faculty areas, one hears of constant problems to do with lack of motivation and commitment, alienation and even 'dropout'. In a limited number of studies where some emphasis has been placed on 'process learning' and interaction in small group work there does appear to be a growth in student commitment. (See case studies on pages 150–68). Although styles of learning and shared values (Gaff and Wilson 1971) may vary from faculty to faculty, the vast majority of students prize the sense of belonging which small groups afford students and the chance to test their understandings with their peers. Both these aims can be put in jeopardy and the student experience in groups can become most frustrating if emotional undercurrents are not recognized and coped with. This is an area where even traditional research evidence and psychodynamic theory are in agreement.

Continually throughout this book we shall be concerned with what Luft (1970) has called 'Habeas emotum' – a recognition that people's emotions are a necessary part of their existence, and that as Rubin (1967) and Jones (1972) argue, if we educate only the rational/intellectual person we do so at our (and their) peril. Behaviour is determined as much by passions, anxieties and convictions as it is by reason, the more so when we are not aware of the effects of our feelings. Negative feelings can be destructive if they are ignored, submerged or displaced into sarcasm and backbiting. Boredom, irritation or fear can interfere with the willingness of a group to engage in the learning process. Moreover, intellectual growth, as we shall see later, is closely linked to emotional development.

It is incumbent upon tutors to recognize all this *and* the part their own emotions may play in the process. This recognition is important therefore not merely for the effective functioning of the group but for the more far-reaching educational aim of developing the student as a congruent person – one who is able to hold together the different levels at which he or she experiences life and to communicate responses genuinely.

Attending to students' emotional needs should not only benefit their intellectual powers but also develop their capacity to tackle the sort of relationships that are so familiar to the industrial sector, not to speak of educational establishments. Contemporary life places a premium on the ability of people to get on with each other, to be able to handle interpersonal problems rather than to avoid them, and to do so constructively and creatively. Nowhere is it more possible to practise these qualities than in small-group work when learning is not subject to purely academic limitations.

INTERACTION THEORY

Whereas psychodynamic theory emphasizes the effect of unconscious processes in the group which exist beyond the awareness of the participant, the interaction approach is concerned with overt interpersonal behaviour between members of the group. This approach has contributed a lot to our understanding of group work, particularly by providing categories for the observation and analysis of different kinds of behaviour in small groups. These categories include qualitative and quantitative considerations, and are designed to comprise all possible types of behaviour. McLeish et al (1973) maintains that the interaction analysis system should include:

- the affective or emotional components of behaviour;
- the cognitive or intellectual components;
- the non-verbal or 'meta-language' components;
- content or message components;
- sociological or personal network segments of behaviour.

Although originally designed as research tools, interaction analyses have been increasingly used for training purposes to provide feedback to teachers, trainee group participants and teams. In describing apparently straightforward and overt behaviour, an interaction analysis makes it possible to provide trainees/participants with increased personal insight through objective and largely non-evaluative feedback. They may also have opportunities to practise different skills and to test them against reactions from their colleagues. In producing a comprehensive analysis of a group discussion, interaction analysis provides information on the differences between participation, and the development of different phases in a group's existence.

The basis of interaction analysis is that everything which a group says or does, including non-verbal acts, may be coded – including items like body posture, facial expressions and tone of voice. The set of categories devised by Bales (1970) is shown in Figure 1.2. It forms a symmetrical pattern and describes different aspects of group functioning. The various categories form complementary relationships. The first three comprise the positive socio-emotional area and correspond to the last three in the negative socio-emotional area. Categories 4, 5 and 6, in the task area, comprise 'answers', while 7, 8 and 9 correspond as 'questions'. Individual categories can be paired off or 'nested'. Categories 6 and 7 focus on problems of communication; 5 and 8 on evaluation and 4 and 9 on problems of control. Categories 3 and 10 are concerned with decision-making in the group, 2 and 11 with reducing tension and 1 and 12 with reintegration, the settling of emotional issues. These combined pairs relate to phases in the evolution of groups too, as they move outwards from communicating the task (6 and 7) through evaluation (5 and 8) to the making of decisions in 3 and 10. It also demonstrates that in the initial stages of a task, the group should be concerned with the instrumental or task components of the interaction, and then, as it moves towards making decisions and achieving agreement, so it becomes more clearly involved in the emotional side of the process.

Theoretically, this is how a group interaction evolves. However, events rarely follow this smooth path and whilst the sequence may be followed in a general sense, the actual group interaction is an unstable, everchanging process subject to all sorts of influences. The analysis assumes that members of the group are not radically affected by external factors such as previous animosities or extrinsic motives in their behaviour in the group.

Bales's position is that if one can outline behaviours in a group as objectively as possible, it will be easier for people to accept what happens and change accordingly to improve group process. Certainly it is my experience that group members are constantly surprised at the feedback they get from an interaction analysis in respect of both the quality and the quantity of what they contribute to discussion. However, it is not always so easy to categorize behaviours in the way indicated by Bales, more particularly in the socio-emotional area where people frequently keep their feelings to themselves or are trying somehow to compensate for various feelings they have towards other people or towards the whole group. The analysis makes no concession to the notion of a group culture but can be a valuable

Social-
emotional
area:

Positive

A

1 Seems friendly

2 Dramatizes

3 Agrees, shows passive
acceptance, understands,
concurs, complies

Task
area:

Emotionally
neutral

B

4 Gives suggestion,
direction, takes the lead,
while implying autonomy
for other

5 Gives opinion, evaluation,
analysis, expresses
feeling, wishes

6 Gives information,
orientation, repeats,
clarifies, confirms

C

7 Asks for information,
orientation, repetition,
confirmation

8 Asks for opinion,
evaluation, analysis,
expression of feeling

9 Asks for suggestion,
direction, possible ways
of action

Social-
emotional
area:

D

10 Disagrees, verbally or by
implication, but without
hostility

11 Shows tension

Negative

12 Seems unfriendly

a b c d e f

Triads

A Positive reactions
B Attempted answers
C Questions
D Negative reactions

Key to problem areas

a Problems of communication
b Problems of evaluation
c Problems of control
d Problems of decision
e Problems of tension reduction
f Problems of reintegration

Figure 1.2 *The verbal analysis of behaviour: Bales's system (1970).*
(All behaviour, verbal or non-verbal, is observed and classified in one or other of 12
categories.)

analytical tool for visible group interaction. It nevertheless fails to reveal some of the more powerful determining forces in a group.

SIX-CATEGORY INTERVENTION ANALYSIS

Another form of behaviour analysis is proposed by Heron (1976 and 1989) and although based primarily on one-to-one interventions, can apply equally to a group setting and particularly to the tutor's role. Heron has modified and developed the categories over the past 15 years, and the analysis that follows in this book represents a selection from his two publications which seems to make best sense for learning in tertiary education. He calls it the six-category intervention analysis and claims that the interventions deal with all 'desirable and worthwhile types of intervention: that is, they exclude only negative and destructive types of intervention'. Six categories are devised in a form which contributes to self-assessment and self-monitoring for group leaders of any kind; to what extent they can be extended to ordinary group members has yet to be seen.

The six categories fall into two main groups, *authoritative* and *facilitative*: authoritative when the leader is in a dominant or assertive role; facilitative where the role of the leader is seen to be less obstructive and more discreet.

Under the authoritative mode the tutor can be:

1. *Directing*
   - Raising an issue for discussion, re-routing the discussion.
   - Suggesting further work to be done.
2. *Informing*
   - Summarizing.
   - Interrelating.
   - Giving knowledge and information.
3. *Confronting*
   - Challenging by direct question.
   - Disagreeing with/correcting/critically evaluating student statement.
   - Giving direct feedback.

Under the facilitative mode the tutor can be:

4. *Releasing tension*
   - Arousing laughter
   - Allowing students to discharge unpleasant emotions such as embarrassment, irritation, confusion and sometimes even anger.
5. *Eliciting*
   - Drawing out student opinions/knowledge/problem-solving ability.
   - Facilitating student interaction.
   - Enabling students to learn and develop by self-discovery and personal insight.

6. *Supporting*
   • Approving/reinforcing/agreeing with/affirming the value of student contributions.

Two of these six categories – eliciting and informing – are of special importance for group work in that they form a spectrum from student-centred learning to tutor-centred learning (see Figure 1.3).

The details of both these categories indicate some of the particular skills the tutor should employ in performing the interventions. *Echoing* refers to the practice of echoing back, without any special emphasis, the last few words a student says before pausing. This invariably encourages the student to expand on his or her thoughts. Alternatively, the tutor may rephrase the last few words. Echoing is a way of conveying to the student, particularly when he or she has paused in the development of an argument, that the tutor is paying attention and wishes the student to continue without interruption in the flow. Various open-ended questions can serve a similar purpose (see page 135). *Selective echoing* is the skill of picking out from a contribution a few words or phrases which seem to carry an implicit emotional charge, or which appeared to cause some sort of agitation in the student. *Empathic divining* is a way of sensing an implicit feeling, thought or intention that is not fully expressed and tentatively labelling it. *Logical marshalling* involves picking up the threads of a discussion, interrelating them and sometimes indicating where they might be leading and putting this back to the group in a succinct way.

Various suggestions for the use of these categories, particularly those in the facilitative mode, are suggested in Chapter 7.

STUDENT-CENTRED

1. Echoing. Open-ended questioning (unfocused, focused, cross-referenced).

2. Selective echoing. Checking for understanding. Empathic divining.

   Eliciting

3. Closed, directive questioning.

4. Paraphrasing/interrelating/ clarifying/logical marshalling.

   Informing

5. Information-giving.

TUTOR-CENTRED

Figure 1.3 *The spectrum from student-centred to tutor-centred learning*

THEME-CENTRED INTERACTION

As much a method as a theory, theme-centred interaction (TCI) is concerned with three constituent factors, each of equal importance: the 'I', the 'we' and the 'it' of group interaction. For productive discussion to occur, the 'I' of individual interests must be balanced with the 'we' of group relatedness and the 'it' of the theme or topic. The theme is treated as common property to which the individuals (which include the 'I' of the tutor) and the group as a whole relate and should include a *gerund* – as for instance '*observing* accurately' – in order to create a momentum and a sense of participating.

These three elements are seen to be enveloped in a 'globe' (see Figure 1.4). The globe comprises the physical, social and temporal environment in which the group takes place. It includes the shape of the room, the arrangement of the furniture and the emotional climate of the group. Each member of the group is expected to act as his or her own chairperson in charge of an inner 'committee' which comprises four members: 'what I want to do', 'what I ought to do', 'how that might affect others' and the chairperson, who has to decide which of these should have precedence.

TCI includes two further principles: that thought and feeling should not be separated and that each person speak for themselves. This latter implies that no one can speak on behalf of others (either the group as a whole or any individual) without checking with them. But more importantly it encourages group members to speak in the first person rather than the generalised 'you'. For example the statement 'when you are in groups like this you can't think what to say' would be preferred as 'when I am in a group like this I can't think what to say'. The nature and tone of the statement usually changes dramatically with the change of personal pronoun.

This basic structure is supplemented by the ground rule 'disturbances take pre-

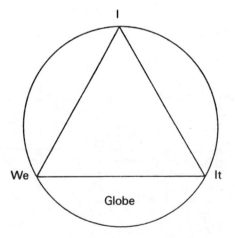

Figure 1.4 *The theme-centred interaction triangle and globe*

cedence': if a group member is unable to focus on the group task because of some distraction – being angry, bored, upset or excited, for example – they should say so. The emotional underlay is thus revealed in a personally responsible way. TCI has strong roots in both existentialism and psychoanalysis. It provides a framework for each individual to internalize and understand his or her own place and function in a group. It is also immensely practical and can be applied to a number of group settings to which other explanatory frameworks may not be suitable. Shaffer and Galinsky (1974) give further details of TCI and compare it with other group methods like T-Groups and Tavistock groups.

DISCUSSION POINTS

- Which of the various theoretical concepts discussed in this chapter make most sense or impact for you? Why might that be?
- Conduct a discussion on authority/dependency, the role of feelings or interaction behaviour in your group. Organize a fishbowl (see page 173) to get feedback on it.
- Choose a problem incident in your group. Which aspects of theory seem to shed most light on what happened?

2 Research into Group Behaviour

Over the past 50 years a wealth of information has been compiled by social psychologists working with experimental groups. Mostly their work has concentrated on the group performing practical tasks rather than processing academic material or experiencing personal growth. Typical criticism of the experimental approach is that the results are frequently trivial and even when put together do not add up to much; that they are frequently conducted with randomly selected students as subjects and are therefore unrepresentative of the population as a whole; and that they have rarely been able to touch upon the sort of complex phenomena of group interactions which appear to dominate the process in many groups.

This form of research has been described by Bronfenbrenner (1977) as 'strange people doing strange things to strangers in strange situations'. However, Argyris (1968) argues that it is more or less what happens in the shop-floor situation; in both, precise instructions are given but nobody is told why. In fact, the goals are quite frequently concealed. The same might be true of the many discussion groups in higher education. There are enormous differences between patterns of behaviour in long-established groups, such as those which exist over a period of time in an academic course or in an industrial environment, and experimental collectivities which are drawn together solely for the purpose of a particular experiment. Patterns of behaviour change as the group develops over a period of time.

Notwithstanding these criticisms, some valuable information does emerge when experimental work in areas of similar interest is compared. Yet we can never be sure of cause and effect in human behaviour: which conscious or unconscious motive does it spring from? What action will a particular motive produce? The task of providing explanations for social behaviour is highly problematical and demands careful evaluation as well as scepticism from the practitioner. On the other hand, it requires an ability to see the relationship between separate bits of evidence, and between those bits of evidence and the practical situation in which decisions have to be made.

Quite apart from the so-called laboratory experiments, we can select from a range of other studies which may loosely be described as field studies. The basic characteristic of these is that the phenomenon under investigation is studied in its natural habitat. Shaw (1977) comments: 'the investigator does not create the situation or situations being studied, instead he or she examines the phenomenon as it occurs in natural on-going social events'. To this extent the evidence derived is based on local events in a special context. For the practitioner they present some problems in interpretation as there is always some uncertainty about the particular effect of the environment in which the experiment takes place – the institution, the personal qualities of the teacher and the students, the external motivating factors such as assessment and social life – all of which can profoundly affect the outcome.

An accumulation of research evidence can, over a period of time, challenge some of our assumptions about what happens in groups and change our understanding of problems. As practitioners, most teachers will need to test the relevance and value of research evidence in their own contexts, usually by incorporating some of the implied principles into their teaching procedures. Everyone must be their own translator.

What this all boils down to is that research evidence has to be interpreted in the light of practical experience with and in everyday groups. That is what Knowles and Knowles (1972) provide a readymade amalgam of research and practice in their succinct review of the common characteristics of group behaviour. The groups they refer to include families, committees and discussion groups; the properties relate to all sorts of groups and situations. All of them are relevant to the learning group and their range and variety perhaps serve to underline the limited view of group interaction we often take in our work with students. The following pages (29–30) are reproduced with the kind permission of Malcolm Knowles.

SOME PROPERTIES OF GROUPS

Background

Each group has an historical background, or lack of it, which influences its behaviour. Members of a new group coming together for the first time may have to devote much early energy to getting acquainted with one another and with the group's task, as well as establishing ways of working together. On the other hand, a group that has often met together may be assumed to be better acquainted with what to expect from one another, what needs to be done, and how to do it. But it might also have developed habits that interfere with its efficiency, such as arguing, dividing into factions or wasting time.

Members come into a meeting with some expectations about it. They may have a clear idea of what the meeting is about, or they may be hazy and puzzled about what it going to happen. They may be looking forward to the meeting or dreading it; they may feel deeply concerned or indifferent. In some cases the boundaries around the group's freedom of action may be narrowly defined by the conditions under which it was created, or so poorly defined that the group doesn't know what its boundaries are.

These are merely illustrations of some of the elements that make up a group's background. Some questions that help to provide an understanding of a group's background include:

- How well were the members prepared to enter the group?
- What are their expectations about the group and their role in it?
- What is the composition of the group – what kind of people, what previous experience, prior friendship patterns and so on? How were they selected?
- What arrangements have been made for their meeting – physical setting, resources, and the like?

Participation pattern

At any given moment every group has a particular participation pattern. For instance, it may be all one-way, with the leader talking to the members; or it may be two-way, with the leader speaking to the members and the members responding; or it may be multidirectional, with all members speaking to one another and to the group as a whole. In a given group this pattern may tend to be quite consistent, or it may vary from time to time. The studies do not indicate that any one participation pattern is always best; it depends upon the requirements of a given situation. But many studies show that on the whole, the broader the participation among members of a group the deeper the interest and involvement will be. Some questions you may ask about a group to understand its participation pattern are these:

- How much of the talking is done by the leader, how much by the other members?
- To whom are questions or comments usually addressed – the group as a whole, the leader, or particular members?
- Do the members who don't talk much seem to be interested and listening alertly (non-verbal participation), or are they bored and apathetic?

It is very easy, and often useful to a group, to chart the participation pattern during periodic segments of time, thus providing objective data about this aspect of its dynamics, as in Figure 2.1.

 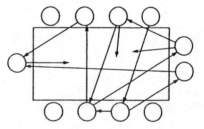

(a) Participation pattern from 3.00pm to 3.20pm

(b) Participation pattern from 3.30pm to 4.00pm

Figure 2.1 *Charts of participation patterns in a group*

Communication

This property has to do with how well group members are understanding one another – how clearly they are communicating their ideas, values, and feelings. If some members are using a highly specialized vocabulary they may be talking over the heads of the rest of the group. Sometimes a group will develop a specialized vocabulary of its own, a kind of verbal shorthand, or private jokes that aren't understood by new members and outsiders.

Even non-verbal communication can often be eloquent. A person's posture, facial expression, and gestures tell a great deal about what he or she is thinking and feeling. Some questions that indicate the quality of a group's communications are:

- Are members expressing their ideas clearly?
- Do members frequently pick up contributions previously made and build their own ideas onto them?
- Do members feel free to ask for clarification when they don't understand a statement?
- Are responses to statements frequently irrelevant?

Cohesion

The cohesiveness of a group is determined by the strength of the bonds that bind the individual parts together into a unified whole. This property indicates the morale, the team spirit, the strength of attraction of the group for its members, and the interest of the members in what the group is doing. In the literature it is often referred to as the 'we feeling' of a group. Symptoms of low cohesion include *sub rosa* conversations between pairs of members outside the main flow of the group's discussion, the emergence of cliques, factions, and such sub-groupings as the 'old timers' versus the 'newcomers', the 'conservatives' versus the 'liberals', and so on. Questions about the group's cohesion include:

- How well is the group working together as a unit?
- What sub-groups or 'lone wolves' are there and how do they affect the group?
- What evidence is there of interest or lack of interest on the part of members or groups of members in what the group is doing?
- Do members refer to the group as 'my group', 'our group', 'your group', 'their group', or 'his group'?

Atmosphere

Although atmosphere is an intangible thing, it is usually fairly easy to sense. In the literature it is often referred to as the 'social climate' of the group, with such characterizations as 'warm, friendly, relaxed, informal, permissive, free' in contrast to 'cold, hostile, tense, formal, restrained'. Atmosphere affects how members feel about a group and the degree of spontaneity in their participation. Atmosphere can be probed by such questions as:

- Would you describe this group as warm or cool, friendly or hostile, relaxed or tense, informal or formal, permissive or controlled, free or inhibited?
- Can opposing views or negative feelings be expressed without fear of punishment?

Norms

Every group tends to develop a code of ethics or set of norms about what is proper and acceptable behaviour. Which subjects may be discussed, which are taboo; how openly members may express their feelings; the propriety of volunteering one's services; the length and frequency of statements considered allowable; whether or not interrupting is permitted – all of these and many more do's and don'ts are embodied in a group's norms. It may be difficult for a new member to catch on to a group's norms if they differ from those of other groups he or she has experienced, since these norms are usually implicit rather than openly stated. Indeed, a group might be confused about what its norms actually are, and this may lead to embarrassment, irritation and lost momentum. Questions about norms include:

- What evidence is there that the group has a code of ethics regarding such matters as self-discipline, sense of responsibility, courtesy, tolerance of differences, freedom of expression, and the like?
- Are there any marked deviations from these norms by one or more members? With what effect?
- Do these norms seem to be well understood by all members, or is there confusion about them?
- Which of the group's norms seem to help, and which seem to hinder the group's progress?

Sociometric pattern

In every group the participants soon tend to identify certain individuals that they like more than other members, and others that they like less. These subtle relationships of friendship and antipathy – the sociometric patterns – have an important influence on the group's activities. Some research indicates that people tend to agree with people they like and to disagree with people they dislike, even though both express the same ideas. Questions which help to reveal the sociometric pattern are:

- Which members tend to identify with and support one another?
- Which members seem repeatedly at odds?
- Do some members act as 'triggers' to others, causing them to respond immediately after the first member's comments, either pro or con?

Structure and organization

Groups have both a visible and an invisible organizational structure. The visible structure, which might be highly formal (officers, committees, appointed positions) or quite informal, makes it possible to achieve a division of labour among the members and get essential functions performed. The invisible structure consists of the behind-the-scenes arrangement of the members according to relative prestige, influence, power, seniority, ability, persuasiveness, and the like. Questions to ask about structure include:

- What kind of structure does the group create consciously – leadership positions, service positions, committees, teams?
- What is the invisible structure – who really controls, influences, volunteers, gets things done? Who defers to others, follows?
- Is the structure understood and accepted by the members?
- Is it appropriate to the group's purpose and tasks?

Procedures

All groups need to use some procedures – ways of working – to get things done. In formal business meetings we are accustomed to the use of a highly codified and explicit set of procedures. Informal groups usually use less rigid procedures. The choice of procedures has a direct effect on such other aspects of group life as atmosphere, participation pattern, and cohesion. Choosing procedures that are appropriate to the situation and to the work to be done requires a degree of flexibility and inventiveness by a group. Procedures can be examined through such questions as:

- How does the group determine its tasks or agenda?
- How does it make decisions – by vote, silent assent, consensus?
- How does it discover and make use of the resources of its members?
- How does it co-ordinate its various members, sub-groups, and activities?
- How does it evaluate its work?

Goals

All groups have goals, some very long-range – for example, 'to promote the welfare of children and youth' – and others of shorter range – 'to plan a parent education programme for the coming year'. Others are even more immediate – 'to decide on a speaker for next month's meeting'. Sometimes goals are defined clearly, specifically and publicly; at other times they are vague, general and only implicit. Members may feel really committed to them or may merely go along with them. Since goals are so important to the group's ultimate accomplishment they receive a good deal of attention in the literature. Some questions about goals include:

- How does the group arrive at its goals?
- Are all members clear about them?
- Are all members committed to them?
- Are they realistic and attainable for this group?

SOCIAL AND TASK DIMENSIONS

It appears at first sight that there are two completely different kinds of groups. Some, such as the bridge circle, the coffee gang and the like, are highly informal, with few rules or procedures and no stated goals. People belong for the emotional satisfaction they get from belonging; they like the people, they are their friends. They tend to think of these as their social groups. Membership in these groups is completely voluntary and tends to be homogeneous. The success of the social group is measured in terms of how enjoyable it is.

In other groups, however – committees, boards, staff meetings and discussion groups – there are usually explicit goals, and more or less formal rules and procedures. People tend to think of these groups, which exist to accomplish some task, as work or volunteer service groups. The membership tends to be more heterogeneous – based on the resources required to do their work – and sometimes brought together out of compulsion or sense of duty more than free choice. The success of the task group is measured in terms of how much work it gets done.

As these dimensions have been studied more deeply, it has become apparent that they do not describe different kinds of groups – few groups are purely social or task – so much as different dimensions of all groups. Most groups need the social dimension to provide emotional involvement, morale, interest, and loyalty; and the task dimension to provide stability, purpose, direction and a sense of accomplishment. Without the dimension of work, members may become dissatisfied and feel guilty because they are not accomplishing anything; without the dimension of friendship, members may feel that the group is cold, unfriendly, and not pleasant to be with.

GROUP MAINTENANCE AND GROUP TASK FUNCTIONS

To understand the way in which various group functions are performed, it is helpful to classify these functions as:

1. *group-building and maintenance* roles – those which contribute to building relationships and cohesiveness among the membership (the social dimension); and
2. *group task* roles – those which help the group to do its work (the task dimension).

The first set of functions is required for the group to maintain itself as a group; the second set, for the locomotion of the group toward its goals. For example, some group-building functions are:

- *encouraging* – being friendly, warm, responsive to others, praising others and their ideas, agreeing with and accepting the contributions of others;
- *mediating* – harmonizing, conciliating differences in points of view, making compromises;

- *gate-keeping* – trying to make it possible for another member to make a contribution by saying, 'We haven't heard from Jim yet', or suggesting limited talking-time for everyone so that all will have a chance to be heard;
- *standard-setting* – expressing standards for the group to use in choosing its subject matter or procedures, rules of conduct, ethical values;
- *following* – going along with the group, somewhat passively accepting the ideas of others, serving as an audience during group discussion, being a good listener;
- *relieving tension* – draining off negative feeling by jesting or throwing oil on troubled waters, diverting attention from unpleasant to pleasant matters.

And the following are some task functions:

- *initiating* – suggesting new ideas or a changed way of looking at the group problem or goal, proposing new activities;
- *information seeking* – asking for relevant facts or authoritative information;
- *information giving* – providing relevant facts or authoritative information or relating personal experience pertinently to the group task;
- *opinion giving* – stating a pertinent belief or opinion about something the group is considering;
- *clarifying* – probing for meaning and understanding, restating something the group is considering;
- *elaborating* – building on a previous comment, enlarging on it, giving examples;
- *co-ordinating* – showing or clarifying the relationships among various ideas, trying to pull ideas and suggestions together;
- *orienting* – defining the progress of the discussion in terms of the group's goals, raising questions about the direction the discussion is taking;
- *testing* – checking with the group to see if it is ready to make a decision or to take some action;
- *summarizing* – reviewing the content of past discussion.

These functions are not needed equally at all times by a group. Indeed, if a given function is performed inappropriately it may interfere with the group's operation – as when some jester relieves group tension just when the tension is about to result in some real action. But often when a group is not getting along as it should, a diagnosis of the problem will probably indicate that nobody is performing one of the functions listed above that is needed at that moment to move the group ahead. It seems to be true, also, that some people are more comfortable or proficient in performing one kind of function than another, so that they tend to play the same role in every group to which they belong. There is danger, however, in over-stereotyping an individual as a 'mediator' or 'opinion-giver' or any other particular function, for people can learn to perform various functions that are needed when they become aware of them.

In groups one can often observe behaviour that does not seem to fit any of these categories. This is likely to be *self-centred* behaviour, sometimes referred to in the literature as a 'nonfunctional role'. This is behaviour that does not contribute to the group, but only satisfies personal needs. Examples of this category are:

- *blocking* – interfering with the progress of the group by going off on a tangent, citing personal experiences unrelated to the group's problem, arguing too much on a point the rest of the group has resolved, rejecting ideas without consideration, preventing a vote;
- *aggressing* – criticizing or blaming others, showing hostility toward the group or some individual without relation to what has happened in the group, attacking the motives of others, deflating the ego or status of others;
- *seeking recognition* – attempting to call attention to oneself by excessive talking, extreme ideas, boasting, boisterousness;
- *special pleading* – introducing or supporting ideas related to one's own pet concerns or philosophies beyond reason, attempting to speak for 'the grass roots', 'the housewife', 'the common man', and so on;
- *withdrawing* – acting indifferent or passive, resorting to excessive formality, doodling, whispering to others;
- *dominating* – trying to assert authority in manipulating the group or certain members of it by 'pulling rank', giving directions authoritatively, interrupting contributions of others.

The appearance of these behaviours in groups tends to be irritating to other members, and they tend to react to them with blame, reproach, or counter-hostility. A group that understands group dynamics is often able to deal with them constructively, however, because it sees them as symptoms of deeper causes such as valid personal needs that are not being satisfied constructively. Often, of course, it is difficult to place a given act in one or another of these categories – what seems to be 'blocking' to one observer may appear as 'testing' to another.

THE ROLE OF LEADERSHIP

In this analysis of functions necessary to the performance of groups, no distinction has been made between the functions of leaders and the functions of the members. This is because the research fails to identify any set of functions that is *universally* the peculiar responsibility of the designated leader. But the fact is that groups in our society typically have central figures with such titles as 'leader, chair, president', and 'captain'. Ross and Hendry (1957) examine various theories that try to explain this institutionalization of the role of leader and, after assessing them as inadequate, give this view as to the current state of thinking:

> Perhaps the best we can say at this point is that any comprehensive theory of leadership must take into account the fact that the leadership role is probably related to personality factors, to the attitudes and needs of 'followers' at a particular time, to the structure of the group, and to the situation. Leadership is probably a function of the interaction of such variables, and these undoubtedly provide for role differentiation which leads to the designation of a 'central figure' or leader, without prohibiting other members in the group from performing leadership functions in various ways, and at various times, in the life of the group.

A classic series of experiments in the laboratory of Kurt Lewin often quoted in the literature of group dynamics bears on leadership style. Their purpose was to measure as precisely as possible the effects of different types of leader behaviour on a number of experimentally-created groups of boys. The three types of leader behaviour tested were 'authoritarian' (policy determined by the leader), 'democratic' (all policies a matter of group discussion and decision, encouraged and assisted by the leader), and 'laissez-faire' (complete freedom for the group or individual decision, with a minimum of leader participation). Their studies produced evidence for the following generalizations:

- Authoritarian-led groups produced a greater quantity of work over a short period of time, but experienced more hostility, competition and aggression – especially scapegoating, more discontent beneath the surface, more dependence and less originality.
- Democratically-led groups, slower in getting into production, were more strongly motivated, became increasingly productive with time and learning, experienced more friendliness and teamwork, praised one another more frequently and expressed greater satisfaction.
- Laissez-faire groups did less and poorer work than either of the others, spent more time in horseplay, talked more about what they should be doing, experienced more aggression than the democratic group but less than the authoritarian, and expressed a preference for democratic leadership.

A mounting body of research on the leadership role since World War II supports the thesis that some situations require authoritarian and others laissez-faire leadership, but that, in the long run, in normal situations, groups thrive best when the *leadership functions are democratically shared among the members of the group.*

GROUPS IN MOTION

So far we have been looking at the complicated elements or variables that make up a group – its properties, dimensions, and membership and leadership functions – almost as if a group stood still in time and space. Actually, a group is never static: it is a dynamic organism, constantly in motion. Not only is it moving as a unit, but the various elements within it are constantly interacting. A change in procedure will affect atmosphere, which will affect the participation pattern, which will affect cohesion, which will affect leadership, which will affect procedure, and so on. Actually, most of the research has to do with the dynamic interaction of these variables in groups in motion.

There seems to be fairly general agreement among the students of group dynamics that groups move through more or less predictable phases of development during their lifecycle. A number of theories about what these phases are have been proposed, as summarized in Figure 2.2. Notice that while each theory focuses on a different theme, they all indicate quite similar phenomena occurring in the early, middle and later phases of group development.

Figure 2.2 *Phases of group development – various theories*

Thelen and Dickerman (1949)	*Phase 1:* Individually centred	*Phase 2:* Frustration and conflict	*Phase 3:* Attempted consolidation of group harmony	*Phase 4:* Individual self-assessment, flexibility of group process, emphasis upon productivity in problem solving	
Miles (1955)	*Phase 1:* Unoriented, restive 'talking about' irrelevant matters	*Phase 2:* Abstract 'talking about' leadership and permissiveness	*Phase 3:* 'Doing level' – discussion and analysis of here-and-now		
Bennis and Shepard (1956)	*Subphase 1:* Dependence–submission	*Subphase 2:* Counter-dependence	*Subphase 3:* Resolution	*Subphase 4:* Enchantment	*Subphase 5:* Disenchantment / *Subphase 6:* Conceptual validation
	Phase 1: Dependence			*Phase 2: Interdependence*	
Schutz (1958)	*Phase 1: Inclusion*	*Phase 2: Control*	*Phase 3: Affection*		
Bion (1961)	*Stage 1: Flight*	*Stage 2: Fight*	*Stage 3: Unite*		
Golembiewski (1962)	*Phase 1:* Establishing the hierarchy	*Phase 2:* Conflict and frustration	*Phase 3:* Growth of security and autonomy	*Phase 4:* Structuring in terms of work task	
Bradford et al (1964)	*Stage 1:* Ambiguity	*Stage 2:* Self-investment and participation	*Stage 3:* Collaboration and learning from peers	*Stage 4:* Motivation for learning	*Stage 5:* Experienced behaviour and feedback / *Stage 6:* Group growth and development

Mills (1964)	Stage 1: The encounter	Stage 2: Testing boundaries and modelling behaviour	Stage 3: Negotiating and indigenous normative system	Stage 4: Production	Stage 5: Separation
Tuckman (1965)	Stage 1: Forming – Testing and dependence	Stage 2: Storming – Intragroup conflict	Stage 3: Norming – development of group cohesion	Stage 4: Performing – functional role relatedness	
Mann et al (1967)	Phase 1: Initial complaining	Phase 2: Premature enactment	Phase 3: Confrontation	Phase 4: Internalization	Phase 5 & 6: Separation and terminal review
Dunphy (1968)	Phase 1: Counterpersonal and negativity — Maintenance of external normative standard	Phase 2 & Phase 3: Individual rivalry and aggression	Phase 4: Transitional – Negativity membership	Phase 5: Emotional concerns — Realization of unattainable Utopian ideals	Phase 6: End of group
Tuckman and Jensen (1977)	Stage 1: Forming	Stage 2: Storming	Stage 3: Norming	Stage 4: Performing	Stage 5: Adjourning
Napier and Gershenfeld (1981)	Stage 1: Beginning – hesitation and testing	Stage 2: Movement towards confrontation	Stage 3: Compromise and harmony	Stage 4: Reassessment – union of emotional and task components	Stage 5: Resolution and recycling

FIELD STUDIES IN TERTIARY EDUCATION

Most of the research into group work in tertiary education is naturally centred on discussion groups. It is interesting therefore to draw comparisons between this and the more general research evidence described above. Beard, Bligh and Harding (1978) claim there is general agreement that some of the more important variables in discussion groups are:

- seating position;
- talkativeness;
- personality of the participants;
- kind of leadership.

They quote Klein (1965) who found that more voluble members of a group tended to be popular, and that a normally silent member giving the best solution to the problem often fails to get it accepted without the aid of one of the more voluble participants. This is substantiated by other research done by Tuckman and Lorge (1962) who found that contributions of members of low status were normally ignored in arriving at a group solution to a problem.

Compare this with Deutsch (1949) who studied the effect of giving different information on the assessment of a group to members of different groups. He noted that where groups were to be assessed collectively, in co-operation, they showed 'more co-ordination of effort, diversity in amount of contribution, subdivision of activity, attentiveness to fellow members, mutual comprehension and communication, greater orientation, orderliness and productivity per unit time, as well as more favourable evaluation of the group and its products compared with groups who were informed that each individual would be assessed independently. Davey (1969) in an experiment with 800 groups of different sizes concluded that with up to approximately seven group members the permissive style of leadership seemed most productive, but above that a controlling style seemed to work better. This leads to consideration of the value of tutorless groups. Marris (1964) found that when staff were absent from groups students felt far less inhibited and frequently discussed their work with each other. They felt that seeking help from staff was viewed as a confession of incompetence. Of course sub-groups within a larger group are a form of tutorless group and Beard and Hartley (1989) point to the success of discussion in pairs (buzz groups) before students raise questions more formally with the teacher.

The presence of a tutor does not of course imply his or her active participation in discussion. Abercrombie (1979), for instance, developed a technique of group work in which the tutor played the part of an onlooker who asked the occasional question or made a comment, rather in the way that a group psychotherapist might do. In this case, the task was specific: to help students consider evidence carefully and to make valid judgements on their observations. The objects of scrutiny were radiographs or an account of an experiment. Some students were clearly unsettled by this procedure and others rejected it out of hand, though nearly all were amazed at the degree to which unconscious assumptions had appeared to influence their judgement. Upon testing at the end of the course, it was apparent that participants in this class were better able to distinguish between facts and inferences, made fewer false inferences, explicitly considered alternative hypotheses more frequently and were less often fixed in their view of the problem by dint of previous experience, than were a control group. This experience had apparently helped them become more objective in making assessments of scientific material.

It thus appears that groups are demonstrably valuable for many of the more sophisticated aims of higher education to do with critical thinking, making diagnoses or decisions, solving problems, and changing or maintaining attitudes to the subject under study. Indeed Bligh (1978), surveying the research evidence on different forms of teaching, concluded that discussion methods are more effective than didactic methods (eg the lecture) for stimulating thought, for personal and social adjustment, and for changes of attitude, and, more surprisingly perhaps, were no worse than the lecture for effectively transmitting information.

There is a vast amount of research evidence on group work and it is in a constant state of expansion and revision. The fact remains that it can be described as 'work done by other people in other places for other purposes' and this provides a ready excuse for teachers to reject it or at least ignore it. The notion of the teacher as researcher therefore has a lot to commend it.

TEACHER AS RESEARCHER

The concept of a teacher as one who is putting into practice ideas developed by others is not an appealing one, nor is it realistic, as Pring (1978) argues. Each teaching situation is governed by a unique set of variables which no general researcher could conceivably take into account: the personality of the teacher, the special characteristics of the students, the effects of the learning milieu in that institution and the structure of the particular curriculum being taught, to name but a few. If teachers are to research their own teaching the question arises: how can the objectivity and rigour demanded by research be obtained? As Pring says:

> being objective is opening to public scrutiny the basis upon which one's judgements are made so that counter-evidence and contrary arguments might, if they exist, be levelled against what one says. I may be correct in declaring at the end of the lesson that things went well, but my judgement is subjective insofar as there is no evidence against which another might test the truth of what I say.

In order to conduct classroom research one would need to formulate hypotheses and choose an appropriate test procedure. Such hypotheses would be unlikely to embrace all the variables, yet as long as they are regarded as provisional and are stated clearly, they can be very instructive. Among test procedures one might use, are:

- an interaction analysis (for example, the one on page 23);

- recording either with audio or video tape;
- recording one's own comments in a diary;
- drawing out the students' perceptions.

None of these would stand up on its own as reliable research evidence, but taken together they could be employed as a 'triangulation' technique in which each account of what happened is tested against the others. This proposal of the teacher as an activator in research, rather than as a recipient, is an exciting one in that it implies a greater sense of direction and self-autonomy for the teacher. It is firmly supported by Rowan and Reason (1981) who propose an interactive style of research in which the mutual influences of researcher and 'researched' are acknowledged.

DISCUSSION POINTS

- Take the sets of questions on pages 29–33 and answer them for, or in, your group.
- Consider the chart on pages 38–9. Which sequence seems most relevant to the way your present group has developed?
- How would you describe the balance between social and task dimensions in your group? What can you do to affect this?
- How would you characterize the role of leadership in the achievement of task goals compared with social goals in your group?

3 Research into Learning

Any scepticism towards research into group dynamics in terms of its usefulness to professional practice applies equally to learning theory and educational research even when it is concerned with student learning. Yet where this research provides a set of helpful explanatory concepts, then its value increases in leaps and bounds. The effect of research is thus indirect.

> Research evidence gradually changes teachers' assumptions, and the way they interpret their role. It 'sensitises' teachers to aspects of the teaching–learning process which had previously lacked significance. It points up anomalies in the existing situation and may provide hints at alternative solutions. But it cannot indicate the single *best* way of tackling either lecturing or studying. (Entwistle 1977)

In recent years several studies of the ways in which students learn have been conducted in Sweden, Britain and the USA. Most of them have implications for the way in which groups are organised and run.

STUDENT PERFORMANCE

The personal characteristics of 1531 students from seven English universities were tested in the late 1960s and early 1970s by Entwistle and others at Lancaster through a battery of psychological tests administered in the first year and again in the final year. A cluster analysis of the characteristics revealed that students achieve success in different ways, with a variety of combinations of aptitudes, attitudes and personality traits. The analysis suggested that there were two contrasting types of student with above average degree results:

- *Highly-motivated; emotionally stable, tending to tough-minded conservatism*; well-organized in study methods, not particularly active in social or sporting life, or in aesthetic interests.
- *Highly neurotic and bounded by the syllabus* (the characteristic of some students who work hard on set work but rarely take the risk of going beyond it); had low self-esteem, no active social life or aesthetic interests.

Though these are but two examples drawn from several possible clusters they appear to display different kinds of motivation – the first looking towards success, and the second fearing failure. These patterns were subsequently confirmed in interviews.

While we may doubt the validity of a 'type-sorting' analysis it does remind us that students differ considerably in their ways of achieving success. The implication for group work is that many quite reticent students may be just as successful academically as those who consistently 'play the system', and even more successful than those whose creative flair we most value in discussion. We should perhaps ask ourselves to what extent our styles and methods of teaching and in particular our assessment system encourage and sustain either of the above qualities and whether that is what we want. There are also ethical issues involved. Are we, by promoting and encouraging the more extrovert and radically-minded student in discussion groups implanting a value which could mislead? Do we allow the tough, goal-orientated students to benefit at the expense of their more inspired, value-conscious and open-minded colleagues? Clearly these are not precise questions as the above research was describing ideal-types and not real, individual, people, but it does at least go part way to explaining the resentment which many students feel – that somehow, though they have 'made all the running' at seminars, it is their quieter, less open-minded colleagues who collect the best marks.

LEARNING STYLES

Rather different aspects of the students' approach to learning have been revealed through a series of studies by Marton and Säljö (1976) and their colleagues at Gothenburg. They identified two distinctive approaches among students in the way they read texts:

- *Surface-level processing* – in which students take a passive approach and are concerned with:
  - covering the content;
  - how much they have learned;
  - finding the 'right' answers;
  - assimilating unaltered chunks of knowledge;
  - learning verbatim.
- *Deep-level processing* – in which students take an active approach and are concerned with:
  - the central point;
  - what lies behind the argument;
  - the whole picture;
  - what it boils down to;
  - what it is connected with;
  - the logic of the argument;
  - points that are not clear;
  - questioning the conclusions.

The surface-level processors divert their attention therefore to the *sign*, and the deep-level processors to which is *signified*. In general those adopting 'deep' approaches are more successful in exams. Surface processors tend to pass only when they manage to overcome the tedium which that form of learning often induces.

Deep processors are more versatile: they find it easier to tackle 'surface' questions than surface processors do 'deep' questions. Strong motivation increases the likelihood that deep-level processing will occur, while anxiety induces a hurried fact-grabbing strategy. This will doubtless be familiar to the experienced tutor, who will have noticed the increasing desperation among students to memorize 'facts' and know 'what is what' as exams approach.

In a parallel investigation in London, Pask (1976) distinguished between two clear strategies among students for drawing up a classification system. *Holists* adopted a broad perspective and looked for a variety of interrelationships, whereas serialists were typified by their attention to details and a pattern of learning by increments. Holists ask a different order of questions too, 'about broad relations and (they) form hypotheses about generalisations' as opposed to serialists whose questions are 'about much narrower relations and (whose) hypotheses are specific'. Lest it be thought that holists are successful in all respects it should be added that they are likely to over-generalize and to make remote and often mistaken connections. Serialists, on the other hand, are often victims of their own caution and their inability to make connections often makes integration of knowledge a difficult task for them. Pask's continuing research into learning strategies has indicated, not surprisingly, a further category – the *versatile* learner who is able to adopt the holist or serialist strategy according to the task at hand. He also demonstrated that holists are not good at learning serialist material; nor are serialists good with holist material, but students whose learning style matched the material learned it quickly and accurately.

INTELLECTUAL DEVELOPMENT

It would be sad if we reviewed student learning solely in terms of processing information and finding ways of 'working the system'. In tertiary education students are free, possibly for the first time, to learn in their preferred way, and to develop their own sense of what is worth learning.

In an interview study of students at the Liberal Arts College at Harvard, Perry (1970) found a coherent progression in the manner in which students approached learning, experienced values and construed the world during their college experience. He identified a sequence of nine positions through which students appear to have progressed as they moved through college. Basically the sequence comprised a development from a dualistic, authority-accepting position, through a relativistic 'anything goes' phase to a final stage of open-minded commitment.

Position 1 *Dualism*	There are Right and Wrong Answers to everything. Authorities, whose role is to teach the answers, know what these are, and if I work hard, and learn the Right Answers, adding more and more to my stock of knowledge, all will be well.
Position 2	Diversity of opinion and uncertainty exist but that's only because Authority is confused or ill-qualified. They set us problems only to enable us to find the Right Answer by ourselves.
Position 3	Some uncertainties and differences in opinions are real and legitimate. But this is a temporary situation for Authorities who are still searching for the Right Answer.
Position 4a	Where Authorities don't know the Right Answers, everyone has right to their own opinion; no one is Wrong!
Position 4b	Some Authorities are not asking for the Right Answer: they are grading us like they do because they want us to think about things in a certain way, supporting opinion with data and so on.
Position 5 *Relativism*	All knowledge and values are relative but equally valid. Everything has to be seen in its context. Dualistic, Right/Wrong thinking is a special case in context.
Position 6	I'm going to have to make up my own mind in an uncertain world with no one to tell me whether I'm right or wrong.
Position 7	I've made my first commitment!
Position 8	Now I've made several commitments, I've got to balance them in terms of priorities. Which do I feel really committed to and responsible for?
Position 9 *Evolving Commitments*	This is how life will be. I must be wholehearted while tentative, fight for my values yet respect others, believe my deepest values right yet be ready to learn. I see that I shall be retracing this whole journey over and over – but, I hope, more wisely.

According to Perry, a students moves into a new phase as the prior one becomes inadequate in coping with the uncertainties and complexities of the world and knowledge. The meanings and structurings attached to the old phase are not lost but contained within the new one to be used where appropriate, and each step is accompanied by a 'joy of realization but also a loss of certainty and an altered sense of self'. The changes and progression appear to be applicable to all ages and to varied backgrounds and situations. Though they do not necessarily develop at the same rate in all aspects of a student's life he or she might well transfer more advanced forms of thinking to less developed areas.

One would hope that most students will enter colleges at a stage beyond position 1 and progress at least to position 5 by the end of a full-time course at tertiary level. However, fewer students appear to reach the stage of maturity implied by position 9. Even the acceptance of relativism as a perception of the world represents revolutionary change in thinking and values for many students and as such is a challenge to some of their fundamental beliefs. It is akin to the restructuring of scientific theory which takes place from time to time in the history of humankind (Kuhn 1973). Such a profound transformation is thus one of great significance in the intellectual development of the student, yet paradoxically it is one which is often the most quietly realized.

Perry also describes forms of 'deflection', or reversion in the process, which offer a way out at critical points. These are *temporizing*, where a student bides time in one position; *escape*, a sense of withdrawn disenchantment; and *retreat*, an entrenchment in the dualist, absolutist framework of positions 1 and 2.

Perry's study raises questions about structure and sequence in course design, about the presentation of knowledge and the ways in whch students are grouped for teaching, about the techniques and skills that tutors bring to discussion, and about ways of assessing students. To what extent is it possible, particularly in group discussion, to assist students to growth points in their development, while allowing for the emotional dispositions to which intellectual forms are often wedded? Is Perry's scheme applicable only to the so-called liberal arts, or is it equally relevant to the learning of science and technology? Whatever the answers may be, and they will doubtless vary according to circumstances, there is little doubt that the studies of Marton, Pask and Perry stimulate thought on the nature of student learning even if they present a somewhat selective picture.

DEVELOPMENTAL PHASES IN THE CONCEPTION OF LEARNING

Säljö (1984) has demonstrated how students may change their approach to learning as they progress in their studies. Gibbs (1990) has summarized this work in a way which represents an integration of the research already discussed in this chapter.

Underlying the approach students take is their understanding of what learning itself consists of. This understanding changes, influenced by the context students find themselves in and by the learning demands these contexts make. Studies have identified five stages in the development of students' understanding, listed here with examples of the kinds of things students who have these conceptions say.

1. Learning as an increase in knowlege. The student will often see learning as something done to them by teachers rather than as something they do to or for themselves.
   To gain some knowledge is learning . . . We obviously want to learn more. I want to know as much as possible.
2. Learning as memorising. The students has an active role in memorising, but the information being memorised is not transformed in any way.
   Learning is about getting it into your head. You've just got to keep writing it out and eventually it will go in.

3. Learning as acquiring facts or procedures which are to be used. What you learn is seen to include skills, algorithms, formulae which you apply etc which you will need in order to do things at a later date, but there is still no transformation of what is learnt by the learner.
   Well it's about learning the thing so you can do it again when you are asked to, like in an exam.

4. Learning as making sense. The student makes active attempts to abstract meaning in the process of learning. This may only involve academic tasks.
   Learning is about trying to understand things so you can see what is going on. You've got to be able to explain things, not just remember them.

5. Learning as understanding reality. Learning enables you to perceive the world differently. This has also been termed 'personally meaningful learning'.
   When you have really learnt something you kind of see things you couldn't see before. Everything changes.

There are other developmental schemes, describing how students change in the sophistication of their perception of the learning tasks they face, which embody very similar descriptions.

Stages 4 and 5 are clearly qualitatively different from stages 1 to 3. Students who understand what learning is at levels 1, 2 and 3 have trouble comprehending what a deep approach consists of and are very unlikely to take a deep approach to learning tasks. Students who are at levels 4 or 5 can take either a deep or a surface approach, depending on the task and their perception of its demands. The connection between these underlying conceptions of learning and the approach students take to specific learning tasks is so strong that it is impossible to predict the quality of learning outcomes directly from students' conceptions of learning. All you need to know about a student is that she has a conception of learning at level 1, 2 or 3 and you can be fairly certain that she will only derive a superficial and fragmentary understanding from, for example, reading a chapter.

For some students, then, their limited understanding of what learning consists of prevents them from approaching learning tasks in a deep way and therefore from learning effectively. Two important questions about such crude and disabling conceptions of learning are: *Where do they come from?* and *Can they be changed?*

As well as being asked about what they think learning is, students have been asked what they think good teaching consists of. Some think that the teacher should do all the work and make all the decisions. The teacher should select the subject matter, present it in teacher-controlled classes, devise tests and mark students on how well they have learnt the material which has been presented. What is to be learnt and what learning outcomes should look like is completely defined by the teacher (a 'closed' conception of teaching). Others think that while the teacher has responsibility for setting the learning climate, for making learning resources available, and for supporting students, all the responsibility lies with the student: responsibility for selecting learning goals, devising appropriate learning activities and for judging when learning outcomes are satisfactory (an 'open' conception of teaching). It will probably come as no surprise to learn that the former, 'closed', conception of teaching is held almost exclusively by students with conceptions of learning at levels 1, 2 or 3, while the latter, 'open' conception of teaching is held by students with conceptions of learning at levels 4 or 5. This relationship is summarised in the table below.

Conception of learning	Conception of teaching
Reproducing (Levels 1, 2 and 3)	**Closed** Teacher does all the work and makes all the decisions
Making sense (Levels 4 and 5)	**Open** Learner does most of the work and makes most of the decisions

IMPLICATIONS OF LEARNING RESEARCH

It is difficult to draw any hard and fast conclusions as to what the research of Marton, Pask, Perry and Säljö implies for teachers at any level of education. Although it is likely that we can equate surface processors with serialists and with those in Perry's dualistic stage (and even with Hudson's (1966) convergers) and the deep processing with holists, realistic reasoning and divergers there are no clear indications of what the teacher should do about it: the research was all investigatory rather than applied. However, we could venture a few working hypotheses based on them:

- Many courses, especially those with high student contact-hours and heavy pressure of exams, are likely to inhibit deep, holistic, relativist thinking and encourage a reproductive, fact-grabbing strategy of learning.
- Deep, holistic, relativistic students are more likely to prefer the openness of small discussion groups to the more formal, distant relationships of highly structured lecture courses.
- The teaching style of tutors will reflect their own way of thinking about knowledge and will vary accordingly.
- A mixture of formal lectures, small group work, individual study and project group work may be best for the majority of students and a course sequence which focuses increasingly on the latter methods will prove acceptable on several counts.
- The most academically successful students will be able to recognize differences in teaching styles and learning tasks and adopt strategies of learning appropriate to them.

There may be implications of a need, as Entwistle suggests:

to think more clearly about the formation of large and small group methods in relation to the particular intellectual skills, or cognitive style, they are expected to foster and whether the assignments and examination questions given to students provide sufficient encouragement for deep-level processing.

Surface processing may be the only strategy possessed by many students when they arrive at college. Whether this is a kind of personality trait or is something more superficially acquired as a means to success in school, and therefore easily shed, is something else over which to ruminate. Certainly, if we can accept what Perry says about the often traumatic nature of change it will follow that tutors require sensitivity and skill in accommodating the variety of student styles within a climate of intellectual growth (not to speak of the tutor's own styles and predilections). Students too readily slip into disillusionment and consequent failure because the range of demands is too great. But are they always the right demands, and is their response to the demands appropriate? What we as tutors must do is to help students understand what choices there are in approaches to learning and to give them the opportunity and support in making their choices. Small groups provide the most suitable environment for this to occur.

DISCUSSION POINTS

- Describe (in writing) what, in general terms, you or your group learns. How?
- In what ways can a group leader encourage deep processing, holistic thinking and intellectual development? Where are *you* in all this?
- How does the balance between different approaches to learning work out in your group and how does that affect the interaction?

4 Communicating in Groups

No amount of understanding of group behaviour is sufficient for successful participation in groups unless each person in the group has the capacity to communicate effectively. It is through communication that people achieve an understanding of one another and are thus able to influence, and be influenced by, others. Only if there is a predisposition to accept and accommodate others will honest communication take place – and this implies a degree of trust and openness between participants. Without these, mutual understanding and influences are liable to distortion: co-operation is unlikely.

THE PROCESS OF COMMUNICATION

Communication is often regarded as little more than the process of passing and receiving information. Concern for improving communication usually centres on the skills of writing, speaking, reading and, less frequently, listening. Typically, the emphasis will be on qualities like clarity, consciseness, precision and logical sequence. Yet many, and possibly most, errors in communication occur because of psychological rather than logical factors. The feelings, attitudes, behaviours and relationships of those involved in communication are more likely to determine whether it is effective or not.

The process of communication is therefore far from being the rational or mechanical exercise (see Figure 4.1) that many people think:

A   B

Sender   Receiver

Figure 4.1 *Model of communication 1*

It involves much more than person A saying something to person B and the latter hearing it, interpreting it and acting on it correctly. Communication is not just about words. To paraphrase Kolb, Rubin and McIntyre (1984): **A** brings to the interaction with **B** not merely the content of the message he/she wishes to convey but much more. **A** brings her-himself as a person. **A** has a self image and, to varying degrees also a set of attitudes and feelings towards **B**. The message to **B**, therefore, in addition to certain content, may well be loaded with cues as to who **A** feels themself to be as a person (eg confident and secure versus tentative and wary), how **A** feels about **B** as a person (eg warm and receptive versus cold and uncaring) and how **A** expects **B** to react to **A**'s communication.

If the issue were even as simple as that we might have a reasonably easy task in communicating. The trouble is we are not always aware of what we are actually putting across. We convey things we do not intend. The message thus gets distorted so that the above picture is transformed into something like Figure 4.2.

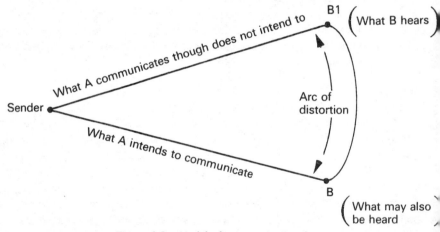

Figure 4.2 *Model of communication 2*

In addition, we often have more than one intention when we communicate something: sometimes the secondary intention becomes the stronger one, and where this is at a less than conscious level the message may well be distorted beyond recognition.

A tutor, for example, who looks 'po-faced' when a particular student speaks, whilst saying 'Yes, that's really very interesting' is communicating a message beyond words. So, too, is the lecturer who though meticulously correct in exposition, shows no enthusiasm for subject or students, and the tutor who always sits as far away as possible from a particular member of the tutorial group. These distorting messages are conveyed by the tone of voice, facial expression, body posture, gesture or physical location. It is the underlying feelings and thoughts which frequently emerge most powerfully through non-verbal cues.

Those on the receiving end of a communication may also be party to the distortion. They have to listen and interpret appropriately and this is not at all easy when they are receiving contradictory messages simultaneously. A common problem in interpersonal communication is failure by the receiving party to attend fully to what is being said and thus miss the important points of a message. Sometimes this is because the receiver is preoccupied, or had a particular way of thinking about something (a mental set) which predetermines the interpretation.

Hearing only part of a message may also serve the receiver's purpose, especially when there are contradictory signals being expressed and he or she has a legitimate choice.

The receiver's part in the hearing and interpreting of messages may be represented by a diagram complementary to Figure 4.2 (see Figure 4.3).

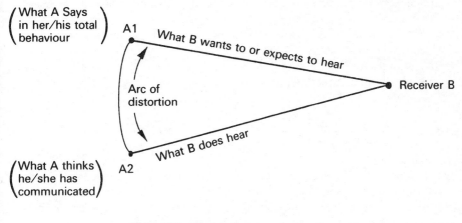

Figure 4.3 *Model of communication 3*

At times, we may *consciously* wish to convey more than one intention at a time. For instance when we express our thoughts in an interview we are usually trying to impress at the same time, to present ourselves in a favourable light. A lot of classroom behaviour is to do with impression: students trying to demonstrate their knowledge, their interest, their regard for the teacher; tutors trying to maintain an aura of objective expertise and control. There is nothing wrong with trying to impress provided it is appropriate and one is aware of it.

We are also likely to distort what we hear because of our personal needs. The need to be liked or to have everything neatly categorized, for instance, may blur our perception of what we are being told. Rather than attending to the complete message, we may block a lot of otherwise important information. Our need to be liked might cause us to be over-sensitive to negative components in a communication: our need for order and neatness or control might predispose us to miss some excellent ideas from students or colleagues who find it difficult to express themselves clearly. What we intend to do with the information when we have it can also cause us to filter and select.

An added factor which may contribute to distorted reception is threat, whether it manifests itself in a direct personal challenge from a group or an individual or in a more general and ill-defined way. The distortion or denial that occurs as a result of threat derives from either the need to protect our self-esteem or from the anxiety which has its roots in early childhood experience. Fear of criticism, reproof, rejection or ridicule inevitably set up defensive barriers, yet because they are at a conscious level they are at least open to scrutiny and change should we so wish. Not so amenable to change are the distortions resulting from childhood conflicts, repressed because of the danger they originally posed, and reawakened at an unconscious level by particular people or events in adulthood. Both of these threats may be revived by a specific thing somebody does or says to us of by an environment which has a high degree of evaluation, control and competitiveness.

Many of the complexities and problems of communication can be tackled through the use of meta-communication: describing the communication that appears to be taking place. For example 'I didn't take in what you said then, could you repeat it.' or 'This seems to have developed into a question and answer session – I suggest you talk me through what you've written on the form for a while.'

THE CONTENT OF COMMUNICATION

The words with which we choose to make our communication are important too, not just for the precision and clarity they offer but because they give colour and light to what we say. Students starting with a group are often at pains to learn how to handle the accepted vocabulary of the subject, and can easily gravitate towards the use of clichés and labels. 'Oh that's a case of X' can cut out the possibility of open discussion when X is a concept which has been invented mainly to box in uncertainty about a phenomenon. More commonly one might hear 'That's a mathematics problem' or whatever the subject in question is, as a way of foreclosing discussion on a topic.

Style and meaning are of relevance too in how people communicate. Statements which begin 'it is' or 'they are' have a more distancing effect than those starting with personal pronouns, especially 'I think' or 'I like'. A psychological distance is also established by the use of theoretical rather than personal understandings. Stanford and Roark (1974) divide the problem into five categories of meaning: theoretical, abstract, objective, personal cognitive and personal experiencing.

Theoretical explanations are the fabric by which we write bits of experience into comprehensive explanations. Psychologically they are impersonal and distant. Theories, abstractions and objective referents can be verified by opinions of others and are thus open to consensual agreement. But personal meanings are open to *our* scrutiny only; we are the sole judge.

Discussion, and even lectures, which focus entirely on 'what is' or 'what other people have said' may help students in jumping academic hurdles but have little personal impact on them.

To quote Stanford and Roark again, teachers often speak as if:

> subject matter has the only 'real' meaning and the students' personal meanings are irrelevant or secondary at best. The effect over a long period of time, especially for students with different experiential backgrounds from the teachers is to drive them away into a world where their meanings are never those of their environment and accepted as having worth.

The effect on students is probably to encourage in their minds and culture a split between that which is acceptable for academic discussion and their more personal experience in the college as a community – a division, that is, between educational knowledge and everyday knowledge. The tendency of many students to seek solace and rewards in the social and political life of their college to the exclusion of academic work may well relate to this 'academization' of knowledge.

IMPROVING COMMUNICATION

As we have already seen, the lack of trust and the existence of threat in any interaction can have a distorting effect on communication. The establishment of honest and meaningful communication can be achieved through these precepts, simple to state but not so easy to practise:

1. Develop a sense of mutual trust and openness.
2. Correct distortions in communication through constructive feedback.
3. Engage in meta-communications; communicating about the process of communication.

The first point demands a willingness to be open to oneself (recognizing and accepting one's own feelings), to others (being able to disclose these feelings discreetly) and to the world around us. The 'Johari Window' (Luft, 1970) is a helpful device for analysing and working on this problem.

The Johari Window (Figure 4.4) is used for increasing personal and interpersonal awareness. It comprises four quadrants:

Quadrant 1: the *free* and *open* area refers to behaviour known to self and to others.
Quadrant 2: the *blind* area, refers to things about us that others can see but of which we are unaware.
Quadrant 3: the *avoided* or *hidden* area indicates things we prefer to keep to ourselves (hidden agendas or personal feelings).
Quadrant 4: the area of *unknown* activity represents the sort of things that are accessible neither to us nor to others, but which may eventually be

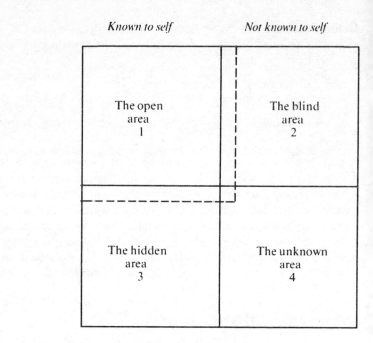

Figure 4.4   *The Johari Window*

revealed. Such behaviours and motives could have affected our relationships, without our knowing it, all along.

Luft suggests that a change in any one quadrant will affect all the other quadrants. By disclosing some of our own feelings or private experiences we expand quadrant 1 into quadrant 3. This makes it more possible for other people to let us know something about ourselves that we were unaware of, for example, 'You always smile when you're angry' which in turn expands quadrant 1 into quadrant 2. This leads to the more open form of communication indicated by the broken line. Exercises using the Johari Window may be found in Pfeiffer and Jones (1974) and Kolb, Rubin and McIntyre (1984), but it is a simple enough tool to use in any group whose members have experienced or observed each other over even a short period of time.

GIVING AND RECEIVING FEEDBACK

The following simple rules about this most sensitive area of communication are likely to promote action and change. The underlying principles are existential: 'I speak of my own experience; I cannot assume yours' and 'I own my feelings.'

Giving feedback

- Feedback is usually better when invited rather than imposed.
- Be descriptive rather than evaluative. Describing what we actually see or hear reduces the need of the receiver to react defensively.
- Reveal your own position or feelings vis-a-vis the other person: For example, 'I get very confused by your questions'.
- Be specific rather than general: for example 'That's the third time you've said one thing to me privately and another publicly.'
- Take into account the receiver's needs as well as your own.
- Direct feedback towards behaviour the receiver can change or control.
- Timing is of the essence: it is usually better to give feedback as soon as possible after the particular behaviour, though one should always take into account the social situation, the receiver's vulnerability and their readiness to listen.
- Check that the receiver has understood; if you can, get them to rephrase the feedback to see if it's what you had in mind.
- When feedback is given in a group allow giver and receiver the opportunity to check with others in the group on its accuracy.

Receiving feedback

- Listen to the person who is giving the feedback; accept what they are saying as genuine and helpful; try to understand their feelings, what they are describing and what they are suggesting you do.
- Give the feedback serious consideration, weigh up the consequences of changing or not changing, express your thoughts and feelings about alternatives.
- Communicate your decisions to the giver.
- Tell her/him what they could do which might help you to change.
- Thank the giver for their concern and help.

Feedback is probably the best way of getting evidence on the effectiveness of our communication. It enables us to learn about how others see us and about how we affect them. It is thus a vital ingredient in the process of evaluation which we shall examine in more detail in Chapter 9.

TRANSACTIONAL ANALYSIS (TA)

The 'superstructure' of the communication process is likely to be accompanied, as we have seen in Chapter 1, by a substratum of emotional forces to do with the relationships involved, whether at a conscious or unconscious level. A simple but powerful model for analysing the processes of human interaction is that devised by Eric Berne (1968) and later amplified by Thomas Harris (1973). Taking Freud's concepts as a starting point, Berne prosposes that each person comprises three basic 'selves' – the Parent, the Adult and the Child – each of which is capable of affecting the tone of communication.

These 'ego-states', as they are called, exist within each of us as a result of our early life experience. They are not – like Freud's superego, ego and id – elements of our inner world operating on each other at an unconscious level. Rather they are conscious experiences of everyday life imprinted in the person as a result of internal and external events encountered during the first few years of life. Transactional analysis addresses itself to the interaction between people, rather than to their inner psyche and is therefore more readily available for a study of relationships in teaching and learning.

The *Parent* in us acts according to how we perceived our mother, father or parental figure behaving. The Parent is often concerned with *prescribing the limits of behaviour, issuing moral edicts, teaching 'how to', protecting, nurturing* and *fostering*; and these functions are typically accompanied by the tones of voice and the non-verbal expressions which partnered them when we experienced them in their original form. For obvious reasons teaching frequently puts us in the position of behaving parentally or at least of being tempted to do so. Institutions provide a broadly parental function (and in view of this it is not surprising that young people often take it out on the physical fabric of schools and colleges). This is not to say that the functions or the Parent are instrinsically either good or bad. The important thing is that we be sufficiently aware of the Parent in ourselves so that we can use it or not (and in any case appropriately) according to our interpretation of what is happening in any transaction.

The *Adult* is that part of us which is concerned with the gathering and processing of information and with rational action in the 'real' world. It derives from the time in our childhood when we began to manipulate objects external to ourselves and to realize we could achieve something worthwhile through our own original thought. The Adult in us is ruled by reason rather than emotion; it is not however synonymous with 'mature'. The sort of functions specific to the adult are therefore the *acquiring* and *sorting* of data (even about one's Parent, Adult and Child states) and the *choosing* of alternatives and the *planning* of decision-making processes. The Adult may thus manifest itself in a variety of ways and is the side of us most concerned with analysing the very transactions it is part of.

The *Child* in us is the residue of emotional responses experienced and recorded in early childhood. These responses are essentially internal reactions to external events. The re-creation of similar events in later life is likely to trigger the corresponding reactions. There are many different 'children' within us and they experience the same feelings now as they did when we were little. Where the feeling derives from parental impositions or restrictions it is likely to be that of *frustration, anger, fear, rebelliousness* or *conformity*. Where it comes from the glorious excitement of first discoveries it is likely to connect with *curiosity, creative delight, desire to explore, spontaneity* and *trust*. Other biographical traces may also include *competitiveness* (from sibling rivalry) and *dependency*.

Each of us comprises all three ego states. None of these states is better or more important than the others. 'Appropriate' behaviour is determined by the situation, the Adult's analysis of it, and the Adult's ability to control the Parent and Child according to perceived circumstances.

Needless to say, the psychopathology of individual human beings is never as simple as this model proposes, but TA is nevertheless a convenient and, at times, telling way of analysing what goes right and wrong in human communciation. It can be important for the tutor to acquire the ability to pick up the verbal and non-verbal cues signifying the existence of a particular ego state. In the world of teaching one might come across cues of the kind shown in Figure 4.5.

Transactions

In diagrams of transactions, the ego states are commonly represented by their initial letter while communication is indicated by arrows in the appropriate direction.

A transaction is *complementary* where the ego state of the responding person is that to which the communication was directed. It is *crossed* where this correspondence is not achieved and *ulterior* where one correspondence is intended but another conveyed. (The broken line in Figure 4.6 indicates the last-named transaction.)

Verbal cues	**Non-verbal cues** (Not directly related to verbal cues)
Parent (P)	
'If I were you . . .'	Pursed lips
'There's no question . . .'	Wagging fingers
'That's ridiculous . . .'	Horrified look
'Well done . . .'	Pat on back or head
'This is the way to do it . . .'	Patronizing smile
Child (C)	
'I'd like . . .'	Delight
'I don't care . . .'	Rolling eyes
'I can't stand . . .'	Shrugging shoulders
'Wow!'	Laughter
'Oh no1'	Teasing
	Raising hand for permission to speak
Adult (A)	
'My view is . . .'	Open alertness
'In what way?'	Giving attention
'Can you say more?'	Interested look
'I think . . .'	Pensive frown
'Why, what, where, etc.'	Frowning

Figure 4.5 *Verbal and non-verbal cues in transactions*

Figure 4.6 *Complementary, crossed and ulterior transactions*

Crossed and ulterior transactions clearly lead to unsatisfied, frustrated or angry feelings. An example might illustrate these three kinds of transation.

A student comes to see his tutor: 'I don't know, I feel like giving up the course – it's all just one big muddle.' This could be intended as a (C) --> (P) communication. For there to be a *complementary* transaction, ie (P) --> (C), the tutor might respond: 'I'm sorry to hear that. Here – take a seat while I make a cup of coffee.' (Nurturing Parent) or 'Now come on, pull yourself together, nothing's that bad.' (Admonishing Parent.)

Alternatively, the tutor might say: ' I see, well it seems to me you've got the following alternatives.' Or 'OK, well what do you see as your choices?' Which would be (A) --> (A) responses. This would constitute a crossed transaction, one in which the sought correspondence is denied. It is therefore likely to be inappropriate as an initial move.

If, on the other hand, the tutor responded: 'Oh, I thought you were going to go and see the counsellor', it might well sound like an Adult response with overtones of critical Parent or even irresponsible Child. Either of these would constitute an *ulterior* transaction typically leading to a tangle of ill-feeling.

To quote another example from teaching; a student might say: 'I'm fed up, none of the articles is in the library like you said they would be.' (C) --> (C), or (C) --> (P).

The tutor could reply either: 'If you were a bit quicker off the mark there would be no problem.' (P) --> (C). Or 'I've got a few copies here you can have.' (A) --> (C). Or 'That's not my fault.' (C) --> (C).

It is typical and proper that teaching should function a great deal at the Parent level. Education does after all involve the setting of standards, advising, guiding, fostering and so forth, but there is always the danger that teachers will direct such transactions indiscriminately to the student as 'Child' rather than providing open choices appropriate to a given situation. A generalized Parent-like posture can easily produce in students a corresponding Childlike response which in turn confirms the original Parental status.

Transactional analysis includes in its orbit several other useful ideas for teaching and learning. For example, Harris (1973) has expanded Berne's original scheme of transactions to include the following 'life positions'.

I'm not OK - You're OK
I'm not OK - You're not OK
I'm OK - You're not OK
I'm OK - You're OK

and these are likely to determine the quality of the Parent–Adult–Child transactions. Many instances of these in education will doubtless spring to the mind of the reader. Needless to say it is the last transaction, 'I'm OK, you're OK', which is the most healthy and creative, though least often encountered.

Another useful TA concept is that of *strokes*. Strokes are the recognition of someone else's existence. Everyone needs them. They are *positive* strokes such as 'Hello John, how nice to see you, come in' or, the sort of knowing wink which evokes a sense of 'I'm OK, you're OK'. Equally there are *negative* strokes like 'I'm not interested in what you want' or the avoidance of eye contact which creates a feeling of 'I'm OK, you're not OK'; *conditional* strokes such as 'I'd be happier if you could come and see me some other time of day'; and *unconditional* ones: 'It's terrific working with you' or 'You look very smart today'. Transactional analysis considers strokes to be necessary for one's emotional well-being. The ability to give as well as to receive unconditional and positive strokes is an important social skill.

One of the strongest and boldest claims that TA brings to the world of human relationships is the belief that people, through self-awareness, are able to change themselves and develop their potential to change others. By recognizing what can cause hurt, misunderstanding and frustration in relationships they are better able to break out of unproductive communication and bring more creativity, enjoyment and freedom into their social environment. This is a large claim and one which needs careful examination through both practice and research. Nevertheless, TA certainly provides a valuable explanatory framework for human interaction, one to which it is easy to relate and to develop in everyday communication.

DISCUSSION POINTS

- What barriers to communication do you notice in (a) your everyday life; (b) your work generally; and (c) groups which you belong to or lead? How do they arise and how might you tackle them?
- What kind of transactions seem to govern your relationships in the various groups you belong to? How does this work out (a) for you; and (b) for the group?
- To what extent do members really listen to each other in the group? Propose a procedure for encouraging more effective listening in your group.
- Are there members of the group who talk more to each other than the rest? Draw a diagram of the most typical flows of communication and compare yours with those of other group members.

5 Aims and Objectives of Learning Groups

Groups in the wider context (the focus of Chapter 2) form and are formed for many purposes: pooling resources, making decisions, mutual support, sharing ideas, creating something, to name but a few. Though the learning group may share some of these procedures to varying degrees, it has two additional distinguishing features. First, the group members are (generally) drawing on knowledge from outside the group in order to process it within, and subsequently use it outside. Second, and this is a particular feature of the traditional seminar, the group includes someone (the tutor) who is responsible for both selecting the external knowledge, supervising its processing in the group *and* checking its use beyond the end of the group through some form of assessment.

This prompts three questions to bear in mind for this chapter:

- To what extent do learning groups have to involve a procession of knowledge from outside to inside and outside again?
- Does it have to be the tutor who controls the input, processing and output of knowledge?
- What can the learning group in its academic world incorporate from the aims and purposes of other kinds of group?

Before we look at these questions, however, let us consider what aims, and educational aims in particular, are all about.

Educational aims seem to appear more often in course documents than in discussion between tutors and students. As a public statement of values, they reflect what teachers, and those who influence them, claim to prize in what they principally do. Some of these values may relate to personal qualities like social skills, or intellectual discipline, and may reach across many fields of study; others are more specific to a subject area and represent what is regarded as important as subject matter for the syllabus.

Several writers have described the use of aims and objectives as instruments of course design (see Taba 1962, Wheeler 1967, Rowntree 1978 and Stenhouse 1975, for instance), and this is not the place to get involved in the weighty arguments of curriculum theory. However, as group discussion is an important part of tertiary education, it is appropriate to examine questions about the place of aims in small group teaching. Such questions as *'What are aims and objectives?'*, *'Where do they come from?'*, *'Why bother to specify them, especially in group teaching?'*, *'What are typical aims for groups?'* and *'How can we make sense of them in terms of classroom practice?'*.

THE NATURE OF AIMS

Teaching and learning are purposeful human activities. That is to say, they may be described in terms of what we as teachers or learners believe we are doing or what we intend to achieve by what we are doing. Of course, as we carry out our day-to-day work we are not always conscious of our intentions or of what our actions achieve. Sometimes we employ, out of habit, a strategy whose origins and true functions are lost in the mists of time; or we imitate what we have seen others do without questioning its value or purpose. In some cases it seems that a teaching procedure exists purely because teachers and students expect it to be there – it has become a time-honoured ritual – and that any attempt to change it will be doomed to failure. The traditional seminar, for instance, comprising groups of ten to 20 students discussing critical summaries presented by one of them may fall into that category. It is used because it is used. Nevertheless, aims are implicit (albeit obscurely) in all teaching procedures and there is no doubt that many students value seminars as a learning technique (see NUS, 1969.)

Aims, where expressed, serve to focus attention on the direction of teaching and act as a reference point in our choice of what we teach. In the words of Dewey (1944), the aim as a 'foreseen end':

- involves careful observation of the given conditions to see what means are available for reaching that end and to discover hindrances in the way;
- suggests the proper order or sequences in the use of means;
- makes choice of alternatives possible.

If we do not make such aims explicit, and therefore negotiable, then participants in a group discussion may be following their own hidden agendas and lacking any common frame of reference. The function of aims therefore may be not only to help establish a direction in learning but to clarify the opportunities offered by a situation. It may also lead to a better sense of collaboration among the group in achieving the aims.

INTRINSIC AND EXTRINSIC AIMS

Some of the aims of group discussion may be viewed as outcomes; they are about what the group may be expected to achieve as a result of the discussion. In this sense they are extrinsic to the process and might possibly be realized by other teaching methods. Such an aim might be 'to attain a deeper understanding of educational theory'.

However, other aims (and these are frequently the most highly valued) are *intrinsic* to the processes: the end is also the means. For instance, if the concern in science education is 'to develop an enquiring attitude towards environmental phenomena' then this, unlike the acquisition of theories, principles and concepts may be achieved only through practising the processes of enquiry and through repeated emphasis on the requisite attitude of mind. A student might make an optimistic attempt at acquiring such skills and attitudes through guided reading, programmed learning and the like, but this would be learning only in the conventional sense: 'learning about' rather than 'learning to be'. It is likely that students would not become committed to these processes without the rigour and incentive of group interaction.

Many of the accepted aims of higher education are of an 'intrinsic' nature:

- developing imaginative and creative thinking;
- developing a critical and informed mind;
- developing an awareness of others' interests and needs;
- developing a sense of academic rigour;
- developing a social conscience;
- developing an ability, and sense of enjoyment, in lifelong learning.

All of these aims have two things in common:

1. They appear to be of more personal interest to both student and tutor than is the acquisition of knowledge and may thus have a greater long-term value.
2. They are processes which are experienced mostly if not totally within well-organized discussion groups.

The aims of group techniques are therefore among the most central aims of tertiary education. Nevertheless, there is no clear way of knowing when a student has achieved the aims, or of measuring their attainment. Perhaps the best that can be said for them in terms of 'behavioural' principles is that the students have been given maximum exposure to the experiences implied by them.

AIMS VIS-À-VIS OBJECTIVES

Objectives are commonly distinguished from aims through their emphasis on what is called 'terminal' behaviour. Where aims in essence indicate broad directions for teaching, are closely related to values and learning processes, and are impossible to pin down in a measurable form, objectives are generally taken to be descriptions of what a student should be able to do by the end of a learning occasion. Though objectives give no indication of how they are to be attained, the achievement of objectives should in principle be measurable.

An example of the distinction between aims and objectives comes from the Open University Course Unit T100/26. One particular aim is 'to discuss methods of objective measurement and subjective assessment of external noise' and two of the objectives arising from this are that students should be able to 'list some physical measurements that may be made on any noise, that distinguish between noises, and that are related to subjective reaction', and to, 'carry out measurements of background levels using the sound indicator'.

Objectives may therefore be similar if not identical to assessment questions. They are also part of what some educationalists would call a rational and systematic approach to the curriculum. Teaching, so the argument for specifying objectives runs, is a rational activity, and one of the conditions of rational activity is the conscious pursuit of a goal or objective. To satisfy the needs of a well-designed course, one must specify an objective, choose the means of achieving it and then measure this achievement so as to evaluate the effectiveness of the strategy.

Objectives, in these terms, constitute a translation of aims into specific behaviours. Aims must necessarily precede objectives even if only in an implicit sense, and serve to guide them. 'Aims provide the ethical standards against which objectives are judged' (Rowntree 1978). Objectives also give us some clues about tasks for so-called 'structured' groups (see pages 84–7 and Wilson, 1980).

THE PLACE OF AIMS AND OBJECTIVES IN GROUP TEACHING

While it is perfectly logical to set objectives, human activity does not in reality follow such a rational pattern. People tend to act on inspiration, on intuitive shifts and changes, and to respond spontaneously to the immediate situation. Nowhere are these unpredictable factors more evident than in discussion groups.

The pursuit of a specific objective in a group discussion could also destroy the possibility of achieving many other equally valuable aims such as those to do with creative thinking, autonomy or democratic learning. In other words, for the educational experience in a group to be valuable, the student must enjoy the freedom to question, to disagree, and to make interpretations and this may take the individual and the group in a direction other than that which was intended by the tutor or the course planner – or the examiner. In the experience of many tutors, what continually happens is that, to quote Pring (1973), 'one's conception of the enquiry or activity is altered in the very pursuit of it . . . the ends in view are constantly changing as one gets nearer them'.

Group discussion is more of a conversation than a one-way programme. What is more, there are few rational connections between means and ends, except where, as previously indicated, the two are coincident. Even if it were possible to select a method to achieve a particular objective, other concomitants such as the group mood, tutor/student relationships or contextual issues like the proximity of examinations could frustrate the intentions of the tutor. This is part of the problem of selecting educational objectives as if they existed prior to and independent of the students and, more importantly, of the group upon whose very existence and energy their achievement rests.

On the other hand, the specifying of aims can provide an intentional framework in which intuitive and spontaneous changes can be made. It enables tutors and students both separately and together to discuss the desirability of a set of aims (and their hidden values). Aims and the means of achieving them can thus be negotiated in the interests of all concerned, and a versatile tutor can propose alternative approaches. All this should contribute to a sense of shared responsibility for learning, particularly because it focuses attention on what the student learns rather than what the tutor knows but also because it releases the students from an over-reliance on the tutor's agenda. In these ways, the expressing, sharing and negotiating of aims in group teaching help to achieve a further aim – that of creating a sense of self-direction in learning.

Nowhere is this more important than in science and technology where mastery of content is often stressed as an end in itself, and little is done to help the student relate to personal goals and frames of reference.

If and when choice *is* exercised in the curriculum it is usually by the tutor. The students are deemed unqualified to select what is to be learned – or how. It may well be, as Entwistle (1981) suggests, that students tend to specialize in subjects where the teachers suit their own personality and patterns of abilities. Yet, as we have seen on pages 45 to 49, there is a contradiction in students being presented with an implacable intellectual authority in subject areas (eg science and technology) where our understanding of the world and the techniques for harnessing its forces are in a constant state of evolution and even revolution (see Kuhn 1973), where change is the only stable factor.

The acceptability of (the vaguer) aims rather than (the more specific) objectives is based firmly on the assumption that the nature of group discussion is discursive and open-ended. However, in science subjects, there are also aims connected with 'mastering the substance of a curriculum', helping students to achieve a firm grasp of principles through discussing them and learning to communicate in the 'language' of the subject. Certain specific content objectives (like those listed on pages 65–6) will be highly relevant to a science course, and these may not be negotiable because of inflexible requirements of the assessment system. Abercrombie (1979) described Blunt and Blizzard's (1973) approach to this problem in an anatomy course where, at each tutorial, student groups were given a set of exercises related to a general objective and its accompanying specific objectives; assessment was closely related to these objectives and indicated the depth of study involved.

Here the idea of setting objectives is applied in an original way, using the group process as a source of motivation. Yet there is a danger that students learning in this way may be exposed to an excessively serialist style of teaching (see page 45). Perhaps the most suitable way of avoiding this tendency to serialism is to use the associative discussion method (pages 107–9) in which students are expected to regard their evidence and arguments critically.

Of course, it is debatable whether this approach is a case of using group process to achieve individual content aims, or of using subject matter as material for learning more sophisticated aims: aims such as 'awareness of others' interests and needs' and 'a willingness to share ideas' or 'the application of interpersonal skills'. In one sense, the task is the means to the end of group process aims; in another, the group process helps the completion of the task.

There are two further circumstances in which the specification of objectives may be particularly valuable for group work. One is where the students undertake a personal or peer responsibility for the conduct of their own work. In some cases this can lead to their assessing their own work. Syndicates and peer tutoring cells (see Chapter 6) may be given a direction by the tutor's specifying objectives for this sort of work. The other is in projects or other self-directed work where students may be encouraged to develop their own individual objectives in groups and thereafter pursue them with group support (see page 162, 'Student planning in the Dip. HE'). In both these cases, the specification of objectives may be seen as a way of investing the authority of the absent tutor in a set of guidelines and standards. Knowles (1986) described a study of personal learning contract in which students decide their own learning needs, strategies for achieving them, evidence of their accomplishment, and criteria and means of evaluating them. The development of the contract is facilitated by the tutor who encourages the students to use various combinations of teamwork in pursuit of their goals.

SOURCES OF EDUCATIONAL AIMS

In general, educational aims are based upon people's conception of what it is to be educated and on the notion of some sort of professional person – 'the engineer', 'the historian', 'the sociologist', etc. Such aims may be described as instrumental or vocational. However, there are others which are essentially part of the educational process itself – the so-called 'intrinsic' aims. The various sources of aims for group work in higher education are depicted in Figure 5.1.

Three basic sources can be identified:

- Society: which includes the personal background of both tutor and students as well as the wider community.
- Students: who draw upon their own background and on their perception of the outside world.
- Tutors: whose aims derive from similar sources to those of the students but who are strongly influenced by the climate of learning in the educational setting.

Although a simplified model, Figure 5.1 is capable of more complex reading. Not only can the aims be seen to originate from *students*, *tutors* and *society* but there are several which occur either through the movement from one source to another or from the direct interaction of one with another – indeed from a belief held by one about the other. For instance, the value of working in small groups derives from a notion that human beings are social animals: most people start their life in

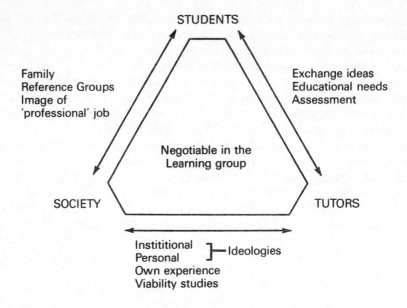

Figure 5.1 *Sources of aims for group work*

small groups, in the family unit, and there is therefore something natural about discussion in groups. Such aims are transported by *students* from *society* into the educational setting. Conversely, the development of teamwork skills derives from the projected movement of students from the educational setting into society.

Let us look now at the base of the triangle. Some of the post-war universities in the UK have been designed both administratively and educationally to give pre-eminence, or at least greater emphasis, to small group work. In some cases, this policy has arisen from a desire expressed in policy documents HMSO (1963) and HMSO (1964) for a change from the old educational order. In other cases it seems that academics have felt the need for students to learn in a democratic environment where critical issues can be faced more openly.

Along the right-hand side of the triangle there are aims which are purely to do with educational needs; those for instance concerned with gaining feedback on student progress, the tutor and student each seeing how the other views the world, and so on. In addition, there are aims and ideas which, although initiated by the tutor, may be modified through interaction with students in group work. An example of this could be the tutor's wish to develop the students' skills in analysing a piece of ecological evidence where the students are more concerned with the ethical considerations of it. Aims like these lie in the open centre of the diagram. It would be comfortable to think that all these aims are naturally subject to a continuing, if not always conscious, revision, as the parties involved identify and reflect on all the contributing sources and the values they imply.

However, aims and their inherent values are not often made explicit. The intellectual rarefaction for which academic life is popularly caricatured may set in, with a consequent risk that the institution will increasingly succumb to the 'ivory tower' syndrome. This could be the result of tutors equating their proper subject expertise with 'knowing what is best for the students' or failing to negotiate their beliefs and values with the flux of ideas deriving from the outside world as it is mediated by the students and through contact with the outside world.

Tutors are often reluctant to make the aims of their teaching explicit, whether because their hidden power is thereby diminished or simply because they feel threatened by change. Small group discussion involves a critical interchange of ideas, opinions, values and judgements. One of the essential elements in any form of education which purports to be adaptable and sensitive to the changes in a rapidly changing world is that the values and judgements implied by educational aims should also be open to discussion.

Another source of aims and objectives for the group tutor can be found in educational theory. Bloom, in what has become a classic educational text (1956, 1964), classified objectives into two basic divisions: knowledge and intellectual skills; and the development of attitudes. Clearly, when it comes to the process of learning, it is impossible to discriminate between these categories of behaviour. Skill is required to learn a piece of knowledge, to apply it or to write about it, and our attitude to both knowledge and its application in a particular environment is important in determining how well we perform these operations or indeed whether we do them at all.

In the UTMU (1978) book *Improving Teaching in Higher Education*, Bloom's classification has been written as a set of associated verbs:

Knowledge: write; state; recall; recognise; select; reproduce; measure.
Comprehension: identify; illustrate; represent; formulate; explain; contrast.
Application: predict; select; assess; find; show; use; construct; compute.
Analysis: select; compare; separate; differentiate; contrast; break down.
Synthesis: summarise; argue; relate; precise; organise; generalise; conclude.
Evaluation: judge; evaluate; support; attack; avoid; select; recognise; criticise.

While we may sometimes feel that the specification of desired behaviour can be an intolerable constraint on the 'democratic' processes of group discussion, a list such as this could provide tutors with a useful focus on two counts:

- each could form an operative verb in the instructions for a group task;
- a tutor could develop a repertoire of questions based on these verbs to have 'up his sleeve' and draw out as spontaneously as possible during the progress of a discussion. For instance the verb 'summarize' might suggest an intervention from the tutor like, 'Would anyone like to put all that together now?' (See page 77 onwards for further proposals on tutor interventions).

WHAT ARE LEARNING GROUPS FOR?

> No-one says anything. You've prepared a lot of work and then find it's taken over by the tutor. Some just talk for two hours solid. You learn to switch off after a while.

Some tutors, as the above student would seem to confirm, regard group work as little more than an extension to the lecture. The so-called seminar takes the form of a monologue in which the tutor expounds the ideas which he or she has been unable to complete or treat in such detail in a lecture. Other tutors, mainly in science and engineering, regard the tutorial discussion as an opportunity to clear up misunderstandings from a lecture; this is perhaps important but could be little more than a compensation for the inadequacies of the lecture method. Still other tutors, more especially in the arts and social sciences, see the seminar as an opportunity for intellectual analysis and the making of critical judgements about the subject, and yet have little concern for the social and emotional aspects of group discussion. Groups run in this manner tend to be highly intellectual and competitive and they frequently descend into an exercise in point scoring (see the student view of seminars on pages 88–90).

Whatever the overt intentions of group work, there is little doubt that learning groups serve purposes other than those stated. Small group discussion provides the opportunity for students not merely to engage in intellectual discourse but also to create a social 'family' to which they can belong and become identified with. It also allows students to learn ways of communicating their thoughts, and occasionally feelings, and of gauging their understanding of subject matter firstly by expressing it and secondly by comparing it with the understanding of their peers. Clearly, the atmosphere in the group will determine whether this can be conducted in an open and co-operative manner as opposed to a closed and competitive one.

How do learning groups compare with the generally accepted basic functions of groups? In terms of group dynamics, the two major areas of aims are those concerned with task and with maintenance. In the academic context, 'task' aims will usually be the so-called intellectual ones such as the exercise of critical judgement, the ability to analyse statements and cases and to question underlying assumptions and values. They will also include those of a pastoral or remedial nature, such as recognizing when students are in difficulties, checking for misunderstandings in reading or lectures, and so on.

Group maintenance, on the other hand, will include aims like creating a sense of belonging in an otherwise anonymous institution, generating a sense of trust and openness, handling conflict in a constructive way and so forth. Maintenance aims may be said to facilitate or underpin task aims. However, 'maintenance', as in its more normal usage, implies repeated attention and adjustment to the running of the group if the task is going to be achieved. Readers may also recall, from the section on group behaviour (pages 18–20), that maintenance aims become increasingly more relevant as the size of the group increases. It is quite common for instance for small groups of three and four to work on a task without concern about who is doing what or any formal leadership role being needed; where a class is divided into small sub-groups (see pages 84–7) the maintenance problem is very much subsumed to the task. However, in a larger group, the opposite is frequently the case. If the task aims are to be achieved, either members of the group must be extremely aware of the dynamic processes within it and be skilled in handlng these, or the tutor himself must take on a firm leadership role.

It will be seen, therefore, that in a large group, certainly one in excess of seven members, the problems of agreeing on how to set about the task and how the distribution of responsibilities within the group should be made will take a predominant role (at least in the early stages) before the group can set about its academic task. Of course it is always possible, especially in the social sciences, for the task and the maintenance aims to be combined. For instance, the explicit task of the group could be to examine the processes of social differentiation or of leadership within the group (though this can become a very difficult and confusing activity to students who are not fully aware of the processes in which they are involved).

TYPICAL AIMS FOR LEARNING GROUPS

It may be important to distinguish between the aims which are achievable by a learning group as a group and those which are principally achieved through the application of the sort of special techniques described in the next chapter. As we have already seen, some group aims of the former kind, the more personal, social and emotional ones, go largely unrecognized. Whether tutors are aware of them or not, however, they will be advanced to some extent in any competently led group. The range of maintenance or socio-emotional aims is well summarized in UTMU (1978):

> Some staff may feel that the emotional welfare of their students really hasn't got much to do with their small group teaching, the essential purpose of which they say is to make sure that students have really understood what they have been trying to get across in lectures. Careful questioning, they argue, can bring out the major misunderstandings and difficulties and many of these can be dealt with by the teacher in a way in which he can be sure that the students have really understood. Under the extreme pressures often felt by both students and staff to cover the ground effectively, such a view of the main purpose of group work is very understandable. But if this purpose is pursued vigorously and efficiently, it may also mean that other purposes will not merely be ignored but will be actively discouraged. Strategies which may produce effective learning within the highly structured formal education system can leave students with little ability, or even desire, to cope with learning and relearning when they leave the formal supportive structures of higher education behind them. Nevertheless, work there will be in structures of a different kind and many professionals now find themselves working in teams.
>
> It could be said therefore that an important function of group work in higher education is to enable students to know enough about themselves and about others to enable them to work independently and yet co-operatively within a team. Such teams may or may not have formal leaders, but the style of leadership is likely to be very different from that of the more traditional seminar leader who controls the activity of the class in such a way

that students learn to feel little responsibility for what happens in the group beyond doing required background reading.

The group experience can, in fact, be extremely important in achieving freedom from dependency if the students learn to play a variety of roles in the group and begin to develop a sense of responsibility for its success or failure. In the process of learning these roles they will need to develop more acute self-understanding, to become aware of their own inhibitions, defences and assumptions, and be able to recognise the difficulties which other students have and begin to help them to overcome them. In learning to become more sensitive to different points of view and ways of thinking and to work co-operatively with others using the varied skills of the group, they may begin to develop a surer sense of social identity, and a feeling of belonging and commitment. This can encourage not only enthusiasm in the subject but a willingness to reveal abilities which are so often effectively hidden, even from themselves. Students' oral skills, moreover, are unlikely to develop very highly simply in response to probing questions.

There needs to be a genuine sense of opportunity for self-expression and this may be very difficult in a context where the main object is to increase understanding and correct misconceptions and faulty reasoning.

There is plenty of evidence both from research and experience that groups of all kinds operate at both a *task* and a *socio-emotional* level. If we look at groups in an academic context we can see that they can also be viewed as functioning within both *intrinsic* and *extrinsic* dimensions (see page 63). Figure 5.2 demonstrates the interrelationships between these four aspects in a matrix format.

The tendency in tertiary education is to give least attention to the intrinsic dimension. Teaching is often solution-orientated rather than problem-orientated and seems to take external requirements as its starting point rather than the needs and interests of the students. Moreover, a lack of attention to the socio-emotional dimension means that many of the task aims cannot be achieved. Without a climate of trust and co-operation, students will not feel like taking the risk of making mistakes and learning from them. To achieve this, the tutor would have to balance a concern for academic standards with a capacity to understand and deal with the workings of group process as well as an attitude of generosity and praise for new solutions to old problems.

The students might correspondingly applaud their tutor's resourcefulness in introducing them to new experiences in group learning.

If, finally, we return to the question posed at the start of the chapter, it will be evident that learning groups are amenable to a much wider range of aims than is commonly supposed and that many of these bear a similarity to the aims and outcomes of groups in the wider world. Insofar as learning groups comprise a meeting of human beings with some shared goals, it seems probable that processes like pooling resources, making decisions, gaining mutual support, sharing ideas, creating something and so on would always exist in the process, at least subliminally. Yet if they could be made more explicit, perhaps by incorporating them into more practical, real-world tasks, not only might they create more stimulation and variety of opportunity in learning for students but also develop their awareness of group and teamwork concerns for their future careers.

	Task	Socio-emotional
I	Expressing selves in subject	Greater sensitivity to others
N		
T	Judging ideas in relation to others	Judging self in relation to others
R		
I	Examining assumptions	Encouraging self-confidence
N	Listening attentively	Personal development
S		
I	Tolerating ambiguity	Tolerating ambiguity
C	Learning about groups	Awareness of others' strengths and weaknesses
E		
X	Follow-up to lecture	Giving support
T	Understanding text	Stimulating to further work
R		
I	Improving staff/ student relations	Evaluating student feelings about course
N		
S	Gauging student progress	Giving students identifiable groups to belong to
I	Giving guidance	
C		

Figure 5.2 *Types of aims and purposes in group teaching*

These practical aims have nevertheless to be converted into acceptable and realistic activities in the classroom. This is the central concern of the next chapter.

DISCUSSION POINTS

- What kinds of discrepancies appear to exist between the express aims of groups you belong to, or lead, and what actually happens? How do they arise?
- Draw up a chart like Figure 5.2 for the aims of your own group(s). To what extent do they vary within the group or between groups? What values and assumptions lie behind the aims?
- How do you think the aims of your group relate to:
  (a) the broader aims of your course?
  (b) what is actually assessed on the course?

6 Tasks and Techniques

If aims and objectives are to represent a bit more than good intentions, they must, as we have already discussed, be related to corresponding *tasks* and *techniques*; each of these demands of the tutor particular skills and the playing of a special role. Tasks specify the activities in which the students individually or collectively are engaged, whether it is to do with a process like 'observe the behaviour of a white rat' or an end-product like 'list ten issues that strike you as important and rank them'. *Techniques* are the ensemble of tasks, rules and procedures which comprise a coherent educational experience. In order to establish and maintain a task or technique, a tutor needs both imagination and skill in prescribing the structure, monitoring what is happening, gently enforcing rules or adjusting them to advantage, and avoiding the risk of being drawn into the sort of relationship with the group which could subvert the purpose of the exercise. Here is an example of the way aims, tasks, techniques and roles might fit together:

Aim: To develop students' awareness of different strategies for solving problems.

A suitable set of group tasks might be:

- to try and solve a given problem;
- to monitor the strategies involved;
- to share the findings and compare them with research evidence;
- to draw up a classification of the findings.

A technique or procedure which could match this might be to organize sub-groups with observers in a 'fishbowl' layout (see page 173). The tutor's job would be to prepare any materials, explain and check agreement on the tasks, monitor their development and control time boundaries.

SETTING TASKS

As already explained, students are often unsure about what to do in groups and might well take up the pursuit of separate individual goals while ostensibly engaged in collaborative discussion. In the traditional seminar the very vagueness of the task often means that students fail to get their teeth into anything substantial and end up with a feeling of dissatisfaction. They are unsure about whether they have achieved anything or even what it was they were supposed to achieve. After several meetings the task might become clear to them, but even then it may well be diffuse and perceived differently by each student. What is more, the rules or conventions of behaviour may not be explicit and may possibly be unrelated to the task. There seems to be tacit confusion about all sorts of things and this creates uncertainty and stress.

Stenhouse (1972) suggests that students evolve a secondary task of their own, which is to study the tutor's behaviour in order to understand the situation in which they find themselves. If this muddled situation is to be avoided, it is important for the tutor to make the task, and her/his role in relation to it, explicit. For a large class working in sub-groups or where students have to do work outside the classroom, it is essential if confusion is to be avoided that the task be carefully worded and written out. On other occasions it may be better to negotiate a task with the group, especially where this is the first time it has been tried.

SOURCES OF TASKS

By placing the emphasis on task, the tutor can partly sidestep the ever-present problem of authority and dependency in the group. In setting a task for a group the tutor assumes authority in order to delegate it to the group in getting on with the task. The tutor may organize any structuring of sub-groups, set time limits, confine his or her authority to a position which is set by agreed rules and procedures, monitor what is happening and make consequent adjustments.

Having set the task the tutor may monitor the work of the sub-groups to check that it is making sense to them and be ready to change or adjust the task to one which is more relevant to the immediate concerns of the group. Sometimes ideas for such changes occur spontaneously with remarkable results. Abercrombie (1979) reports the experience of Felicity Baker (1974) who converted the uninspiring experience of a group studying French prose into a 'small new awakening' by giving responsibility to the students for the assessment of each other's work as a group task.

Boredom in a group can often be relieved by a change of task and with remarkable results. The boredom may be due to a lack of 'grounding' in the discussion: that is, it is not rooted in the personal experience of the students. The sort of real-life process encountered in case study, role play, or marking each other's essays can reactivate the dormant energy of the group. On the other hand, the boredom may comprise no more than subdued anger which can arise from the group being trapped in an authority/dependency tangle (see pages 15 & 17), and a tutor may be wise to spend time getting the group to look at its assumptions about the teaching/learning relationship.

The problem of how to relate group discussion to personal experience or real-life

processes is discussed by Parker and Rubin (1966) who argue strongly for the introduction of real-world experiences (as opposed to academic artefacts) in the classroom. One model they suggest for this purpose comprises four stages:

1. Creating and acquiring knowledge: students observe phenomena, read exposi-
   tory material, collect evidence and listen to presentations.
2. Interpreting knowledge: students derive meaning from what they have
   learned; they relate new knowledge to old. The necessary skills include analysing, reorganizing and experimenting with information and relating it together.
3. Attaching significance and communicating knowledge: students infer generalizations, relate information to new situations and learn or reorganize the information in new ways. These activities precede communication.
4. Applying knowledge: students use information to recognize, clarify and solve
   problems.

Several of these processes could be converted into group tasks and elaborated as
the discussion progresses. Parker and Rubin's approach reminds us that we can
learn a lot about ways of education by considering 'natural' activities in the outside
world. Many of the tasks and techniques listed on the following pages are derived
in this way.

It is worth mentioning here that, while any task or technique may embody a
unique complex of aims and objectives, any one aim could be achieved by a number of
tasks or techniques. Tutors who can build a repertoire of tasks and techniques should
thus find themselves more versatile in the pursuit of all sorts of aims.

TYPES OF TASK

The possibilities and permutations of tasks are endless. All we can do here is look
at some broad categories and suggest some specific examples.

Tasks for groups as a whole, or sub-groups

- *Argue* with tutor/students – disputation.
- *Discuss* presentation.
- *Discuss* misunderstandings.
- *Draw up a list* of similarities and differences.
- *List* items from experience.
- *List* items from observation in group.
- *List* items from reading.
- *Mark* own or each other's essays.
- *Set criteria* for essay marking.
- *Generate* ideas.
- *Make* categories.
- *Clarify problem*/solve it/evaluate it.

- *Enact*.
- *Discuss* critically.
- *Diagnose*.
- *Argue* relative merits.
- *Share* anxieties.
- *Share* essay plans.
- *Share* study methods.
- *Watch* video.
- *Read and evaluate* text.
- *Report back* on previous session (see page 174).

Tasks for individuals followed by discussion in groups

- *Mark off* checklist.
- *Rank* or *rate* and *compare* values.
- *Make desisions/proposals* about case.
- *Construct* model, etc.
- *Observe* group process.
- *Make* choices.
- *Analyse* text.
- *Allocate* individual tasks –project work.
- *Suggest* thesis and argue it.
- *Solve* problem.

Tasks for peer tutoring (see page 95–6)

- *Teach*.
- *Question* to check learning.
- *Prepare* questions.
- *Prepare* tasks.
- *Counsel*.

Resourceful tutors will doubtless dream up a host of other tasks as they consider the ways in which knowledge in their subject is created, interpreted, communicated and applied.

STRUCTURING TASKS

As we have already seen, large groups (ten or over) find some difficulty in working cohesively on a task and will tend to split into sub-groups unless held together by strong leadership. When it is important to mobilize a sense of commitment and immediate purpose among a largish group of students, therefore, it may be sensible to capitalize on the group's desire to divide into smaller units by 'doing what comes naturally'. As tutors, we might for example invite the students first to work individually on a listing task for five minutes, share their ideas in pairs for ten minutes and finally, in groups of four to six, write up categories on a large sheet of paper followed by 25 minutes of open discussion between groups. We could explain our role as that of wandering round to check that everyone understands and accepts the task and is doing it in an appropriate way, and to help students in formulating categories. The nature of the students' encounter with each other would thus vary over a period of time, and with each change would come a different kind of learning experience.

The *skills* required of the tutor in setting up these 'task-oriented' groups differ somewhat from those required in tutor-led groups. They are more to do with a considered negotiation of a mutual contract than a sensitive response to the unfolding group process. These skills are discussed in more detail in Chapter 7.

Group tasks alone do not lead to integrated learning. They have to be co-ordinated into a schema which not only pinpoints roles and relationships within the group, but also puts them in a valid and coherent learning sequence. Though the following task from Nisbet (1966), and quoted in Rudduck (1978), is elaborate, it is a nice example of such integration. The amount of detail thought necessary may be an indication of the number of pitfalls inherent in the traditional seminar which must consciously be avoided if new structures are to take shape. The course is in theory of education.

Each student chooses a field of study and has a two-and-a-bit meetings in which to complete the task. At the introduction meeting, the tutor explains the procedure. Within each field the student responsible must first *produce six statements worth making*. What this involves has to be clearly understood: a 'statement worth making' (worth making, that is, in the context of this seminar) is one which is clear, succinct and important; which is controversial enough to require careful decisions before it is accepted or rejected; and which represents the personal belief, based on study, experience and reflection, of its author. To put it negatively, statements not worth making are high-sounding platitudes, trivialities, vague abstractions whose acceptance or rejection would make no observable difference in practice, disingenuous 'OK' phrases, inadequately grounded opinions, or assertions that no one is likely to dispute. Each statement must consist of only a single sentence but the author will in due course be given every opportunity of providing supplementary details and explaining why he chose to formulate each statement in its present form. No attempt must be made to 'cover' the whole field. The six chosen are to be regarded as a selection from the hundreds he could presumably produce in the given area of study if called upon to do so. When a student has made up his list he is expected to provide enough copies (with recommended references to relevant literature appended) to go round the group.

The second meeting begins with the distribution of the copies of Student A's statements and a short talk by that student to introduce them. The remainder of the meeting is devoted to free and informal discussion. 'Spontaneity and freedom are the characteristics of this meeting.'

At the third meeting the statements are quickly reintroduced; in an atmosphere of *discipline* and *urgency* (in contrast to the previous meeting), Student A tries:

to obtain unanimous agreement for each statement in turn. Whenever this is not immediately forthcoming he and the other group members, including the tutor, suggest
amendments which might (a) satisfy the critics and yet (b) retain the support of those
who approve the statement as it is and (c) still leave 'a statement worth making'. If, after a
long discussion, a compromise proves impossible, the dissident member(s) will be left to
compose a 'minority view' on the statement in question. Each member of the group,
including the tutor, knows that when the first is promulgated in its final form his name
will appear as one of the supporters. At the end of the meeting [Student A] takes home the
group minute book to write up the official account of the two meetings for which he has
been responsible.

These minutes are checked with the group at the beginning of the next meeting.
What seems particularly interesting here is that the task is similar to that of the
traditional seminar in which a student presents views on prior reading, yet it places
a very explicit and more comprehensive set of demands on the students. Above all,
decisions have to be made and this almost invariably draws out values and beliefs
into open conflict – they cannot in this case be avoided by mere verbal felicity. The
alternating of free and disciplined styles of discussion is a structure worth looking
at also. Too often a group vacillates between the two styles, so that the benefits of
neither are convincingly achieved.

In these seminars then, the broad ground rules for discussion are clear and
explicit (we shall return to this matter later on page 128). The role of the tutor is
also made clear:

> The method makes it easy for the tutor to sustain his rightful role ad *primus inter pares* –
> 'primus', in that he is chairman, and is responsible for the conduct of the meetings,
> occasionally supplying factual information, tactfully bringing in the less vocal members,
> keeping an eye on the clock, and exercising self-restraint by remaining silent where nec-
> essary, even when he would like to say a lot; 'inter pares' because he participates in the
> discussion on the basis of equality, criticising and being criticised, asking and answering,
> revealing his own personal values as well exploring those of the students.

These tasks, rules and roles are of vocational benefit to the students, the writers
claim. For post-graduate students (average age 27), the practice of shaping a consensus view and reconciling opposing positions has direct relevance to their professional work on committees and the like. They are also of great value to the tutor
who cannot fail to be stimulated by the flux of new and unexpected ideas and con-
frontations (see also Wilson, 1980). The above tasks emphasize processes of discussion and decision-making. Another fruitful task field is evaluation and assessment.
Students may be asked to do one of the evaluation exercises described on pages
173–6 or to assess what they have learned (in perhaps a general sense) and what
they have contributed to, and got from, the course. This latter task can be given a
keener edge by asking students to rate themselves on a numerical scale according
to agreed criteria on work or performance. These criteria can be worked out by the
class as part of the exercise. Following this, the students might rate each other and
compare their self-ratings with the mean of the peer ratings. If these are then put

alongside the assessment of the tutor, a fascinating discussion can ensue as a result of which students begin to internalize some of the criteria and standards of academic learning. This task is yet another which could equip students for more autonomous learning and self-appraisal in their subsequent careers. It also introduces the idea of triangulated assessment (self–peer–tutor) in which a degree of objectivity is obtained by having three separate judgements on the value of the student's achievement.

Clarifying tasks and roles can be enormously helpful to group project students too. Projects (in this context) consist of several successive and overlapping tasks. Choosing a problem or topic, choosing partners, researching solutions, analysing results, writing a report, doing a presentation and so on, all occur with varying degrees of overlap and weight. Pervading all of these is the task of group maintenance – how to get the best out of a collection of students with disparate experience, skills, knowledge and personal qualities. One task for the tutor in this regard is therefore to alert students to leadership issues and decision-making processes as the project progresses. Kuiper (1977) suggests an 'internal' contract for project groups which comprises aims and values on which members can agree and an 'external' one which describes the practical purpose to which the project is to be put. The external contract involves a third party possibly outside the institution whose aims and needs may differ from the educational ones required inside. We shall return to the subject of projects later in this chapter.

GAME TASKS

Making rules and procedures clear is important enough in group teaching but sometimes it is useful to introduce some imaginary scenario into the task, as in a role-play or simulation. In an engineering laboratory several years ago, I introduced three new experimental tasks:

- Dear Sirs,
  I am designing a series of submerged pipelines to cross rivers in different parts of the UK (details given). I am in urgent need of a reliable check on the forces I might expect them to withstand and would be most grateful if you could test various models in a wind tunnel in order to give me some working data. Please send me your report within three weeks from this date.
  Yours, etc.

- The first year students are currently interested in the differences between static and dynamic forces. Could you please conduct the following experiment to check on the nature and magnitude of these differences and, having undertaken suitable rewording, write out a set of explanatory notes for the first year students?

- 'The valley of Erehwon (map and relevant data enclosed) is being considered as the site of a huge new dam and reservoir. You are to divide into three professional groups: engineers, technicians and journalists. The engineers must conduct a feasibility study on

(a) dam structure;
(b) water supply; and
(c) hydro-electric power.
The technicians must determine measuring techniques for [a list of purposes given] and the journalists must compile a public relations brochure on the study. Your written reports should be submitted two days before the meeting of the study commission where they will be formally introduced and discussed.

In these three cases, and especially the last one, the rules and procedures, though not very explicit, are no longer embedded in the teacher/student relationship but are invested in understanding of everyday life *outside the educational system*, to do with the consultant/client relationship, students in a teaching role and feasibility studies respectively. Approaches like this are admirably suited to group-teaching in subject areas which have low intrinsic interest and need some imaginative boost to get them going. Games and simulations are indeed most valuable in this regard. Many examples of their use in Language Teaching are given in *Take Five* (Carrier, 1981).

However, we must not conclude that this approach lends itself only to 'remedial' purposes, where a subject is basically boring. Games and simulations appear to be of enormous benefit in developing professional, communication, and problem-solving skills, in integrating learning at different levels and across disciplines and in achieving unexpected insights into other people's views. We shall return to this topic later (page 101) but the interested reader might like to note the existence of the Society for the Advancement of Games and Simulations in Education and Training which publishes a quarterly journal containing many helpful ideas on games.

Chapter 8 provides further examples of various group tasks in the context of the curriculum.

A VARIETY OF TECHNIQUES

Thus far we have looked at aims and tasks and the educational and psychological principles that support them. When these are integrated into an established pattern of rules, roles and procedures, we have an ensemble of means – a *technique*. In this section we shall look at some of these techniques and the principal aims they are designed to serve. Subsequent chapters describe the skills required of the tutor in preparing and operating these techniques, and how they may be organized into the curriculum.

Neat classifications of social processes are generally a futile venture and make for lazy reading. The following descriptions of group techniques are therefore organized within a fairly loose framework. Any reader interested in reclassifying them according to different criteria might find it a helpful way of getting new insights into their further use. The way the various techniques are used will vary enormously from group to group. Some, like *synectics*, a creative problem-solving technique, are fairly specific in their format; others, like the seminar, are infinitely variable. Some are incorporated with others. Whichever category system one uses there are always too many exceptions.

The techniques are grouped in three categories:

- those concerned with mainly cognitive objectives (knowledge, comprehension, application, problem-solving, analysis, evaluation);
- those involving creative objectives (seeing new relationships, connecting the emotional and the intellectual, producing imaginative solutions);
- those developing individual or group awareness, personal growth, communication skills, participation and the breaking-down of interpersonal barriers.

Within each of these broad categories, there is a progression from *tutor control* to *student freedom*, though even these terms are quite clearly problematical: one of the most creative and liberating techniques, *brainstorming* has a set of fairly strict rules for discussion in the group.

The open intention of this chapter is to encourage tutors to break out of the mould of traditional seminars and tutorials and to recognize the range of variations and alternative techniques or methods they can use; techniques which are less frustrating, more enjoyable, which challenge and stimulate the minds of students and which give credit to that under-used faculty of mind – the imagination. Many of these less-than-familar techniques may be included within the bounds of what is, for timetabling purposes, called a 'seminar'. Others may need to be pursued in their own right.

The first two techniques are of particular relevance for larger groups where the communication of knowledge is clearly directed through the tutor. Others, like 'syndicates', indicate the tutor's role in relation to several groups, but say nothing about what happens within each of the syndicates. In other words, some are to do with the inner processes while others define external features. The nature of the experience in each group will in any case be determined to a large extent by the points at which control is applied and the manner of its application.

Controlled discussion

This technique is commonly used as a means of checking for knowledge and understanding of presented material. Discussion is controlled by the tutor; either students ask questions or make comments, or the tutor fires questions at students in a manner of a Socratic dialogue.

Advantages: convenient to organize at the end of (or as a follow-up to) a lecture; quick feedback; large and 'economical' number of students.
Disadvantages: inhibiting to open communication; reticent students not heard; little peer discussion.

Step-by-step discussion

Though similar to controlled discussion in its communication pattern, this tech-niques is based on a prepared text, audio or video tape that provides a sequence of subject matter. In leading the students through the sequence, the tutor draws out and guides the students' developing knowledge in discussion and, by using open-ended questioning skills (see page 135), allows students some freedom to explore the realism of their own knowledge. The input for step-by-step discussion may be a sheet of notes, or a text shared by tutor and students alike, or even a video/audio tape where a 'stop–start' procedure can be employed (see page 176). This technique brings together several of the qualities of the lecture and the seminar.

Advantages: economical use of large groups; 'authority' can be invested in shared text or tape – students not dependent on tutor for content; combines information-giving, processing and feedback aims.

Disadvantages: as for controlled discussion, but to a lesser extent; sequence and structure of discussion pre-ordained – may not correspond with students' needs.

The next four techniques are ways of achieving the same basic aims as the previous two, but within a much more 'democratic' climate.

Buzz groups

Frequently, where the group is large, there is a need for a break in the more formal proceedings in order:

* to provide a stimulating change in the locus of attention;
* for the tutor to gain some idea of what the students know;
* for the students to check their own understanding.

If, therefore, during the course of a lecture or other one-directional communication, students are asked to turn to their neighbours to discuss for just a few minutes any difficulties in understanding, to answer a prepared question, or to speculate on what they think will happen next in the proceedings, a sense of participation and some lively feedback are quickly achieved. Buzz groups enable students to express difficulties they would have been unwilling to reveal to the whole class without the initial push of being obliged to say something to their neighbours. Taken by itself, the buzz group technique has little meaning. Yet in the context of a lecture or other large group event it can rekindle all sorts of dying embers. Its incorpor-ation into a pattern of teaching events is described on pages 145 to 147.

Advantages: can be used in any teaching situation for as short or as long as desir-able; helps students and teacher check on misunderstandings; cre-ates a stimulating break.

Disadvantages: can destroy intellectual and emotional cohesion if timed wrongly.

Snowball groups (pyramiding)

Buzz groups can easily be extended into a progressive doubling in which pairs join up to form fours, then fours to eights which finally report back to plenary session. This developing pattern of group interaction is known as a 'snowball'. It is amazingly effective in ensuring comprehensive participation, especially when it starts with individuals writing their ideas in the first stage before sharing them. Lest students become bored with repeated discussion of the same points, a sequence of increasingly sophisticated tasks is often desirable (see Figure 6.1.)

Advantages: good for encouraging the creation of well-integrated ideas: allows students to think for themselves before discussing; generates full and lively participation in plenary discussion.

Disadvantages: breaks up cohesive feeling in some groups; takes time to unfold.

(1)	*Individuals*	O	Write down a list of problems in writing essays (2 minutes)
(2)	*Pairs*	O O	Share their lists with each other (5 minutes)
(3)	*Fours*	O O O O	Share lists and classify (15 minutes)
(4)	*Eights*		Propose a set of solutions and agreed intentions (20 minutes)
(5)	*Whole class*	Plenary session report back (20–30 minutes)	

Figure 6.1 *Snowball of pyramid groups*

Crossover groups

One continual problem with the division of a class into sub-groups is how to avoid a tiresome plenary session when each group reports publicly to the others. In the crossover technique, students are divided into groups such that the number in each group is approximately equal to the square root of the total number participating. There are then two (and possibly more) ways of proceeding, each requiring group members to meet at least one from each of the other groups. If we take a group of nine students organized as in Figure 6.2 and hand each a card marked A1 B2 etc as in Figure 6.2, the two distinct procedures are:

* After a given time, all suffix '2' people move to their 'home' tables (ie A2 goes to table A, B2 to table B and C2 to table C) and then, after a similar period of time, suffix '3' people move to their 'home' tables.
* At a given time all As join each other, all Bs and Cs similarly.

TABLE C

TABLE A

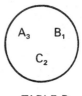

TABLE B

Figure 6.2 *Cross over groups*

Alternatively, a colour coding rather than a numerical one can be employed. The task of each student as he or she moves into a new group can be to report what has been said in the previous group before discussion in the new group proceeds. This technique is helpful in mixing a new group of students and, according to Bligh (1981), is of particular value on part-time courses where the circulation of ideas is never very rapid.

Advantages: excellent for mixing people and information; simple to organize; students enjoy it; avoids plenary discussion.
Disadvantages: can lead to confusion about learning outcomes; can break up absorbing discussions.

Horseshoe groups

This describes a way of organizing a class so that it can alternate with ease between the lecture and discussion group formats. Rather than the students facing the front in serried ranks, they are arranged around tables in a horseshoe formation with the open end facing the front as in Figure 6.3.

Figure 6.3 *Horseshoe groups*

A tutor can thus talk formally from the board for a time before switching to give the groups a task such as a problem or an interpretation; the task should of course be one demanding collaboration among the students. The horseshoe formation can be of great benefit in science and engineering exercise classes if students are given problems at the start and then the tutor circulates round the groups, listening and asking or answering questions. Should any general problem emerge, an explanation can be offered by the tutor or indeed by any student to the whole class.

Whether the groups are given identical, similar, or entirely separate problems there is always the opportunity to open up discussion of a sticky point or to ask groups to explain their solutions or decisions to each other. If a sense of inter-group competition can be infused into the situation, not only can the level of interest and work be heightened but also the cohesion in each group.

This format may also be used for syndicate meetings (see page 93).

Advantages: students can clear up misunderstandings, share uncertainties and teach each other; tutor has flexibility of talking or listening; students help each other.

Disadvantages: some students do little or nothing; tutor cannot easily identify students in difficulty (unless 'remedial' exercise set up); many 'problem' tasks not suited to group work.

Seminars

Though often presented as a formal title for a timetabled group session, the word 'seminar' is generally taken to mean a group discussion with fairly intellectual aims, led formally or informally by the tutor, and focused on issues arising from the subject matter rather than student difficulties (cf tutorials). The number of students is usually in excess of eight and less than 20; traditionally, one of them will be asked to present a critical analysis or other preparation to introduce the discussion. Seminars, and the tutors' leadership of them, have been the butt of much criticism in recent years. An education student, Treadaway (1975), described eight types of seminar which served to illustrate some of the common problems.

- The monologue or 'sitting at-the-feet of the master' type.
- The highly structured or 'I know what you want to say' type.
- The duologue or 'wrestling match' type (one bright or forceful student wants to impress the tutor and a duologue ensues on areas which no one else knows about).
- The anecdotal or 'Did I ever tell you?' type.
- The essay-reading or Oxbridge type.
- The article-summary or 'We've all read this anyway' type (if a student summarizes without making critical comment then his or her colleagues may not bother to read it; the tutor may not have read the article for years and the discussion can thus become sterile).
- The examination-cramming type (the tutor seems concerned mainly with the students passing the exam, sometimes more so than the students).
- The 'I don't believe in structured discussion' type.

Treadaway continues his analysis of seminar problems at the London Institute of Education as seen through the students' eyes:

The first necessity is that the leader of the seminar should be clear what his purpose is and should ask himself whether a seminar is actually the best way to achieve this. If his purpose is merely to impart information, to put forward a particular point of view or to cram for an examination he may, and I think probably should, decide that a seminar is not the best method for doing this. The fault of many seminars, therefore, lies in trying to use the method for purposes for which it is not suited.

The next problem is size. There is no rule, of course, but my experience both as tutor and student suggests it is difficult to have a discussion in which everyone takes part fully, if the group is larger than ten. In an hour or so, even the actual time is against you – six minutes per person is not very much to develop a serious argument. But, more important, observation in this Institute and elsewhere has shown me that a significant proportion of people find it difficult to speak easily and confidently to a larger group. This may be due to personal inhibition, unfamiliarity with the Institute, the country or the language or a combination of these. It is very noticeable, for instance, how overseas students may be silent for a whole seminar but may be leading the discussion in a small informal group afterwards. The size of the group is, of course, an administrative problem and staff/student ratios often make large groups inevitable. But, if the group is large, the answer is not, I suggest, to attempt discussion in spite of the size but to spend as much time as possible in smaller sub-groups. I have found that it is in these groups, especially when given a particular problem or project, that most learning takes place. At the same time, if the tutor feels he has particular information or ideas to put across, there is nothing wrong with spending part of the time in the larger group while the tutor gives a lecture or holds a question-and-answer session, provided he plans it as such and realises that this is different from a discussion seminar.

The second basic organisational factor is the physical one. You cannot expect a discussion if people are facing each other's backs, if they are miles apart across a huge room or table or crowded into a tutor's small room all facing his desk, or even if the room itself is dirty or cold. All these problems cannot always be solved, of course, but at least tutors should be aware of the importance of the physical arrangement and should not be surprised if discussion fails to develop when they neglect it.

The next decision is who should lead the seminar, and how. There are no rules about this, of course, and equally successful seminars can be led by tutors or students. Most tutors seem to feel, probably rightly, that it should be led by a student, as the student himself gains a great deal from having to lead it. On the other hand, few students have much experience at leading seminars and it is essential that they should be given guidance on this. This is rarely done and the result is sometimes a waste of time for the rest of the group. Whoever leads, however, the most important thing to remember is that a seminar is supposed to be a discussion. This means that the introduction should be fairly short and should deliberately raise points which will be the basis for discussion, rather than merely summarise an article or other material. The actual material for discussion should have been distributed and/or read in advance and without this a good seminar is unlikely. Sometimes, of course, the object of the seminar is to discuss a particular article. More often, however, an article or book is meant to be the *starting point* for discussion of a wider topic. If so, this should be stressed to the leader and he should be encouraged to use the article as a starting point to bring in his own viewpoint and experience. Often the seminar becomes a discussion of one article when it was supposed to cover a whole topic. It is up to the tutor to decide this, however, and to make clear to the leader what is needed. In some cases, he may have the delicate task of stopping students who go on too long or summarise rather than discuss. Many tutors, quite naturally not willing to offend, fail to do this when necessary; but is it worth destroying a whole seminar by being unwilling to risk offence to one student? Advice to all beforehand should in any case make the choice unnecessary.

The most crucial factor in a seminar is, of course, the role of the tutor. This is very difficult. He has to provide sufficient guidance and structure to give the seminar a meaningful shape without dominating it and forcing it into a shape he has predetermined. Ultimately, there are no rules and a seminar can only be guided intuitively as it progresses. The problem is that students get the impression that some tutors are not sensitive enough to the difficulties. A good seminar leader has to ask himself constantly whether he is leading too strongly or talking too much; whether everyone has made a contribution or a few students are dominating and others need to be encouraged by careful questioning; whether some time in small groups might be useful; or even whether he should withdraw altogether for a while and let the group continue on its own. An unstructured seminar is usually as unsuccessful as a tutor-dominated one. To strike the balance successfully is a difficult skill. I would suggest it really needs some definite training. I know this would have helped me considerably when I started to lead discussions amongst trainee teachers. Perhaps we too easily assume that teachers need training while tutors who teach them do not?

There may be occasions in a seminar, of course, when tutors can help best by their absence. Whether they like it or not, tutors are seen as authority figures and some people will be reluctant to speak, and perhaps show lack of understanding, when they are present. Sometimes a whole group can be inhibited in this way, with everyone silently thinking they are the only one who does not understand. I have often found, therefore, that the best way to get a discussion going is to leave the group, or even the room, for a while. Often a group who seemed to have no ideas of their own when I was present were almost at the point of fighting each other when I came back ten minutes later, and had by then gained the self-confidence to continue the discussion with my participation. There are some occasions, therefore, when a seminar, divided for at least part of the time into a number of small groups with a peripatetic tutor, works much better than a single group with the tutor present all the time.

It would be very valuable if official encouragement could be given right from the beginning of each course towards forming small informal groups for projects or discussion. It is often more useful, for instance, for a seminar to be prepared and led by a group who meet together and discuss the topic beforehand. Similarly, it is useful for groups to meet together after the seminars to follow up, practically or theoretically, some of the ideas raised by the seminar or some of their difficulties. This will usually only happen with some encouragement by the tutor.

My ideal seminar, then, would be one prepared by a small group of people who had met in advance, discussed the topic and distributed any necessary material to the whole group. They would present the topic to a group who had already read something about it and would emphasise points for discussion rather than just summarise. Depending on the size of the group there would then be discussion by the whole group or by sub-groups with the tutor moving from group to group guiding rather than leading the discussion. There would probably be a short summary at the end by the tutor or the group leaders and encouragement for those particularly interested in the topic, or with any difficulties, to get together for further discussion later.

Finally, my definition of a seminar as learning through discussion should not preclude the use of other teaching methods, where appropriate (within the boundaries of the seminar). Treadaway (1975).

Treadaway's analysis of the 'seminar experience' highlights problems about both group teaching in general and the traditional seminar. We should remember that the word seminar is as often used to describe a timetabled discussion period of any kind as it is the sort of intellectual battleground described by Treadaway. The three unconscious problems of the latter seem to be:

- the weight of academic authority and expertise invested in the tutor;
- the inability of tutors (and students) to recognize and try out alternative approaches rather than sticking with a respected tradition;
- a pervading anxiety about assessment with a consequent feeling among students that they should speak only when they have something 'safe' to say.

The seminar at a research or postgraduate level, as Bligh (1981) remarks, can be very useful, particularly when new ideas and proposals for research are being discussed. In such a case, it is a discussion among equals. Bligh is singularly critical of the seminar as a general method of teaching. He describes it as 'simply inappropriate'. Its success is dependent on too many chancy factors: the 'lead' student may not do a competent job either in preparing or presenting: the essay is often not a good way to introduce a topic for discussion; there may be collusion among the students not to criticize a colleague in front of a tutor; the balance of dynamics in the group with a student leader *and* a tutor may be a precarious one.

In a survey conducted by the British National Union of Students in 1969, students nevertheless regarded the seminar as being particularly valuable for the following purposes: 'To encourage learning and to facilitate the interchange of ideas'; 'To provide a stimulus for creative thinking'; and 'To improve students' self-expression'; but less so: 'To provide an occasion to study in depth'.

On the other hand they were critical of seminars in the following respects: 'Tended to be dominated by one or two students'; and 'Students tend to wait always for a lead from the staff members'; and 'Students avoid doing sufficient preparatory work'.

The students were also of the opinion that the maximum working membership of the seminar was six to ten (NUS, 1969).

These views reflect the same type of problem, and the consequent ambivalence among students, that Treadaway describes. Potentially, seminars provide an intellectual stimulus that is difficult to match. In practice, the dynamics of the group and the way tutors commonly handle it make this technique an unsatisfactory experience for many students. The exceptional tutor may succeed in elevating the seminar to a memorable level of intellectual ferment. Mere mortals might be better advised to try alternative means of achieving the same educational objectives and, in the process, achieve some which they had not previously considered.

Advantages: procedures accepted by general convention; intellectual atmosphere stimulating when well run.

Disadvantages: task rarely clarified; leadership roles confused; often results in mini-lecture; little regard for social and emotional dimension.

Tutorials

Where the seminar is usually devoted to a critical and searching discussion of subject matter, the tutorial, at least as distinguished by the Hale Report (HMSO, 1964), is concerned with the development of the student's powers of thought. The tutor's task is to 'use the subject to what he considers the best advantage to promote that development'. This distinction is one of emphasis rather than of strict demarcation. The tutorial is aimed towards teaching the subject as well as the students and the seminar increases the students' intellectual powers as well as teaching them the subject. Numbers, however, do seem to be important. In a one-to-one tutorial the tutor may focus attention entirely on work prepared by the student. When the number of students increases, less and less time tends to be devoted to each individual concern and correspondingly more becomes applied to the subject matter as a way of spreading the focus. The tutorial is thus transformed into a seminar: the Hale Committee chose four as the critical number for this to happen.

Readers may well recall that four to six students appears to be the critical number in other situations, particularly in leaderless groups. Below that sort of number, no leader is considered necessary for certain defined tasks. With more members, unless a leader is designated, a group may break into disarray as leadership conflicts are fought out. What function then does a tutor serve in a group whose size does not necessarily justify a leader? If the answer is none, then it follows that the tutor's presence in any tutorial is likely to be a superfluous and therefore a visible and possibly dominant one. This is not to suggest that there is anything inherently wrong with such a dynamic – it may be very necessary for certain purposes – but if as tutors we wish to avoid over-direction of student learning, with its concomitant problems, we may want to consider other techniques which allow the students more autonomy. This is never more true than in the one-to-one tutorial where, in the words of the Hale Committee, 'the inequality of intellectual power and attainment between tutor and pupil is often too great for any real discussion'. One-to-one tutorials are also extravagant in the use of tutors' time – but that is self-evident.

Tutorials appear to serve three main functions: a regular meeting ground for the checking of student progress, a means of locating misunderstandings in lectures and an opportunity to give special scrutiny to a piece of the student's work. In two, if not three, or these respects the tutorial conforms to a teacher-based pattern of learning. However, the pastoral role of the tutor should not be under-valued; in this capacity some tutors manage to combine all the above functions quite happily. They hold a regular meeting with three or four 'tutees' where they look at a piece of written work (not necessarily for submission to them), check what difficulties the students may be experiencing in particular areas, and relate this to any reports they have of students' progress. If they are able to use the group potential skilfully – for instance by getting students to assess each other's written work – they may increasingly divest some of the responsibility for these concerns to the students to the point where the tutorial group becomes a sort of 'learning cell' with the tutor as a resource. In this setting, learning can develop into a more mutually supportive exercise than is typically the case in tutorials.

In science and engineering the word 'tutorial' is often used to describe an exercise class of up to 30 in which students work individually on set problems while the tutor circulates. In a way the exercise class is a form of rotating one-to-one tutorial with all the virtues and drawbacks that entails. The tutor does have a chance to check how students are getting on but many students will be wary of admitting mistakes or lack of effort to the tutor, and can quickly acquire strategems for avoiding him or her during the all-too-short one-hour period that is conventionally allocated to the class. The alert tutor may well choose to divide the class into sub-groups with tasks demanding collaboration between the students alternating with individual work (see horseshoe groups on page 87). Readers may also find some interesting references on problem-solving in Polya (1957), Wicklegren (1974), Frazer (1977), Woods et al (1977).

Advantages: focuses attention on individual student work and ways of think-

ing; helps tutor keep an eye on student progress; provided continuity in tutor/student relationship.
Disadvantages: can be expensive of tutor time (especially with one-to-one); tutor
in dominant role.

Syndicates

A dilemma which commonly faces tutors in seminars is how to exercise control
over the content while at the same time giving students room to express their own
ideas in their own terms; to a great extent this is resolved in syndicate learning.
The technique is described by Collier (1968, 1969 and 1983). The students in small
tutorless groups (five to six members in each) are given joint assignments which
require reading, discussion and written work. The tutor's first task is to prepare the
assignments; these may cover the same ground as a lecture course and comprise a
developing sequence of questions and references. Here, by way of illustration, is
part of one of the assignments Collier describes as it is presented to the students:

Organisation Structure: Principles of Interpretation

1. What are the characteristics of the 'organic' and 'mechanistic' forms of organisation
   described by Burns and Stalker? In what circumstances does each have advantages?
   What features of the organisation of Plant Y unders Messrs Stewart and Cooley's
   methods of administration do *not* come within Burns and Stalker's analysis? See
   Burns and Stalker: *The Management of Innovation*, Chapters 5 and 6.
   Revans: *Standard for Morale*, Chapters 1, 8, 9 and 10
   Guest: *Organisational Change*, Chapters 2 and 5
   Thelen: *Dynamics of Groups Work*, Chapter 4.

Some assignments may be considered sufficiently important to be worked on by
all the syndicates on behalf of the class as a whole. The students distribute the
reading, discussing and writing tasks among themselves with the groups, and meet
during what would otherwise be a lecture period, to work on the tasks while the
tutor circulates among them. Plenary discussions are held at various points during
the course. The collection of student views emerges in either a written or an oral
report; dissenting opinions, where they arise, are included. The tutor summarizes
the reports in a formal lecture suggesting any changes and improvements in the
work produced and extending ideas beyond the students' material where appropriate. A final plenary session follows.

The students are thus given both the security of specific content and a clear
task, and the freedom to exercise their own skills and judgement in analysing and
synthesising information. Collier claims that syndicate learning cuts across any of
the fundamental assumptions about teaching and learning which the educational
system may have established in the students:

• the students are placed in a situation where, in the first instance, they form views derived from their reading and experience and from discussion with their peers, rather than from the teacher;

- the students form bonds within their syndicates which give them some support in the face of the teacher's authority;
- the relations are no longer controlled by the naked confrontation of the teacher with a number of separate individuals and can thus become more easily personal and informal.

In this way, whereas the tutor's authority in respect of discipline and procedures within the group is either ignored, or rejected, his or her authority as subject expert is, if not intact, a separate issue to be treated on its own merits. This may of course raise problems for some students who find it difficult to function in groups without the guiding hand of a tutor, but it is equally possible that it is liberating to those students who have problems in expressing themselves freely in the presence of a tutor. Syndicate learning also appears to combine the two ingredients of high motivation – competition between groups with the consequent cohesion and purpose within them. There is nevertheless a tight prescription of task, and the boundaries of knowledge are firmly controlled.

Advantages: combines control of content with freedom in discussion; authority is clearly delegated; groups take pride in achievement, work harder; disparate knowledge is integrated.

Disadvantages: not all students able to cope in tutorless groups; discrepancy between kind of learning and assessment methods; overall control of what is learned tends to be un-negotiable.

Case studies

A standard technique of teaching in management and business studies, the case study is in a sense a kind of simulation of a real-life situation in which the experience is secondhand and probably condensed. The important merit of the case study is that it allows a problem to be studied in a complex form, including elements of real-life events which it might be impossible to reproduce in the classroom. Typically the students are provided with case notes in advance and are expected to prepare their own solution to the problem or problems presented. Case studies open up opportunities for role play (see page 106) where it becomes necessary to shed light on particular encounters rather than general issues. In some ways, case studies have the edge on simulations in that students are not tempted to trivialize; there is, however, little of the sense of risk-free competition and personal involvement which appears to be an inherent part of games and simulations.

The main virtue of case studies is the way in which they can efficiently integrate a wide diversity of subject matter. They are mainly used in applied social sciences but there is no reason why they should not be used to advantage in science and engineering, for instance in respect of socially related issues and design failures.

The Open University 'Open' files of written material on their technology foundation and man-made futures courses are excellent examples of this approach.

Case studies can also be used as examination questions in order to test a student's power of synthesis (Easton, 1982).

Advantages: · integrative – encourages a 'broad view'; develops a sense of objectivity; demands tolerance of several points of view.

Disadvantages: requires some maturity and prior experience of students; makes heavy demands on the tutor in holding the discussion together; can be time-consuming.

Peer tutoring

It is clear that a lot of teaching is done in courses by the students themselves – perhaps more than many teachers would wish to recognize. In laboratory groups for example it is quite common to see students explaining points to each other and helping one another over basic misconceptions and more advanced problems. Not quite so apparent is the mutual help and support which exist outside the curriculum in the refectory, the halls of residence or in the library.

Peer tutoring is a way of harnessing these valuable processes within the bounds of the curriculum. According to Goldschmid and Goldschmid (1976), peer tutoring can be supported on the following grounds:

socio-psychological – it offers close personal contact in an otherwise remote environment;

pedagogical – students are active as learners, teaching enhances learning for the 'tutor', and there is increased co-operation, motivation and self-esteem;

economic – a saving on staff time and energy;

political – it helps students effectively adjust to the curriculum as a 'system'.

Examples of different models of peer tutoring are:

- senior students acting as regular seminar leaders;
- 'proctors' who help test and guide more junior students through a programme of individualized instruction;
- self-directed student groups;
- the learning cell, in which students in pairs alternately ask and answer questions on commonly read material;
- parrainage*, where older students counsel new students firstly over practical matters to do with settling in, and later over study problems.

Because they have long been trained in the passive 'reception of information' and in 'success through competition' students may need to be inducted to the academic and social skills necessary for peer tutoring. Moreover, not all students will

---

* The nearest translation from the original French is 'sponsorship'

be suited to the role of peer tutor and in some of the above schemes care may have to be exercised in both role choice and training. In others, everyone will perforce be involved in the operation. For further reading on peer tutoring see Cornwall (1979), Boud (1981) and Goodlad (1989).

Students can also practise a form of peer tutoring in learning teams – groups of four to six which have the following tasks:

- to maximize the learning of its members;
- to provide the incentive, the opportunity and the ability for its members to learn;
- to learn about teamwork through the conscious experience of working in a team;
- to develop the ability of its members to work in a team;
- to organize tasks and roles for each learning activity within an agreed set of rules;
- to rotate tasks and roles so that each member has a range of experiences;
- to monitor, and report on, their individual and collective progress.

The role of the teacher with learning teams is to negotiate appropriate rules to provide team training for the sharing of group tasks and opportunities.

Advantages: students actively involved – learn by teaching; integration of students into course facilitated; inexpensive.

Disadvantages: students require training – needs regular monitoring; not all students good at it; may demand constant staff supervision for success.

Projects

Put simply, a project is a learning task in which the students have a choice of topic and direction and whose outcome is therefore unpredictable. It demands initiative, creativity and organizing skills of the students: they are required to produce a report, plan or design which comprises the solution to a problem. In pursuit of this goal the students have a considerable amount of time to develop their own learning strategies according to where the project takes them and generally rely on a supportive relationshhip with a tutor/supervisor.

Projects are thus more of an educational strategy than a technique, as they involve a comprehensively different philosophy of learning. Students are responsible (to a greater or lesser extent) for the direction and range of the work they undertake, which may carry them beyond the tutor's own area of subject expertise either in breadth or depth. Consequently projects are likely to create all manner of anxieties in both tutor and students as to direction, progress and personal competence. Various studies of project work (SRHE, 1974 and Jaques, 1980 and 1981) show a fairly consistent pattern of events. Goodlad (1978) summarizes these in *Improving Teaching in Higher Education*:

First, students should be actively involved in the choice of the subject; this increases their involvement with the task. Secondly, the student should be encouraged to discover for himself the implications of the constraints of conceptual fruitfulness in the discipline, availability of resources (library information) or institutional arrangement. It is a delicate task for the tutor to strike a balance between over-direction of a student's work (which can destroy the distinctive benefits of project methods) and under-direction (which can lead the student into muddle and frustration). Thirdly, some teachers have found that a student's enthusiasm is closely related to the production of documents – high at the beginning (when an outline and bibliography are being prepared) and at the end (when the final presentation is being fabricated), but low to the point of despair during the period of gestation. It has been found wise to arrange an input of teaching (presentation of ideas at a seminar, brainstorming sessions, simulations, discussion of rough draft, etc) in the middle of the lifespan of a project and just at the beginning.

Group projects present students with two additional problems. One is that the choice of partners is often confused with the choice of topic and tutor and this may be too much for students to unravel – a bit like choosing who to marry and where to work at the same time! It is not unusual to find a group project resolving itself into a collection of individual, if related, tasks.

One procedure for tackling this problem was operated at the City University, in electrical engineering (Edwards, 1980), where groups are organized as follows:

1. Topics of interest to the class are listed.
2. The topics are whittled down, through discussion, to a small number.
3. Each student ranks the topics in order of personal preference.
4. The course tutor then allocates topics to students according to these preferences: the groups are thus constituted.
5. Tutors' names are not revealed or allocated till the groups are established.

In another rather different scheme at Worcester Polytechnic Institute, Massachusetts, the tutors advertise the projects they are prepared to supervise, or a starting point from which they will negotiate, and in some cases attach persuasive posters to their doors.

On the other hand it might be preferable to allow the project to emerge as an expression of the combined interests of preselected groups. The tutor in this case might, having formed the groups, give them a file of papers covering a range of issues (eg Open University files*) and then assist them in the formulation of a problem to be solved, perhaps using another OU resource, the PIG Problem Identification Game (OU, 1975). Of course this presupposes there is no 'hassle' about who teams up with whom. Either the grouping must be done arbitrarily according to some principle (eg random selection or heterogeneous mix) or the students must take part in a team-building exercise such as 'Card Exchange' described on page 208.

The second problem about group projects arises both logically and psychologically out of the first. Notwithstanding the use of a clarifying procedure for selecting topics and projects, it may in many circumstances be too much to ask a group

---

* Several 'Files' or 'Case Studies' have been produced by the Open University, on problematical issues, as 'supplementary' material to their course units.

of students to handle both the uncertainties of project work and the problems of working in a team concurrently. Aware of this problem, tutors at Delft in Holland offer their project students in town planning a prior training course in group dynamics and teamwork. However, prior training has to be followed up with procedures for monitoring the unfolding progress of the group if it is to be of enduring benefit. If learning about teamwork is one of the critical aims of the project then students might learn much through monitoring the group process, not merely about the personal and collective problems of teamwork, but of their priorities as individual learners. Various checklists and exercises (see page 198 et seq) should be of help in this respect. So might the keeping or a group diary or logbook which could form the basis of a commentary on the work of the project to be submitted, but not assessed, with the project report. If, on the other hand, the students are being asked to learn about teamwork issues 'the hard way', one may wish to give them some help with their programming of the work – it is all a matter of time and priorities. A more elaborate form of the diary idea is the portfolio: 'a permanent record of a personal journey' and 'a basis for continuing reflection' (Boud et al 1985). The portfolio can include ideas, pictures, cuttings and reflective comments on these. It works best when treated as confidential.

Two other sourcebooks of ideas for project tutors are my own (Jaques, 1988 and 1989).

The actual scheduling of progress through the project also requires attention. The following planning guide is used at Mount Royal College at Calgary in Canada.

On page . . ., you find a graph containing a breakdown of the approximate percentage of time taken by each major project phase. Although the percentages will vary, depending on the amount of research necessary and the type of medium chosen, the graph will give you a general idea of how much time to spend on each phase. Use this graph to complete the 'flow chart' on the next page [ie Figure 6.5].

Before you begin phase I of this guide, determine specific dates for the completion of tasks noted in the flow chart. Do this in consultation with your instructor. The use of the flow chart in the planning process will virtually assure you of completing your project on schedule. *A Word of Caution*: You may not have time to do certain tasks which involve complex productions. If you are not sure, check with your instructor.

There follow the phase group and flow chart given here as Figures 6.4 and 6.5.

Projects offer students a unique chance to develop skills and capacities that might never be apparent in other kinds of learning. They give students feedback on their ability to handle freedom in relation to the constraints of the outside world, to cope with real problems, and, if all goes well, to build up a continuing interest in them beyond the completion of their studies. The learning potential of projects is therefore enormous. Group projects add the further benefits of pooling resources, division of labour and the enjoyment of interpersonal learning.

However, assessment, yet again, presents a problem. It is very difficult to compare one student with another when the report is the result of a group effort. Students differ in their skills, their rates and levels of working, and their styles of learning.

Phase IV –
Presenting your project
- Selecting equipment
- Presenting your project
- Follow-up

Phase I –
Planning your project
- Choosing your topic
- Determining your audience
- Developing a goal statement
- Determining method of
  approach

Phase III –
Producing your project
- Storyboarding
- Scripting
- Producing audio and visual
  components

Phase II –
Designing your project
- Developing content
- Research
- Organizing content
- Selecting media
- Developing evaluation

Figure 6.4 *Phase group for project work*

Who is to say the student who held them together and constantly inspired the group yet contributed nothing to the report should receive no academic reward? One method in use for dealing with this problem is described on page 164. It makes sense nevertheless for a group project to be assessed according to criteria that demand a co-operative effort and that these criteria should be clearly negotiated with the group near the start of the project or, at the very least, before irrevocable decisions are made. Gibbs and Habeshaw (1989) give a clear example of an assess-

Deadline	Project phase		Instructor's initials
	Phase I	*Planning your project*	
	Step 1	Choosing your topic	
	Step 2	Identifying your target audience	
	Step 3	Developing a goal statement	
	Step 4	Determining your method of approach	
	Step 5	Developing your content material	
		Stage A – Determining relevant questions	
		Stage B – Selecting appropriate resources	
		Stage C – Researching your project	
		Stage D – Writing a content outline	
(Research Completed)			
	Step 6	Selecting the most appropriate medium	
	Step 7	Evaluating your project	
	Phase III	*Producing your project*	
	Step 8	Preparing your storyboard	
	Step 9	Writing your script	
	Step 10	Preparing audio materials	
	Step 11	Preparing visual materials	
(Production Completed)			
	Phase IV	*Presenting your project*	
	Step 12	Selecting your equipment	
	Step 13	Presenting your project	
(Presentation Date)			
	Step 14	Following up the presentation	

Figure 6.5   *Flow chart for planning project work*

ment proforma that requires a project group to distribute its tutor-determined grade to members of the group according to their individual contributions.

A clear step forward in clarifying goals, relationships and responsibilities in project work is the use of a learning contract. Knowles (1975 and 1984) describes contracts for self-directed learning which are evolved through a set of class discussions. The contract comprises learning goals, strategies and sources, evidence of accomplishment and criteria and means of measuring accomplishment. Heron (1981) proposes a scheme for self-monitoring and assessment which, though less clearly prescribed, is clearly worth considering in projects where one of the critical aims is for students to learn about themselves as learners. The tutor's (as supervisor's) role in promoting group experiences in project work is of course considerable. If students are to gain full benefit from working together there must be a *demand* in the project design for collective effort, *training opportunities* for the students in teamwork, a clear *monitoring* of the students' team dynamics and an *assessment* that emphasizes group effort. Each of these features requires leadership from the tutor, but external to the group: in other words a clear definition of authority and boundaries (see Chapter 1). Further reading on the role of the project tutor may be found in Jaques, 1987 and 1989.

The kind of learning that can be achieved in project work, given commitment, energy and imagination from all concerned, is potentially vast in both variety and depth. Our understanding of the processes and their scope nevertheless has a long way to go.

Advantages: freedom to study in depth and breadth; chance to tackle real problems, provide solutions that can be tested in 'real world'; learning active; comprehensive challenge to students.

Disadvantages: things can go radically wrong; challenge and freedom may prove too much for some students – some tutors not able to function in non-directive role or outside area of subject expertise; assessment may be a problem.

Games and simulations

There is a growing interest at all stages of education in techniques which allow students to act out the problems and issues under discussion and make decisions about them based on a more personal understanding of their nature and implications. If we were to take a cynical view this interest might be viewed as a response to the sense of alienation among students towards the learning of knowledge as if it existed independently of them and for purposes (eg examinations) extrinsic to the knowledge itself. From a more positive standpoint the interest in games could result from a recognition that enactment of issues can serve to integrate even pedestrian knowledge into the framework of values, beliefs and personal behaviour of students. The medium for this 'gestalt' is the imagination, that faculty of mind so often written off because of its association with fun and the supposedly childish connotations that holds. The assumptions which underpin this argument were exposed three-quarters of a century ago by Dewey (1916):

> The difference between play and what is regarded as serious employment should not be a difference between the presence and absence of imagination, but a difference in the material with which the imagination is occupied. The result (of overlooking this) is an unwholesome exaggeration of the fantastic and 'unreal' phases of childish play and a deadly reduction of serious occupation to a routine efficiency prized simply for its external tangible results.

It appears that among those students who get most out of games and simulations are those who are able to maintain a delicate balance between play and reality. They can commit themselves wholeheartedly to what they are continuously aware is an exploratory device, and the energy seems to be released through the creative interplay between fantasy and reality. The experience of games and simulations therefore brings a further meta-dimension to the experiential cycle, that of play, a factor that in a successful game with suitable players is likely to suffuse all parts of the cycle. It allows people to imitate and experiment safely with new behaviour in the context of a prepared situation and to gain instructive feedback on it in the knowledge that the boundaries between the imagined world and the real one are safe.

Games and simulations and their concomitant debriefing provide an excellent example of the experiential learning cycle (shown on page 10) in action.

Before we discuss the games and simulations as techniques, a few definitions are called for. The word *game* is usually taken to describe a group exercise in which players co-operate or compete towards a given end within a regime of explicit rules. Players behave as themselves (even if they do display exceptional behaviour at times!). Cricket, chess and charades are obvious examples of popular games; educational games include 'The Colour Game' (six people with hidden agendas have to agree on a colour), 'Back to Back' (where a drawing is described so that a back-to-back partner can draw a copy) and 'Starpower' (players trade tokens to acquire power). Games are generally given no real-life context and people act as themselves.

A game becomes a *simulation* when a scenario is provided – it thus constitutes a simplified representation of life. The scenario might be a public meeting, a classroom or a radio station. If play is not prescribed by rules then it is usually shaped by *roles*, and the roles may be fixed – such as 'You are the city architect who has been fighting a losing battle over the provision of pedestrian precincts' – or free, where people act themselves in a given situation. Sometimes roles are written as aims: 'Your aim is to become chair of this committee.' What is described as *role play*, is often therefore an exercise in which interpersonal encounters can be explored with some degree of freedom. Whereas in games the interplay occurs within a pattern of clear and often artificial rules, in role play what happens is governed by the implicit rules of everyday life in a defined situation.

All of these definitions are a matter of degree and balance – combinations abound. It is possible for instance to have a simulation in which communication between groups is governed by rules, where the activity in the groups is determined by roles and where each group has a singular objective to fulfil in competition with the others. Most simulations are depicted in the diagrammatic model shown in Figure 6.6.

The model in Figure 6.6 may be contracted or expanded to suit. As depicted here it comprises a number of groups – A, B, C and D – each with a goal and possibly a shared role (eg a pressure group). The intergroup communication may replicate what happens in real life (eg if there is a hierarchical relationship there might be more communication channels available 'downwards' than 'upwards'). The relations between each group may be ordained by roles. Each group's attention is focused on a model which may be a concrete object (eg a 'Lego' town), or map, or an imagined problem scenario. The task of the tutor in a simulation/game is usually that of referee (though this may be delegated) who plays a benign 'God', and who supervises the setting up, smooth running and debriefing of the exercise. All of these operations require qualities often ascribed to a deity – prediction, an ele-

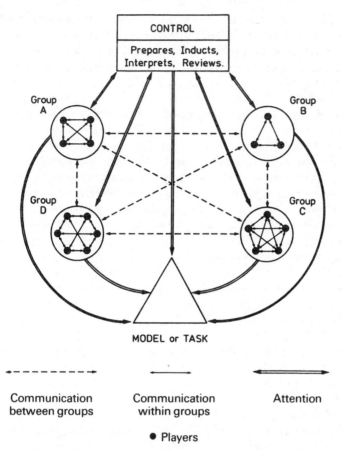

Figure 6.6 *Diagrammatic model of games and simulations*

ment of mystery, apparent control of the elements, the creation of ad hoc roles and rules, and a tendency to ignore requests.

Debriefing, the review of a game or simulation, is the most important part of the task educationally and should last for at least half the duration of the exercise itself in most cases. Abstract games often require double or triple this amount. This reflective discussion helps students to generalize from their particular experience and to think beyond the immediate experience. The following pattern for debriefing is one which seems to put the students' learning into perspective.

1. How are you feeling right now?* (Often this needs to be asked in order to tap some of the emotional charge of the exercise.)
2. What was going on in the simulation? Who achieved what? What different perceptions were there of what happened?

---

* These are particularly important questions to put when, by accident or design, a lot of intense feelings have been aroused.

3. What did players learn about themselves, each other, social groups, social systems, limitations of science and so forth?
4. What did the simulation tell them about the 'real world'?
5. How did it parallel the 'real world'?
6. How could the simulation be improved?
7. How is everyone feeling now?*
8. What might you do differently as a result of your experience in the simulations?

The debriefing discussion, though typically conducted as a plenary, can often be enlivened by dividing the class into sub-groups, especially ones whose membership cuts across the grouping in the simulation. Following the debriefing the often loose and variable learning can be better tied up and consolidated with students in syndicates or task-orientated groups with tasks like:

• Discuss and report back on generalized insights.
• Make links with learning from more traditional sources: lectures, reading, for instance.

Or, if it can be video-recorded:

• Use a video-playback to look at the why's and wherefores of interaction in the simulation (a *step-by-step discussion* (qv) works well here).

Games and simulations are considered to be particularly valuable in promoting social and professional skills such as communicating, role-taking, problem-solving, leading, decision-making, and so on, not to speak of their less academic but more affecting function in opening the eyes of participants to what it feels like to be in someone else's position. Games and simulations are also claimed, with good justification, to increase the level of motivation and interest in the subject matter, develop a greater sense of self-awareness and personal power, and create a freer and more democratic climate. As for cognitive learning, apart from the impact of all the above in energizing the learning process, games and simulations can facilitate the understanding of relationships between separate areas of subject matter, particularly those where personal action is demanded. Nevertheless, without the consolidating effect of debriefing and further tasks a lot of this learning may remain only half realized.

The number of possible permutations of the game and simulation format is vast: as varied, one might suppose, as life itself. Ready-made and tested exercises with full instructions for the tutor/organizer are available from a variety of sources. Reference to these may be found in books such as Christopher and Smith (1991), Jones (1991), Davison and Gordon (1977), Krupar (1973), Taylor & Walford (1972) and Pfeiffer and Jones (1972 through 1990). The Society for the Advancement of Games and Simulations in Education and Training (SAFSET) includes many examples in its journal, *Simulations/Games for Learning* and produces resource lists for different subject areas. Should readers want to design their own exercises, some helpful advice may be found in Stadsklev (1974), Davison and Gordon (1977), Chesler & Fox (1966) and Jones (1988). Such an exercise could come under any of the following categories, or combinations of them:

- public meeting;
- assessor's panel;
- communication network;
- competitive or co-operative interaction in group;
- committee role play;
- critical interactions role play;
- board game;
- in-tray exercise;
- card game (usually with Rummy rules).

Finally, as an indication of the scope of games and simulations, here are descriptions of three exercises covering different formats and subject areas.

Star River Project

Eight interest groups, including industry, the local authority and residents, are involved in a series of joint meetings to prepare and negotiate their cases on the planning development of a river estuary. They must also process a lot of scientific and technical information (political, economic, social, historical, biological and chemical) in order to present their case at a final public meeting. A newpaper covers events and keeps all informed on policy trends.

This simulation aims to develop an understanding of the conflicting issues that arise in planning a community's environment. It requires upwards of 20 participants and lasts anything from three to eight hours.

Moco

Four players in competing pairs choose various elements of an engineering structure which are represented by plastic magnetic pieces designed to stick on a metal board. Each pair then tries to complete as high-scoring a structure as possible using some or all of the elements according to specified conditions. The first pair to finish score an extra point, but must submit their structures to inspection by their opponents. Participants are thus compelled to apply their understanding of the 'nature' of structures to the problem in question without involving themselves in the detailed and more remote analytical calculations. The duration of Moco depends on how many rounds are played.

For a full description of the game see Cowan & Morton (1973).

Role-reversal

This involves an improvised role play. Participants are invited to recount an incident or continuing problem to do with their social or professional life. The problem might, for instance, be that a student going to see his/her tutor gets the feeling of not being welcome and ends up tongue-tied and frustrated. In the role play the student would first be asked to describe the encounter, and then invited to play the role of the tutor in question; another student is asked to be the one with the problem. The roles are thus switched which enables the 'student' to experience the nature of the problem from the tutor's point of view. The original student, it is hoped, will gain insight not only into what her/his own behaviour may provoke in the tutor, but also into the frame of mind of the tutor and how as a student to tackle the problem more constructively.

Variations on this strategy may be the introduction of the 'alter-egos' who either advise or take the place of the role players at agreed junctures, or the re-enacting of critical moments, perhaps using video playback in order to explore alternative tactics. The tutor/student relationship is but one sample of this kind of role play. It can be used for any number of encounters where things are perceived to go wrong. Any role play may be conducted either by the central players only, with the rest of the class watching, or simultaneously by several small groups.

Role play is a particularly helpful technique when, in discussing a social or professional issue, it becomes apparent that interpersonal behaviour is a signifcant and causal factor.

Role play used in this manner can sometimes be a bit threatening to participants. In a sense they are on stage and the rest of the group or class is watching them. Gibbs (1984) describes a peer learning method in which participants, working in *tutorless sub-groups*, take full responsibility for their own role play and debriefing. For the scenario described above for example, the roles of tutor, student and observer(s) would be designated and rotated in groups of three for as many cycles as needed. The observer(s) would be responsible for the time boundaries and the debriefing.

It is sometimes said that games and simulations are manipulative in that they constrain people to behave according to the designer's model of reality with all its attendant values. This is an indisputable danger, but can readily be countered through a proper debriefing in which such issues are brought out.

Games and simulations can, as may already be apparent, be used within a scheduled group meeting or at a specially convened, extended, session. As such they can be of great value as a stimulus for further discussion or in illuminating particular issues. Alternatively, they may be used to bind together the disintegrated elements of a course either in the form of a grand finale or by constructing the whole course as a 'partial' simulation in which students participate only at certain scheduled times and otherwise work on tasks demanded by or related to the simulation. For the imaginative teacher there is no end to the possible variations in the style and scope of games, role plays and simulations.

Advantages: experience is first hand and concentrated; motivation intrinsic to activity, learning well retained; high level of interest; removes teacher/student polarization; learning occurs at sundry levels.

Disadvantages: time-consuming, can demand a lot of preparation; some students don't or won't participate; colleagues regard games as trivial; materials often expensive, learning unpredictable and difficult to evaluate; dangers of hurtful stress in some, especially where not carefully handled by tutor.

As a footnote, readers may like to learn that three publications, Lewis and Mee 1981, Jaques in Cryer (1982) and van Ments (1983) give clear counsel to tutors in the handling of role play and similar 'experiential' exercises.

Free or associative discussion

The benefits of giving people freedom in a controlled environment to talk about whatever comes to mind have long been understood in psychoanalysis and group therapy. The therapist is trained to listen and generally refrain from comment while the patient 'freely associates', thus revealing underlying patterns of thought and feeling. Free discussion operates on a similar principle. The tutor says very little but encourages spontaneity of speech among the students. What the tutor does say is by way of directing students' attention to anomalies and inconsistencies in what they have said, pointing out patterns and relevances in what might otherwise seem a vague and rambling discussion, and helping them 'to see themselves as capable of change' (Abercrombie, 1979).

Although free discussion may comprise a great number of apparently random exchanges, its permissiveness allows the student to become increasingly aware of some of the habitual attitudes and assumptions which to a large extent determine his or her ways of thinking about the subject. McLeish (1973) states that:

> Students discover, in the course of discussion, that they have highly specific, even idiosyncratic reactions to problems, to situations, to individuals; that they always slow down their ability to solve problems. An understanding of the nature of knowledge, and self-insight, is given them in a manner no other teaching method can provide. It is first-hand, personal experience of the shifting character of experience, the ambiguity of evidence, the tenuous nature of our most profound convictions.

In these senses free discussion is a means to intellectual growth – the sort of personal development that Perry (1970) describes as students move from the dualistic to the relativistic phases, and even onward to commitment (see page 46).

The tutor's job is not to correct mistakes (other participants quickly pick up this task) but, with a good sense of timing, to inject comment on the nature of the argument; otherwise to listen attentively. By clearly specifying the aims and by intermittently restating them in the context of what is being said, the tutor sets a direction. By occasionally expressing feelings – 'I don't know what I've done to shut you all up' – the tutor encourages a recognition of the important part that emotions play in our thinking; by referring to his or her own habits when students are talking about theirs, and encouraging 'oscillation of attention between different contexts', eg from the present group to the whole class or profession, the tutor promotes the transfer of learning and a reflexive understanding of problems. The tutor's role is therefore to clarify the field of discourse and set its boundaries as well as to draw associations within the general aim. For this reason Abercrombie expresses preference of the word 'associative' rather than 'free' to describe the group discussion.

In her earlier book *The Anatomy of Judgement* – a classic text which merits study by all teachers and students – Abercrombie (1969) describes tasks set to groups of medical students. The tasks were designed to elucidate 'for the participants some of the factors that had affected their judgement on scientific matters'. Each of the tasks was undertaken in the climate of free/associative discussion.

Task 1 Students were shown two similar but different radiographs and asked to 'list the differences you can see between the two hands'.

Task 2 Students were given a short extract from a book in which the words 'normal' and 'average' occurred. They are asked to 'Write what you think the author means by these terms and give all definitions of "normal" you can think of.'

Task 3 Students wrote a short essay on classification and discussed in the group.

Task 4 Students first read a scientific paper reporting an experiment and its conclusions. They were then asked to answer the following:

(i) Quote a statement which summarises what the author claims she has discovered.

(ii) Compare this with observation actually made.

(iii) How could you set out to test the hypothesis that [author's hypothesis stated]?

The students were thus being asked to reveal how they interpreted, ordered, commented on and judged scientific information, and to improve in and through the process. Several students claimed this caused them to think seriously and to continue doing so well beyond the group session. In some cases it appeared that the time effect was delayed by months. One student claimed that it was two years after he had finished the course before he understood it. It was remarked that the course helped students express themselves clearly, to understand what others were saying and to listen. The last, as Abercrombie remarks, is a much neglected skill.

A variation of the free/associative group model was used by Smythe and Besly on a basic biology course in Sydney. The tutor was originally placed *outside* the group and the students were told she was present only as a resource and would not enter discussion unless the whole group agreed it was necessary. Later, a five-minute limit for 'non-intervention' by the tutor was introduced. Tasks ranged from the arrangement of specimens, diagrams or cards to intriguing questions such as 'Was Jack's Beanstalk possible?' Two of the themes that come through strongly in all the literature on these groups are the somewhat painful silences from a state of dependency into one of responsibility, and the need for some sort of training for tutors in what is a very unnatural role for most. The authority/dependency conflict is deeply rooted in the culture of teaching and learning. It takes a lot of courage, care and personal insight to handle it successfully.

Advantages: promotes intellectual growth, greater student responsibility for learning; encourages flexibility; has long-term value.

Disadvantages: apparently rambling kind of discussion; time needed for adjustment to process; learning difficult to assess by traditional means
as often very internal; difficult role for many tutors.

Brainstorming

This is the best-known and most frequently employed procedure to stimulate creative thinking. It was devised by Osborn as long ago as 1938 in reaction to much of
the cramped thinking he saw being applied to the solution of problems at business
meetings. In fact, it is only one part of a creative problem-solving procedure: that
designed to generate ideas. The full procedure includes the stages of fact finding,
idea finding and solution finding.

* *Fact finding* involves the definition and preparation of problems; definition in
  the picking out and refining of the problem; preparation in the gathering and
  analysis of relevant data.
* *Idea finding* deals with the production and devleopment of ideas through brainstorming.
* *Solution finding* relates to the evaluation of tentative solutions and the choosing and implementation of the agreed one.

The two main principles of brainstorming are the 'deferment of judgement' –
evaluation and criticism inhibit the freedom of creative thinking – and 'quantity
breeds quality', based on the premise that we have to work through conventional
ideas before we can get to original ones.

During brainstorming sessions four rules operate:

* *Criticism is ruled out* – any attempt at evaluation must quickly be ruled out of
  order; this also includes discussion as it usually raises doubts and qualifications.
* *'Free-wheeling' is welcomed* – the wilder the idea the better. 'It is easier to tame
  down than to think up (ideas)' (Osborn).
* *Quantity is wanted* – the more ideas suggested, the greater the likelihood of an
  original one coming up.
* *Combination and improvement are sought* – participants are encouraged to
  build on and improve each other's ideas and combine them to form new ideas.

The participants in a brainstorming session should ideally have knowledge of
the problem areas though not be too close to the problem, and be of such a mix as
to provide a variety of experience and personal style. Osborn regards the ideal size
of group as 'about a dozen' and this is the experience of most practitioners. The
leader must be both alert and pushing yet be able to maintain a friendly and informal atmosphere. A typical session might proceed as follows:

1. The leader makes sure that the problem has been properly defined and background information prepared.

2. Having arranged everyone so that open communication can take place, the leader runs a warm-up session (especially for novitiates). For this purpose, the leader may place an object, eg a plastic beaker, brick, paper clip into the middle of the floor and invite a quick generation of ideas on possible uses of the object. In order to free members from the usual inhibitions he or she might throw in some less conventional ideas: very often those of a lavatorial, aggressive or sexual nature have an astounding effect!*

3. The leader reminds eveyone of the rules and principles and prepares to write up on a board or large sheet a title for each of the contributions; constantly pushes for more, proposing own ideas where necessary, stimulates further lines of thought by asking how the 'thing' could be changed in terms of colour, shape, motion, etc.

In a brainstorming session on the problem of 'How to remove oil slicks from the surface of the sea' the dialogue might go as follows:

- Burn it
  (write 'burn it').
- Let it get washed ashore and scrape it off the beaches
  (write up 'scrape beaches').
- Sink it with sand
  (write 'sink with sand').
- Blow it out to sea
  (write 'blow out to sea').
- That won't get rid of it
  (reprimand for evaluating).
- Soak it up with seagulls
  (write 'soak with seagulls').
- Harness it to seagulls
  (write 'harness to seagulls').
- Train seagulls to dive down and suck it up into straws and drop these into a waiting tanker
  (what shall we write down for that? – sucking gulls!).

And so on.

5. The ideas may then be evaluated by the same group, a completely different one, or a mixture of the two. As a first step it is often fruitful to ask 'What is the wildest idea on the list?' and try to translate this into a practical proposal. The above list might, for example, throw up 'sucking gulls' as the idea to develop, and this could lead to the more practical proposal of helicopters holding the suction end of a pipe onto the slick with the delivery end held in an adjacent tanker.

* This arises from the taboos which commonly operate in these areas.

6. Finally, discussion focuses on the implementation

Brainstorming has been well tried and successfully pro
creative solutions to all manner of real-life problems. In
which generally pays much lip service to creativity but does
mote it, the very simplicity and quickness of this technique m.
try, especially in design, project work or other areas where ope
are of consequence.

Advantages: simple, easy to learn; good fun; can easily be ⸻ ⸻ized to include many aspects of life.

Disadvantages: can be facile and unproductive; some people unable to function in it.

Synectics

A more structured and thorough scheme for creative problem solving was developed by Gordon (1961) and Prince (1970). Synectics is built around many of the psychological states known to be helpful in overcoming blocks to creative thinking. It uses analogues and metaphors, encourages a wide range of ideas, and pays particular attention to the role of the leader in this. The psychological states are:

- *involvement and detachment* – an oscillation between close personal resonance with the problem and detachment from it;
- *deferment* – avoiding the danger of the quick and superficial solution;
- *speculation* – the freedom to let ideas flow easily;
- *hedonistic response* – a recognition that the feeling aroused, as a solution is approached, is an indication of where the discussion should go.

These psychological states are induced through a series of 'operational mechanisms' which serve to 'make the familiar strange' – people are distanced from the problem in order to free them from their prior concepts of it – or 'making the strange familiar' in order to bring them closer to it. The operational mechanisms are as follows.

Personal analogy
Each person is invited to imagine themselves to be the object under consideration, to merge themself with its physical existence. In the case of a concrete object such as a spring, or an oil slick (the problem being considered) the individual would attempt to feel the tension, the glutinousness, or whatever. With personal and social problems, role play may do the same thing.

In personal analogy, group members are asked first to describe the facts about their identified-with object, its everyday experience and how it feels about its existence.

Direct analogy
Now the group thinks of instances where comparable modes of operation, function or movement exist. The oft-cited case is that of Brunel getting his idea for the design of caissons from seeing shipworms tunnelling into wood.

analogy

the emphasis is on finding a visual or metaphorical image which helps to free the mind from the constraints of literal thinking. One group used the Indian rope trick as a symbolic analogy for the design of a jacking device to fit into a box four inches square.

Fantasy analogy

The value of fantasy is in the way it can act as a releasing mechanism for the unconscious motives and wishes we all have. Fantasy analogy is based on Freud's notion that creative work is the result of 'wish fulfilment'. It is an effective way of making the familiar strange. The group is asked to abolish their rational under-standing of the object or problem and indulge in daydreaming. For instance, members might be asked, in tackling the problem of inventing a vapour-proof closure for space-suits, 'How in your wildest fantasies do you want the closure to operate?' Alternatively, the group may be led into a story fantasy based on how the initiator of the concern senses the problem. The 'hedonistic' responses (see page 111) are picked out to see what they reveal.

In a synectics session on how to design a training workshop for administrators, a fantasy story led into the notion of poodle dogs floating down from the sky by para-chute. This was quickly 'forced' into the somewhat more practical proposal that random individual tasks be 'showered' upon participants at the beginning of each day.

Unusual techniques abound in synectics. Because creative thinking is essen-tially a free-flowing and undisciplined process, structure has been built in to help clarify and emphasize what is happening. The interested reader should refer to Stein (1975) for a review of all the procedures of synectics as well as the original work of Gordon and Prince.

Apart from its use for stimulating creative thinking, synectics has potential for more general learning purposes. For instance, in metaphorical thinking for 'unsticking' discussion (see Pirsig, 1974), students are encouraged to suggest what something is like – perhaps the influence of Socrates on the Athenians could be likened to a river cutting into a bank of clay – and to play with that for a while. This approach seems to have been particularly successful with under-achieving students. It has even been used with success in the teaching of philosophy.

The role of the synectics leader in facilitating the creative process is illuminat-ing to a host of group-dynamic problems. Prince is concerned, as is Osborne, about the effect of prematurely evaluating ideas in a problem-solving group and in avoid-ing comment on their negative aspects. He offers the following advice to the leader:

- 'Never go into competition with your team' – everyone else's ideas have preced-ence over the leader's.
- 'Be a 200 per cent listener to your team members' – in order to understand some-one's view the leader might paraphrase or build on it.
- 'Do not permit anyone to be put on the defensive' – there is value in what every-

one offers and the leader's job is to find it; those seeking negative aspects should be asked what it is they like or would prefer.

- 'Keep the energy level high' – the leader should be alert, interested, involved and demonstrate this with body movements; he or she should use humour, challenge and surprise.
- 'Use every member of your team' – verbose members should be thanked rather quickly after a contribution, their eyes avoided when inviting a response and if all else fails, talked to frankly; quiet members should be brought in.
- 'Do not manipulate your team' – whatever ideas of his or her own the leader may want to have adopted he or she should work towards the group over solutions being reached; the leader's job is to keep them informed on their stage in the synectics process.
- 'Keep your eye on the client' – the person presenting the problem should be constantly referred to.
- 'Keep in mind that you are not permanent' – the leader is the servant of the group, and must keep lines of communication open and emphasize imagination and flexibility; assuming that traditional leaders accrue power and that everyone wants the role, the leadership should be rotated.

Synectics is both a problem-solving technique and a means of training people to be more creative. In utilizing so many of the conscious, preconscious and even unconscious psychological mechanisms of human ability it appears to stimulate hard work, spontaneity and a happy connection between the rational and the emotional. For these reasons some of its procedures carry lessons for us in the more straight-laced context of tertiary education.

Advantages: taps subconscious mental processes, stimulates creative thinking, people work hard and intensively; provides clear procedures;
Disadvantages: demands considerable skill and time; is unusual – not usually germane to academic learning.

WHY HAVE VARIETY?

As explained at the beginning of the section, this list of techniques is by no means exhaustive and there are undoubtedly many others which could lay claim to inclusion. Nevertheless the techniques do embody a multitude of principles and procedures for group work, many of which might be combined or used in sequence by the versatile tutor. Their inclusion within the repertoire of a tutor is no guarantee of success – external issues and personal factors may be paramount. Yet the value of acquiring a repertoire of tasks and techniques seems undeniable for the following reasons, if not more:

- Students' learning styles vary, and implicit in each of the activities described is a different approach to learning (Ramsden in Marton et al, 1984).

- Each student needs variety of stimulus and experience.
- As students develop intellectually and emotionally, a change in their relationship to knowledge and its 'agent', the teacher, is necessary.
- It is possible to cast the teaching and learning net over a wider range of aims than would otherwise be feasible.
- Students who have experienced a variety of approaches to learning and to human interaction should achieve increased choice and awareness in ways of working in later life.
- It is impossible to predict the way any teaching/learning interaction will go: a tutor therefore needs to be adaptable and resourceful to maintain interest and momentum.
- In making choices and exercising a wider range of skills the tutor becomes more alert.
- Evaluative feedback is easier: students can make critical remarks with less embarrassment when the tutor is not closely identified with any one procedure.

But perhaps more important than becoming skilled in a variety of tasks and techniques is a resourcefulness in any specific situation. How do we handle the knotty problems? Can we recognize the part we are playing in any interaction? Are we able to find time, space and a clear head to make decisions about what to do and when to do it? We shall make some progress towards answering these questions in the next chapter.

DISCUSSION POINTS

- List as many group tasks as you can that might encourage people to understand and apply the ideas in this book.
- Draw up a chart of the various techniques described in this chapter according to aims, tutor's role, special skills, etc.
- What would you look for as evidence of success for each of the techniques described? Why?
- Take the techniques described on pages 83 to 113 and list the principles of group behaviour that each seems to embody.

7 The Tutor's Job

Translating sound theory or research evidence into practice is a complicated and tentative process. Good intentions are often difficult to put into effect even where we know what is necessary to achieve them. In the process of realizing our aims we may find ourselves stuck in patterns of communication and interaction which fail to unleash the full energy and potential of a group.

To write about the practice of skills in groups is in some ways self-contradictory in that it is making 'content' out of 'process'. Nevertheless, in this chapter, I propose to offer some specific ideas about what the tutor, and in turn the students, might positively do to enhance the effectiveness of group learning. In some cases the tutor may choose to keep a low profile and merely respond to the ferment of discussion at suitable times. I shall call initiatives of this kind *tactical*.

While many of the variables affecting behaviour are ephemeral and even capricious, there are on the other hand some which the tutor can influence, if not control, by decisions taken before the group actually meets. I shall call this kind of action *strategic*. 'Strategic' therefore refers to planning the overall structure and content of group teaching where 'tactical' refers to the handling of events as the discussion itself progresses. In acting strategically (for this purpose), knowledge and understanding of group dynamics and of the characteristics of the particular group may suffice. For tactical purposes, however, the more elusive qualities of skill and sensitivity are demanded and these cannot be acquired without some training, practice and reflection.

STRATEGIC CONSIDERATIONS

As the organizer of a group meeting or a series of meetings, the tutor has an opportunity to influence the course of events in at least three areas of decision: group size, group membership and the physical conditions in which the group meets. The tutor might also wish to plan for possible exigencies and prepare a small list of self-questions to ask such as 'What am I trying to achieve and what do I have to do to achieve it?' (see Chapter 5) and 'What courses of action should I be prepared for?' (see the previous chapter for some possibilities).

Though we often tend to make such decisions alone, there is a lot to be said for drawing on a friendly colleague's help to check out our thoughts. If this can be done happily and on a reciprocal basis, then so much the better. Care taken in the preparatory work can reap many later rewards and pre-empt several of the common problems of learning groups.

Group size

The number of students in each group has a profound influence on the kind of interaction that can be attained. The smaller the size, the greater is the likelihood of trust, close relationships and consonance of aims among members; these advantages may however be offset by the lack of variety, and the greater probability of a 'poor mix'. In the larger group, though a better mix and a more favourable student/staff ratio may be achieved, a sense of competition, and a greater differentiation of role might be expected to occur. Not only does the opportunity for each member to contribute diminish in inverse ratio to the number of people in the group, but the discrepancy in level of participation between high contributors and low contributors is disproportionately greater. There are thus quite significant differences too in the style, frequency and length of spoken contributions, not to speak of non-verbal behaviour, in groups of three to six compared with those of 12 to 15 students.

If timetablers and course tutors have not already determined the size of group for us, we might ask ourselves the following questions:

- What is the optimum range of group size socially and educationally for a given set of aims and tasks (assuming we can predict these)?
- What, apart from educational aims, do I hope the groups will achieve socially?
- What mix of sex, nationality, age, etc do I want to have?
- Do I intend or need to be present as tutor with all the groups all the time?
- What limitations does the meeting room(s) impose on the total group size and the kinds of activities possible?
- How does it all fit into the scheme for the whole course?

Figure 7.1 may give some indications of the dimensions to be taken into account.

Although decisions about group size may be predicated upon several variable factors, more often than not the tutor will be stuck with two fixed ones: the total number of students and the room in which they meet. However, with a little initiative, we can, whether with six students or 96, create a variety of group sizes for different purposes. For instance, it is possible by pairing the students in *dyads*, to encourage the sharing and development of half-formed or tentative ideas, the airing of anxieties, or merely to provide a break in the pattern of participation.

In many ways the size of total group most amenable to a variety of aims and techniques is 20 to 30. In recent years this sort of number has achieved popularity in management and teacher training as the most suitable for *workshops*. Workshop formats allow a variety of group techniques to be practised. Apart from the universal

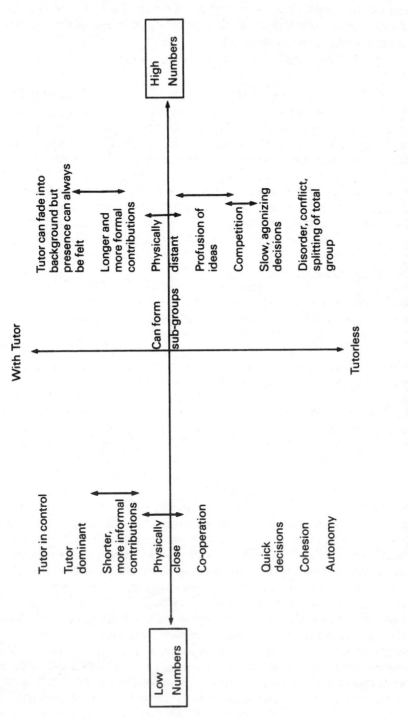

Figure 7.1 Characteristics of groups in relation to size and tutor's influence
Note: The short arrows indicate possible variations of that characteristic on the chart

facility of organizing dyads, they provide for either three to five groups of six to 18 with or without a tutor, or plenary sessions; workshops thus combine the advantages of small and large group experience.

Group membership

The way in which students are assigned to groups likewise depends on the purposes, both educational and social. As a general rule a heterogeneous mix of students in each group provides the best chemistry for interaction and achievement of task. Such qualities as age, sex, nationality and personality can be taken into account. One procedure for accomplishing effective mixes is as follows:

1 Divide the total number of students by the possible number of groups to estimate the rough size of each group.
2 Decide on criteria which might be used to differentiate one student from another, eg sex, age, background, expressed interest, exam results, nationality.
3 Go through all the notes and assign a code to each according to these criteria A, B, C, etc.
4 Then, starting with group 1, take one person from each of A, B, C, etc until this group's complement is made up. Repeat this if the complement is more than the number of qualities. Do the same for the other groups. Finally, check that each group has a similar mix and adjust if not.

Intellectual differences may also be taken into account. If the main purpose of discussion is to solve problems or to clarify or elaborate matters which have already received attention, then there are both commonsensical and research reasons (Amaria, Biran and Leith, 1969) why it may be wise to mix the better progressed or more quick-thinking students with those who are either behind with their work or slower thinking. Provided the given task demands co-operation, the former will find themselves teaching the latter. In this way we can kill two birds with one stone: the quicker students learn the subject matter themselves and the slower ones are provided with the opportunity to query misconceptions without embarrassment. Suddenly there are as many 'tutors' as students.

It would be a mistake, however, to think of group composition solely in terms of individual qualities. Of equal concern is the *sociometry* or likely pattern of emotional links among the members (where these can be known beforehand). In every group, personal likes and dislikes for fellow members soon begin to grow and can have an important influence on the way the group functions. Again, research and common sense tell us that people tend to agree with the individuals they like and disagree with those they dislike, even though both might express the same opinion.

Cliques may present another problem. There are good reasons for separating groups of students who have such close affinity with each other that they form an exclusive sub-group which could easily destroy the cohesive fabric of the larger group. On the other hand there may be pairs or threesomes who somehow trigger or inspire each other in more productive ways. The tutor needs considerable skill and sensitivity in watching out for cliques and taking appropriate action, which, though an extra chore, can deflect so many subsequent problems.

If the choice of group partners is to be left to the students (as happens often with projects) it is advisable to adopt a scheme which allows them to find partners with whom they prefer to work yet avoids the risk of some feeling left out or not chosen. A sociometric device suggested by Stanford and Roark (1974) is as follows:

Give each student a card and ask them to write their name in the upper left hand corner. Then ask each to list two members of the class with whom they would like to work. If a student can think of only one or wants to list more than two, that is perfectly acceptable.

The cards are then handed in to the tutor who uses the information on the cards to assign students into groups containing at least one colleague for whom they expressed preference.

Even with preparation like this the tutor may need to be alert to the dangers of friends falling out or of exclusive cliques developing as the life of the group develops. What the tutor might subsequently do about such happenings is suggested later.

The elegance of the workshop format described on page 116 is the facility it offers for varying the mix of people and affinities in groups while still allowing for planned changes of group membership both for the sake of variety and in order to monitor the progress of each group (though any such decision must be tempered by knowledge of the disruptive effect of breaking up groups).

Physical conditions

It is in the physical arrangement of chairs that many of the most basic yet influential problems in group discussion can occur. Who sits where and at what distance from whom will affect the social roles and relationships pursued by members. The cardinal rule is, if you want full and democratic participation, play down any prior differences of role and reduce the likelihood of their becoming firmly established. A closer sense of sharing in a common task is thus more readily achieved.

A starting point in organizing the physical arrangements is to ask:

- What associations does the room have in the minds of the students?
- Is it the tutor's room, a classroom, a 'neutral' room?
- Is the room a regular venue, is discussion vulnerable to noise or interruption?

Then it may be sensible to consider the seating arrangements:

- Is everyone equally spaced?
- Does anyone have a special position, eg behind a big desk; at the head of a table?
- Can everyone make eye contact?
- How possible is it to rearrange the groupings of chairs and tables?

It is remarkable how often tutors maintain an evidently dominant position for themselves by sitting behind their desk, with students grouped round in front, without being conscious of the effect it has on participation. Figure 7.2 indicates

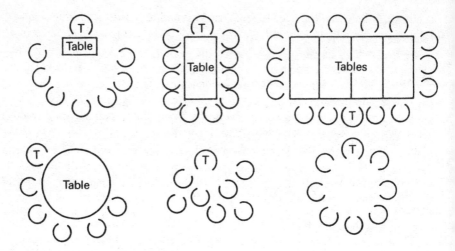

Figure 7.2 *Optional arrangements of furniture in the classroom*

some of the layouts commonly used in tutor-centred discussion groups. I leave the reader to make judgements on the level of participation and the sort of communication pattern likely to occur in each case.

Although an awareness of the effects of the physical position of students and tutor may be highly desirable, there may nevertheless be a limit to the amount of self-conscious juggling of furniture that a group of students will be prepared to undertake. Sometimes there is a sense of 'Why can't we just stay as we are?', and perhaps the tutor should bow to this feeling rather than make a self-conscious effort to 'structure the environment'. If the configuration of chairs and tables is strange to the students, the tutor may have to explain the rationale, particularly when the students themselves are invited to help in the operation. An obsession with rearranging the furniture can indeed unsettle students.

Even in such an apparently 'impersonal' task as arranging furniture, some sensitivity to the underlying feelings of students may be necessary. Students can become oddly unsettled by unexpected and unexplained changes in the physical environment of the classroom.

Such a change, or the prospect of it, might precipitate other changes too. At a recent class with a group of students who were accustomed to my moving the tables out of the way and the chairs into a circle, a fascinating but tense discussion about an unrelated issue developed as we stood by the door on the way into the room.

This led in turn to an enthusiastic switch of interest by the students into an unexpected field of study. In my judgement, the cliff-hanging conversation would have collapsed had I then killed the moment with: 'Look, before we sort this out, could we just rearrange the furniture?'

The physical scenario of teaching is something which requires careful handling and its effects are not always predictable. As with all manoeuvres connected with group study however, the need to reveal reasons and to be attuned to the resulting feelings can not only make things easier but be of unforeseen benefit to the learning process.

Planning what to do

It is never easy to decide in advance what will catch the imagination of a group of students or to anticipate what kind of learning might occur through a one- or two-hour session. To some extent, the learning may be gauged by the level of subject matter implicit in the prior reading. Nevertheless, to rely on a factor external to the dynamic of the group and its stage of development might have a stultifying effect. Both theory and research inform us that both the evolving dynamic of a group and the intellectual growth of students require that the sophistication and the spectrum of aims and tasks should change and develop both within each meeting of the group and as the group progresses through a course.

The choice of aims and tasks will be largely predetermined by what is feasible for a particular group and its physical environment, and also by its state of preparedness. Prior reading is a clear case in point; group discussion frequently falls down or lapses into a mini-lecture as a result of inadequate preparation by the students. If this is likely to happen, the sensible tutor will have some alternative strategy in readiness. Here are three possibilities:

- Have copies of a few seminal paragraphs, discussion points, or critiques related to the text which the students can quickly read in the group (for the tutor to talk through what the students have not read puts the tutor in a lecturing role).
- Discuss with the students why the work has not been done and perhaps agree a firm contract henceforward on preparatory work.
- Cancel the meeting on the grounds that nothing useful can take place until the students have fulfilled their part of the (implied) contract.

As we saw in Chapter 5, specifying aims in group teaching carries with it several hazards mainly because of the unpredictability of the outcome. Nevertheless, depending on the overall purpose of the group meeting, there are good reasons for improving our capacity to understand the tutor's job better through a process like the one shown in Figure 7.3. It indicates how we as tutors might take time out to anticipate, monitor, reflect and revise procedures.

As with all cycles, one can engage in the process at any point, though logically one might be expected to start at 'BEFORE'. The proposed activities under each stage are:

- *Before* – consider what you want to achieve (aims);
  - decide on how you might do so (techniques/tasks);
  - write some notes on these to refer to after (read up any notes on previous sessions);
  - try to anticipate incidents or developments which might occur (start with 'the worst thing that could happen is . . .');

Figure 7.3 *Monitoring strategy for group tutors*

- imagine what you might do to meet such eventualities;
- decide how you might monitor what happens in the group during its progress.

- *During* – monitor what is happening; this will at the very least require you to set yourself slightly apart from the discussion at times, even when you are directly involved;
  - ask yourself how your intentions compare with what you observe happening and what that implies;
  - whenever the opportunity occurs take 'time out' either by yourself or collectively to take stock of progress.

- *After* – jot down notes on what you did and what you didn't do that you wished you had (while the memory of them is still vivid);
  - check back with the notes you wrote before the session;
  - review the session – if possible with a colleague – and in any case jot down further notes on what you want to do differently next time;
  - look at any other information you have gleaned, eg video or audiotape, questionnaire, informal chats with students outside.

- *Interim* – mull it over;
  - read books like this one for new ideas;
  - revise as you see fit;
  - prepare new material.

While this model can be viewed as a 'macro' cycle of thought processes and experiences, most reflective tutors will be carrying out a series of 'mini' cycles in which the process of anticipation, decision, action and assessment are quickly, if not subliminally, rehearsed during the group session.

A more representative diagram might therefore be that of Figure 7.4.

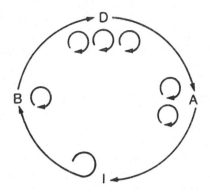

Figure 7.4 *Modified strategy for monitoring*

This whole procedure may strike the busy tutor as far too self-conscious and elaborate for practical purposes. Yet it is merely making explicit a process of thinking that commonly exists at a subliminal level which, because it is conducted unconsciously, is prey to the vicissitudes of emotional blocking and denial. In other words it is an attempt, as is much of this book, to apply academic canons and procedures to our everyday practice: and by and large we are notoriously poor at doing just that!

The practical value of any of these catechisms is probably as great as those of a more religious intent: they depend on some commitment to the faith and on a kind of dedication to the task. Yet they do require honest checks against first-hand experience. A 'meta' cycle might therefore be added – a check on the whole procedure and its revision or replacement according to personal needs.

The simplest adaptation might be to reduce the 'catechism' to two simple questions which, though self-evident, are most helpful to ask oneself prior to each meeting with a group of students:

- What do I want to achieve?
- What do I need to do in order for that to happen?

It is to the second of those two questions that we now turn in looking at the tactical aspect of tutoring.

TACTICAL CONSIDERATIONS

Roles

As soon as tutor and students encounter each other at any meeting, mutual sets of expectations about personal behaviour begin to hold sway. As explained in Chapter 6, the tutor, like it or not, is invested with some of the authority of the institution as an organization inasmuch as it defines the rules and requirements of courses for the students, and this is compounded by the tutor's authority as judge and assessor of the students. In this sense the tutor will be an authority figure no matter how he or she may try to minimize it.

However, one must distinguish between being 'in authority', being 'an authority' and being 'authoritarian'. As tutors we are *in authority* for the reasons described above and because we have ultimate responsibility for the time and space boundaries in the meeting: that is, we are (usually) deferred to over questions of starting and finishing, and who may join or leave. We will also be perceived as *an authority* in respect of our expertise in the subject matter. When either of these aspects of authority is challenged there is a possibility that we will fall into an *authoritarian* style of leadership in order to preserve the only image or role we are able to conceive of ourselves. What sort of threat such a challenge poses depends on either our point of view or on how we personally experience the problem. Fears of losing control or (at the level of unconscious fantasy) of being destroyed, are common in such situations.

The virtue of acquiring a repertoire of options is again evident. The authority role is not the only one available to us. We can adopt one or more of several roles according to how we define the need and the educational aims. The following set of leadership roles present some options for the versatile tutor.

Leader/Instructor
This is the traditional role which is easily adopted through the preconceptions of both tutor and students though it frequently leads to dissatisfaction on the part of both. Typically, the tutor initiates proceedings and demonstrates control over content and process with a short statement or summary and then tries to draw out students' thoughts, periodically linking them together and redirecting the content of discussions as appropriate. Often the tutor's task in providing the initial stimulus is taken by a student, but in a sense only as an 'alter ego' for the tutor. There is a great danger with this role that the students may become over-dependent and feel constrained by what *the tutor* demonstrates as acceptable knowledge, ways of thinking and academic standards. In educational terms, at least, the tutor may thus establish an authoritarian or autocratic atmosphere. Sometimes students behave as if this atmosphere existed, even though they would hotly deny it.

Neutral chair
This is a variation of the leader/instructor role in which the tutor controls procedure but does not contribute to the content in any determining way. It is thus possible for the tutor to create a 'democratic' atmosphere (see page 37).

Facilitator
A difficult role for the 'traditional' teacher in that it involves careful listening and eliciting rather than giving of one's own knowledge. Both tutor and students may find this regime difficult and even painful to adapt to. It should not be supposed that the facilitator role represents a 'laissez-faire' style of leadership: rather is there

a sense of shared or developed responsibility for learning. It usually requires that the tutor be student-centred, helping students to express what they understand by respecting them for what they are rather than what they 'should' be.

Counsellor

If the personal or social needs of the students demand it, or if a tutorial is designated for such purposes, the tutor may wish to draw out some of the students' emotional problems on the grounds that sharing anxieties can be both relieving and reassuring, and may provide valuable feedback for the tutor. The tutor may also have some tentative suggestions for tackling the problems. Small, more 'intimate', groups are of course preferable for these purposes.

Commentator

The tutor sits outside the perimeter of the group and comments from time to time on the dynamic of the group interaction or on the kinds of arguments being used by members. In this way, though students may be aware of the tutor's presence and influence, they are not constantly using her or him as a reference point or focus of attention in discussion. (See also pages 107–8.)

Wanderer

Where the total group is split into sub-groups (as in a workshop) who are working on a set task, the tutor can helpfully infuse influence by circulating round the groups:

- to check their adherence to the task and identify any teething problems;
- to help them out of any unproductive patterns of thinking or interaction they have got into;
- to pick up trends in the discussions for use at any subsequent plenary discussion.

In this way we may as tutor perform several roles in our travels according to what is currently taking place in any group we happen to drop in on. Here again, the tutor's authority is in general evidence but should not be obtrusive within the groups.

Absent friend

Many of the best virtues arise from necessity: tutors who find it necessary to absent themselves from the group for reasons of nature or administration are often surprised at the intense buzz of conversation which greets them on their return. It is an interesting test of the effect of one's authority to make a video tape before, during and after one's temporary absence from a group. The essence of this 'role' is physical withdrawal from the room, and this applies equally to situations where sub-groups have been formed as to the integral group. For instance, it is not unusual for a tutor to sense that her or his presence is causing some sort of 'stuckness' in the group, especially where students are being asked to make a decision which requires them to reveal some of their doubts and uncertainties. There is a danger nevertheless of the group(s) disintegrating unless a task (implicit or explicit) is generally agreed for the duration of the tutor's absence.

The choice of role for the tutor may be determined by:

- the declared aims and objectives of the meeting or the course;
- the kind of task undertaken; or
- a summary assessment of the dynamic of the group.

Clarification of the role can help polarize activities more purposefully than is typically the case when the relationship between students and tutor is tacit and obscure. Several of the roles could be combined and varied over time. With a project group, for example, the tutor may first act as a chair, then as a facilitator, followed by consultant and, because of the students' withdrawal to work on their project, an absent friend.

It is arguable that as competent tutors, we are in and out of these roles continually and the above discussion merely confirms established modes. That is possibly so, but the muddled and often uneasy nature of some teaching relationships may need sorting out at times in order to make the transactions more straightforward and explicit. Students can thus reorient themselves to what the tutor offers and respond accordingly.

While the spelling out of roles may seem in general to be valuable there may be occasions when, for good reasons, the tutor may wish to leave things opaque; when for instance, the aim is to examine the students' response to the tutor in the traditional leader role in order to dig out some of the deep-seated assumptions they may have about teaching and learning. Richardson (1967) describes the resounding silence which frequently followed her proposal to a group of students that they decide for themselves the form and content of the discussion. She claims it is important to discuss this reaction on the road to achieving a better comprehension of crucial relationships in the group and particularly the most problematical one, that of authority.

If we look again at this question of authority in the group, it may now be apparent that some aspects of it are an unnecessary encumbrance to the creative tutor who may decide to devolve the leadership role among the members. Hill (1969) proposes a set of roles and functions which enable this devolution to take place. As the lack of satisfactory experience of democratic discussion makes it difficult for students to adopt such roles readily he proposes a list of criteria for gaining a common understanding of what effective discussion can be like. These criteria are that:

- a happy, non-threatening atmosphere prevails;
- learning is accepted as a co-operative exercise;
- learning is accepted as the object of discussion;
- everyone participates and helps others to take part;
- leadership functions are distributed;
- material is adequately covered;
- members attend regularly and are prepared for the discussion;
- evaluation (assessment) is accepted as an integral part of the discussion group.

This list corresponds in many respects with the University of East Anglia 'contract' (see page 191) though it does not mention the central issue of assessment. It does nevertheless clarify certain functions which group members may perform, when the occasion seems to demand it, in order to assist group process:

- initiating – starting the discussion, proposing new ideas, activities, resuming it after a lull;
- giving and asking for information;
- giving and asking for reactions;
- restating and giving examples;
- confronting and reality-testing – restating others' messages and checking their examples;
- clarifying, synthesizing and summarizing;
- timekeeping and holding groups to discussion plan;
- encouraging participation by others.

Readers will notice the similarities with Knowles's list of functions for group maintenance and task (page 35), though here the maintenance roles are somewhat underplayed. Obviously, these functions are not required at all times or in equal measure in a group. Indeed, as Knowles remarks, if a function is performed inappropriately it may interfere with the group's operation. But it can be helpful when a group is working unsatisfactorily to pause and consider which of these functions might be lacking and to remedy the situation before moving on. Whether the functions should be allocated to individuals or shared and used as necessary by the group as a whole is a moot point and will depend on the skill of its members. What is fairly certain is that members should be discouraged from playing just one role at every meeting, lest they become stereotyped in it. If possible, roles should be reallocated as and when individuals feel able to perform them adequately.

One might expect the competent tutor to realize all these behaviours in the leadership role, yet the value of sharing them round the group can be immense as then students are able to learn the skills for lifelong participation in groups. These positive or helping functions would, however, be of little use if due recognition were not also given to some of the 'negative' behaviours, which Hill lists as:

- aggressing (being aggressive);
- blocking;
- self-confessing;
- seeking sympathy;
- special interest pleading;
- playing around;
- status-seeking;
- withdrawing;
- dominating.

The appearance of these behaviours in individuals tends to be irritating to other members. They may be tackled most constructively through regular reflection on, or evaluation of, group process, but, always bearing in mind the need for a consistency between them and the group task.

NORMS OR RULES

Whereas roles describe the positions taken by individuals in a given context, norms or rules define the context.

Norms, except in particularly formal settings (eg committees) are internalized, implicit and generally unstated. Nevertheless, it is usually clear when they are broken: if disapproval is not openly expressed the 'offender' may feel a sense of exclusion.

In general, the norms of everyday interaction work for groups as long as they appear to be productive, or evidently maintain stability. Yet from our understanding of some of the unconscious processes to which groups regularly fall victim, it is apparent that in some cases the unexpressed needs of members may be satisfied only through somewhat destructive behaviours.

Everyday norms are often more ambiguous than many would like to believe, and there may be hidden disagreement about them anyway.

Many of the problems that students feel in expressing themselves in groups stem from either uncertainty about what the 'rules of the seminar game' are, or from their feeling overly constrained by assumed rules to do with authority and competition. For instance, it is frequently assumed that it is the tutor's job to fulfil most of the roles listed on pages 126 and 127 and it is not for the students to propose objectives, topics, changes of direction, or procedures. Often there is also a norm against expressing one's inner feelings or against interrupting anyone making a presentation. Several of the rules of behaviour in seminars are drawn by students from their school experience and have no great relevance in tertiary education. It is sometimes important therefore for a tutor to formulate with the group members some explicit ground rules which, though they may appear more constricting in some ways, can generate a sense of freedom as students begin to understand what is and is not 'OK' with the added knowledge that they are free to propose changes if they wish. It is the very fact that such ambiguities and confusions are hidden that leads some tutors, and more especially 'growth group' facilitators, to propose ground rules for discussion.

Making explicit rules can help students avoid distracting pressures and better concentrate on the learning task. Such 'ground' rules may be:

- that existing norms be changed or revoked, eg students may initiate and redirect discussion;
- formalistic – for example: no one speaks a second time before everyone else has spoken once; comments begin with 'I' (I believe, I imagine, I have read, etc); the tutor speaks only in answer to direct questions; no evaluative comment may be made, etc;
- meta-rules – everyone takes responsibility for the process (see Hill's list on pages 126–7); 'time out' may be called at any time to review progress and efficacy of the rules; all rules may be changed by a consensus.

It is clear that the more ground rules that are introduced, the nearer the discussion gets to a game (see page 101) and many students may take legitimate exception to that as a regular feature. However, there is a lot to be said for encouraging a group to explore its own norms and to consider which of these it means to keep and which to change in order to determine whether any improvement in the group climate takes place.

Leadership interventions

> Of a good leader, when his task is finished, his goal achieved, they say,
> 'We did it ourselves.' (Lao-tse)

Encouraging interaction

For several of the reasons already described, students are often strangely inhibited in discussion and at best seem prepared to make only rather formal contributions. As one student remarked:

'People ask questions and this stimulates the group. I feel we don't mind if a friend asks a question, but if a lecturer asks you, you dry up. A member of staff will always have the answer at his fingertips. I've always resented making an idiot of myself.'

Students who are remarkably talkative outside classes are often reluctant to contribute to group discussion when a tutor is present, and we have already noted how a tutor's leaving the room quickly stimulates a resurgence in conversation among the group, even on academic topics. What can a tutor do while present to induce a similar sense of open discussion among students without abdicating a leadership role? The necessary skills or behaviours are not difficult to acquire, though it may not be easy to produce them always when most wanted. They are nonetheless worth including in our repertoire even if we do need to perform them self-consciously in the first instance.

Glancing round the group: It is generally considered rude not to look at somebody when they are talking to you. Yet to do so as a group leader will quickly create the sort of communication pattern illustrated in Figure 2.1 (a). It is not easy to pick up the habit of scanning the group when we are talking, let alone when students are contributing. Though we will want to catch the eye of a student as he or she talks from time to time we can, by looking around, encourage them to follow suit and so cause the whole group to give that person more attention, thus discouraging the common tendency for discussion to drift into a series of one-to-one duologues.

Looking for signals: If, when one student is talking, we glance round the group, we will find ourselves picking up cues from others who are puzzled, or anxious to check something. As the contribution ends, we will be in a better position to draw in some of the less vocal students.

Often the cues are not more than an indrawn breath, a snort of frustration, a shifting of position, or a puzzled frown. To have noted them and to be seen to have done so, is usually helpful to us in the role of tutor in deciding what to do or what not to do at the next stage in the proceedings. We will also be better appraised of the group climate. In fact we may even be contributing to a more positive climate through the very act of glancing round the group.

Using non-verbal communication: Sometimes it may be difficult to interrupt a discussion without sounding critical or punitive. A non-verbal intervention can work wonders in this situation. On some occasions, this might consist of catching a student's eye and giving an encouraging smile or an invitation to speak by raising your eyebrows. On others, the connection may be through gestures – an extended palm to suggest 'Would you like to come in now?' or using two hands to indicate 'What does everyone else think?' Of course, these non-verbal signals are natural partners to verbal invitations but are generally less intrusive and just as productive. Two non-verbal gestures which are often used but seem to work effectively are the 'traffic cop' signals designed to bring students into a discussion and to block them out (see Figure 7.5.)

Bringing in and shutting out: The gestures in Figure 7.5 highlight two complementary purposes. In order to encourage a student to talk, it may be necessary for the tutor to invite him or her into the discussion, either verbally or non-verbally. By the same token, it is sometimes necessary to exclude more vocal members or to stop them before, as often happens, both their less vocal colleagues and they themselves have become fed up with what they are saying. This becomes a sort of 'rescue operation'.

Sometimes a verbal stimulus is also needed. For example, when a student silently smiles, looks puzzled, rolls their eyes you could say 'What are you thinking Liz?' or 'You smiled, John'. This usually has the desired effect of drawing a student into discussion.

However, the opposite problem may prevail: how to shut out someone who constantly talks or interrupts. Provided we can do it supportively and straightforwardly

Figure 7.5 *Hand signals for bringing in and shutting out*

– 'Could you just hold it there Brian, it would be interesting to know how the others respond to that' or 'Let's put that on ice for the moment, Gill, while we hear what everyone else has to say' – the student should not feel unduly put out. The problem is rather on the tutor's side, as it can feel extremely awkward consciously to interrupt someone in the sure (but often erroneous) belief that one could be hurting their feelings, and we may well feel that the risk is too great to take in a group of students. Should this be so, the solution might be to practise these skills within the safer company of colleagues in a 'practice' group (see Chapter 10).

Turning questions back: Of the many temptations open to the unsuspecting tutor, one is the supplicant question from students which places us on our authority pedestal: 'Can you tell us what you know about . . .?' 'What should the answer be?' for example.

The question can simply be turned back with: 'Well, what do *you* think?' on the grounds that:

- the student probably has an inkling of the answer anyway or would not have asked the question; and
- it is usually better to get students to formulate their own ideas in the first instance.

This is not to say that there are not many occasions when the tutor may be the only person present who could possibly know the answer to a particular question, or where a refusal to answer could slow down proceedings. The judgement in all these situations must be based on a recognition of the dynamic and the learning needs of the group.

A very useful and more comfortable variation of 'turning questions back' is to redirect or *deflect* them. For instance the question from a student: 'I don't understand what the author is trying to say. What does it all mean?' could be met with 'Well, what does anybody else think?' or 'Does everyone else have the same problem?' or 'Do you have *any* ideas about what it means?'

Supporting and valuing: Thus far we have considered some very quickfire, though not always easy, tactics for the tutor in a leadership role. However, it is easy to overlook an important ingredient of effective group discussion: the creation of a feeling of security and belonging; an atmosphere of trust and openness where people are valued for what they are and have no need to fear making a fool of themselves. Now this is easily said, but not so easily done in the thick of a hectic term's work where teaching and assessing become an almost undifferentiated continuum. The temptation to correct discussion contributions in the same way as one might write comments to an essay is great. Perry (1970) describes how tutors typically view the discussion as 'an opportunity to develop initiative and scope in their own thinking', at least initially.

No sooner do the students get started, however, and some error or inexactness is voiced, than the older form of responsibilities imposes on the tutor the imperative of 'correcting'.

In the time where this tendency gets in motion, three to five corrections of this kind appear sufficient to defeat the students' initiative for search and flow of their exploration. The initiative for conversation then falls back on the instructor who then finds himself in a monologue or lecture, with the sensation of being somehow trapped, compelled, by powerful forces, in himself and the students, to do what he had never intended to do.

This is not to say that the correction of 'errors' is an unacceptable sin. The question is not one of 'whether' but rather of 'when' and 'how'. To reject or correct the first contribution a student makes would generally be counterproductive. Apart from inhibiting expression, as in the above quotation, it is likely to lock the students into the first four stages of Perry's scale of intellectual development (see pages 45–6). Nevertheless some kind of corrective action may be called for – but this can be achieved in a less inhibiting and intellectually more elevating way:

- 'Is that *really* so?'
- 'Could you think about that again?'
- 'Let's just look at that more carefully.'
- 'How does that tally with what you said before?'
- 'Would anyone else like to comment on what George just said?'
- 'Uh-huh!'
- OK so what does everybody else think?'

and so forth.

Students will doubtless pick up that they have said something irrelevant or inconsistent but be encouraged to discover their own way out.

Checking and building: Students (not to speak of tutors) are not always as lucid as they would wish to be when formulating ideas for the first time. Some of the most imaginative contributors to a discussion may find it difficult to express their half-formed ideas clearly at first. Lest the whole group continue in a state of confusion the tutor can quickly check for understanding by simply asking: 'Let me check that I understand you. Are you saying . . .?' The student is often grateful for the clarification. What the student *does* say may well relate to a line of argument pursued earlier in discussion or contradict something he or she has said earlier. In each case, the tutor can help to make links with comments such as: 'That ties in with what you were saying before – it sounds as though you have a coherent view of it' or 'Does that contradict what you said a few minutes ago?' or 'So it would be fair to say that whilst you disagree with the functionalist view, you have not yet . . .'

Ideally, it would be preferable if the students were left to make the interpretation for themselves: 'How does that connect with what you said before?' 'Is Julie being consistent there?'

Sometimes the tutor may go further in putting several emerging themes together and formulating a new coherent picture of the topic under discussion. But again – how much better it would be to allow the students to do so for themselves!

Re-directing The initiative required of a tutor in acting on the physical environment, which we discussed on pages 119–21, is just as valuable when it comes to changing the social interaction. Again it is a matter of knowing when it is important to act and when the prevailing climate is too good to destroy. It is never easy, especially when the tutor has a planned schedule of discussion, to decide whether students would be glad of a change in the direction of the discussion or would feel cheated of a rewarding line of interest. Yet sometimes it *is* necessary to take command and say: 'Hang on to that but let's switch our attention to another aspect . . .' or 'I think we've reached the point where we could turn our attention to . . .'

More often than not, it is difficult to be sure of the climate and also of one's own motives. A safer way of approaching the problem may once again be to test the group: 'Are you ready now to . . .?' 'Do you think we've worked on that one for long enough now?'

It may be even more valuable to check the process as well as content: 'Could we stop at this point and check whether we're going about this the right way?' This intervention is almost identical with the basketball term *'time out'* in which teams take a break from the game to review progress and discuss tactics.

There is nothing unusual about all these leadership interventions. They are practised quite frequently in everyday life but are somehow forgotten in the culture of a discussion group. We must, however, use them with discretion, not in pursuit of our own needs, but in response to what our growing awareness of the group process tells us.

Asking questions

Supposing a tutor were to open discussion with:

'Do you think the assassination of Archduke Francis Ferdinand was intended as a precipitating factor for World War I, even though none of the schemers, if schemers they were, could have had any notion of the consequences in terms of both the extent of hostilities and the degree of suffering that resulted?'

Pause. Ten seconds' silence.

'Let me put it another way. On the evidence we have, was the war a typical example of intentional cause in international conflict? Or was World War II a better one?'

Pause. Another ten seconds' silence.

'Did nobody read the papers I asked you to look at last week?'

What, if anything, went wrong here? Were the questions too complicated? Did the tutor wait long enough for an answer? What sort of answer was expected? This imaginary dialogue (based on two real transcripts) is intended to demonstrate at least one of the common traps in asking questions: posing a multi-part, highly academic and leading question at the start of a session, not waiting long enough for a response and then rephrasing it as another question. We all do this sort of thing from time to time and we usually wish we could 'unask' the question rather than become more deeply enmeshed through our own wish to appear clever. Yet having got ourselves into this fix perhaps we could learn from this tutor by waiting a little longer for a response, using our 'third ear' to reflect on the way the question came out, and possibly checking with students: 'Do you want me to re-phrase that?' or 'Was that question too complex/obscure/involved to answer?'

Questions serve at least three purposes in discussion: to test the students' knowledge, to clarify information, and to stimulate students into expressing ideas and constructing arguments. Very often the same question can satisfy all these purposes, though that will depend on the group climate and any underlying message in the question.

There is perhaps a further purpose served by questions: the opportunity they give the tutor, or anyone else in the group, to make a link between what they and the others are thinking. The choice of question will depend very much on when it is put and the purpose of the discussion. If, however, we take the above three purposes of questioning, we can look at the different types of questions which relate to each and leave the decision as to their practical application to the reader.

Testing questions: These will mainly begin with words like 'what', 'where', 'when', 'which' – and will therefore be essentially convergent as they are intended to elicit specific information. They are concerned with:

* checking knowledge – 'What is the best catalyst for . . .?' 'Which critics have described *Godot* as a comedy?'
* comprehension – 'How do you justify that . . ,?'
* application – 'How do you predict that would work in . . .?' 'What relevance does that have in . . .?
* analysis – 'What qualities do these have in common?' 'What would happen if . . .?'
* synthesis – 'How does that connect with . . .?' 'Could you summarize what we've discussed so far?'
* evaluation – 'Which do you think is best?' 'How do you feel about that?'

Such questions are clearly linked with Bloom's taxonomy (see page 69) and the accompanying list of verbs might prove a helpful reference. However, they can, as part of a *probing* exercise (Hedley and Wood, 1978) be combined in a way which is searching and vigorous.

Clarifying questions: Whether a question is defined as a clarifying or as an elaborating one will often depend on the expression on the questioner's face and what has preceded the question. However, these sorts of questions could be used to clarify:

* 'Can you rephrase that?'
* 'What did you mean by . . .?'

- 'Can you give me an example?'

Where the last question fails we might follow it up with: 'Might this be an example . . .?' and provide one of our own.

Elaborating: Elaborating questions are essentially a gentler way of enquiring than the other questions we have discussed. They are concerned with helping students express themselves more fully, both in thought and feeling:

- 'Can you tell me more?'
- 'Could you elaborate on that?'
- 'Uh-huh, what else?'
- 'How does that make you feel?'

Echoing and selective echoing (see page 25) while not strictly a form of question, have an important place here. For example:

Student: 'I've been thinking that, if you take the phenomenological argument to its limits then you end up with nobody helping others to make sense of their own world. There would be no point in teaching, for a start.'

Tutor: 'No point in teaching.' (Echoing)

or

Tutor: 'Take the argument to its limits.' (Selective Echoing)

It is easy to see how, with a little inflexion, these 'echoes' could sound like quite threatening questions. It is essential therefore that they are said in a *neutral tone* as though one was ruminating over the particular phrase.

There are also questions which are intended to rouse the curiosity or the imagination. For example: 'I wonder if that really would happen?' or 'If you were in that position, what would you do?'

Often questions like these are best kept ambiguous, though this could be very threatening for a new group.

Let us not forget, too, the principle of personal relevance mentioned already in the section on communications. A question like: 'How did it seem to you?' or 'What did you like about it?' is much more acceptable as a starter than: 'What is your assessment of Y's Theory?'

It is clearly not in the best interest of discussion that the tutor should spend most of the time asking questions: this would quickly set up a focal pattern of communication. The more students can competently take over the task of asking each other questions the more responsibility they will be taking for their own learning. However, it is quite properly the tutor's job to explore and probe further into students' understanding of issues.

The following counsel to tutors who want to avoid getting stuck with unproductive questioning processes comes from UTMU (1978).

- Try to have some idea of the mental processes students are going through, and adjust your questions to the way they respond rather than thinking up good questions beforehand as though the quality of a question was independent of the time, place and person involved.
- Try to avoid questions which suggest one answer is expected more than another, eg 'Do you think Wordsworth had a great influence on Coleridge?' Rather ask: 'What sort of relationship do you see between the works of Wordsworth and Coleridge?'
- Try to avoid playing the game, an elaboration of the above, in which you invite the students to guess what is in your mind, as in the children's party game 'Hunt the Thimble'. If you do not want students to arrive at a predetermined answer or you have your own favourite solution, it is probably better to draw out a range of possible answers from students and then encourage discussion of their merits. This often produces ideas which you had not previously not thought of. You may then reveal your own list for comparison.
- Try to ask questions which give informative answers. Avoid verbal checklists: 'Did you calculate the mean?' 'Did you subtract the mean from each reading?' Rather ask: 'Tell me exactly what you did', followed by 'What about . . .?' 'What else?' 'Uh-huh?'.
- Ask questions which elicit responses at the higher end of Bloom's Taxonomy, (see page 69) eg 'Could you put those ideas together for us?' 'How does that theory compare with the other?' 'How important do you think this scheme is?' 'How do you feel about it?' or 'How committed do you feel to that?'
- Be very cautious about showing approval and disapproval in evaluating answers. Sometimes it may help reticent students to have their one and only contribution approved, but disapproval is likely to change what a student is willing to say. An honest attempt to contribute should be welcomed. If you feel a comment is irrelevant to the discussion (remember it may not be irrelevant to the student concerned or to the other students), you may respond with 'That's very interesting – could we come back to it later once we have settled the issue of . . .? It is important to recognise that the apparent irrelevance of a comment may be an indication that the student is feeling out of depth or has had to wait so long to speak that the contribution has become out of date.
- Once you have asked a question, be prepared to wait for an answer. Short silences are not necessarily a bad thing – they often get students talking more freely in the long run once they know you require (and appreciate) an honest answer to an honest question. If every question is greeted with silence then it might be of value to discuss with the group why this may be so.
- If you find you do not get the answer you want, consider the possibility that the answer a student gives may be the answer he or she wants, or that you have asked the wrong question!
- Sometimes it can be useful to encourage individual thought about a question by asking students to write some brief notes which might then be compared with a neighbour's. As well as allowing students to stand back from the discussion for a while it can encourage participation by quieter members. Notes may sometimes be transferred to a board or overhead projector so that they may be shared more easily.

Remember you can often ask questions with little more than the raising of an eyebrow (if you can do it!). Facial expressions are frequently a more direct and less threatening means of querying someone's contribution.

DISCUSSION POINTS

- What prior planning is done in order that the groups to which you belong run successfully?
- What assumptions lie behind the various interactions, roles and rules described in this chapter? To what extent might *students* employ them?
- Write one or two ground rules that might improve interaction in your group. Invite the group to try them out in order to gauge their value.
- Make a note of the number of times you exercise the function on page 127 in your group. Invite others to do the same and compare notes.

8 Learning Groups in Context

THE LEARNING MILIEU

Although the institutional setting in which a learning group occurs may not be seen by the group itself to have a significant influence over their deliberations, it is evident that students can be profoundly affected by aspects of institutional life outside the formal curriculum. Parlett (1977) contrasts the educational foreground of lectures, tutorials, courses, examinations and so on with the relatively unchanging background of buildings, traditions, local customs, geographical features, etc.

> While students are concerned – inevitably and properly – with attending to the foreground, much of what they do and think about while in the institution is governed by the background. That this is ever present, 'taken as read', and rarely examined systematically is no guarantee it is educationally insignificant in its long-term impact.

The view that a department has of itself is a kind of foreground which may conflict with the background of learning norms among students. Indeed the more loudly trumpeted the self-image, the more likely is the presented picture to be a false one with consequent disillusionment for students. Self-image is often revealed at induction talks designed to orientate students to their studies. Parlett reports one department that adopted a tough and austere image, warning the students of the hard work ahead, that some would fail and that the control of knowledge and its dissemination lay firmly with the department. Another conveyed a more open attitude to learning; the department chair talked about University as: 'a time during which you should take a critical look at yourselves and rethink things – it should be a most stimulating time', and later broke the meeting into small groups to discuss the course. He cautioned: 'Don't let the work get on top of you.' A third department set the tone by immersing students in their work from the start with experiments involving measurements of each other, while staff circulated and instructed students on techniques.

Nevertheless, it is more than possible for student norms to prevail in spite of staff intentions. Students can be reluctant to discuss academic matters outside the organized class – there is often a taboo on it. Further, there may be strong disinclination among students to follow what they agree are desirable educational goals but which conflict with more immediate pressures to do with assessment. In physical sciences for instance, some students are likely to look for 'correct' answers to tutorial problems rather than engage in a more open intellectual discussion even though they may accept this as valuable in a more professional sense.

Many of these features of student life become part of the folklore that is passed on from one influx of students to another. Folklore can, as Parlett suggests, support the status quo so much more powerfully when the departmental sub-culture becomes insulated from the wider culture of the institution and the outside world through the self-confirming nature of its academic ideology and the

> progressive retrenchment of certain ideas that all within the organisation adhere to and take for granted, and which are not exposed to any bracing challenge from the outside. (Parlett, 1977)

Students also draw comparisons between experiences of different groups and between the learning milieu in different departments and these often serve to underline the prevailing folklore.

The physical environment

Whatever the aims of a curriculum or the motives of individuals, the physical arrangement of teaching rooms, staff offices, corridors, social and domestic amenities and constraints of the timetable will be a significant factor in determining the pattern of communication and relationships in an institution. To some extent, powerful drives such as the need for personal affiliation can mitigate many of the physical barriers – distance for one. However, where the desire to learn is (as it often seems to be) a less than powerful drive, physical proximity and frequency of encounter may have a marked effect. The nearer one lives to somebody, the greater the likelihood that chance meetings will occur and even where they do not, their likelihood may also exert a strong influence. Of course, the very fact of meeting does not ensure that effective communication will occur; nor does the lack of meeting mean that it will not. Festinger, Schachter and Back (1950), quoted in Smith (1973), reported in a study of friendship patterns in The Massachusetts Institute of Technology, that students whose rooms were relatively inaccessible had fewer friends and those whose rooms were more accessible had more friends and they tended to be from nearby.

A similar situation exists where the proximity of a 'significant' person or object causes a person to attend to them more readily than another at a greater distance. People are always more alert to immediate demands. It is likely, therefore, that frequent casual encounters with tutors and group colleagues will serve as a regular reminder of agreed tasks and a spur for new ideas for the group. The frequency of group meetings will determine the extent to which the group ethos will prevail over other priorities.

To some extent the total size of the institution will also affect the sense of group identity because the likelihood of chance meetings is lessened both with physical distance and with a larger population. It would seem likely that the anonymity and the sense of alienation that may grow in bigger institutions would push people into small (and perhaps deviant) affinity groups and discourage participation in organized group activities. This hypothesis is supported to some extent by Barker (1968) who found that with the increasing size of a school, students tended to become audience rather than participant in many of the school activities.

In the same way, it is probable that the physical shape of the environment will influence the nature of casual interaction. A building designed as a set of rooms leading off long corridors limits encounters to hasty exchanges in the corridor or specially arranged meetings in designated places, neither of which promotes spontaneous communication. A conveniently situated open area or refreshment facility can offset this sort of environmental drawback to some extent, but there is so substitute for rooms arranged round a central area with refreshments immediately available.

The problems of communication and relationships in the environment appear to echo those experienced in the learning group. Size, physical layout, personal proximity and so forth all play their part. The style of interaction present in a learning group could also be influenced to a large extent by its general environment. The implication of these considerations is that whether one is thinking of the learning group or its environment, physical arrangements must be taken into consideration if the kind of educational and social relationships we desire are to occur.

EDUCATIONAL MATTERS

The design of a course, or curriculum, involves many value judgements about styles and techniques of teaching and learning and the order in which they should occur. Ideally these judgements should be subsumed under a general educational style or philosophy agreed by the teachers and even the students. However, the limits imposed on educational procedures by logistics, such as disposition and availability of rooms and timetabling of other classes, frequently make the reality of curriculum development an untidy compromise. More often than not, educational ideals are decimated by timetables which organize course programmes into a fragmented collection of learning experiences for the student and give a similar sense of disconnectedness to the teachers.

However, it would be unfair to place the blame for this kind of course entirely on timetabling committees. Teachers themselves are prone to equally myopic tendencies in at least two ways. One is connected with course content or subject matter, which is frequently regarded as a sort of academic territory to be established and defended against the encroachment of other warring tribes of academe. The second is the way in which the subject content is transmitted and the apparent need to control its dissemination and boundaries. It is normally the teacher who determines what is to be learned, and how, and what counts for an acceptable standard of learning. However, beneath all this there may exist a hidden curriculum; one in which the teaching is geared to the interests and levels of achievement of only the brighter students to the neglect of the majority whose main, and perhaps only, concern is to qualify competently and get a job. What Stenhouse (1975) describes as:

> Official policies which tend to encourage those (school) teachers who turn away from the practical and vocational realities of their pupils and turn to higher things

acquire even more significance in tertiary education where the power of abstract reasoning, in which many otherwise able students are not proficient, is highly valued.

Tutors usually define what they regard as reality and 'acceptable' knowledge in discussion groups and can quickly and firmly establish norms about the kind and level of knowledge that may be discussed. Many of these norms are determined by the style of tutor intervention. Sometimes, the style can be inhibiting; for example, where tutors open a seminar with a learned introduction or where their eloquence sets too high a standard for students who are still struggling to put their half-formed ideas together, never mind express them.

On the other hand, tutors can equally well set standards whilst still drawing students into the discussion. They can, for instance, pick out what they consider loose or 'incorrect' thinking and reflect it back either to the contributor or to the whole group using some of the interventions given in Chapter 7 and in Rudduck (1978).

In their capacity as both leaders and organizers of learning groups, tutors are involved in mediating the values, requirements and ultimately the authority of the institution which, willingly or not, they will be seen to represent. They also have the quasi-administrative role of passing on and collecting organizational information: small groups provide an effective means of ensuring that some of the more difficult administrative guidance is given and properly understood. How a tutor carries out the administrative/organizational function can be crucial to the relationship established with a group. However, there is one organizational role which can have a much more critical effect on the atmosphere of the group: that of assessor. Whether the concern is with setting exams, marking essays/lab work, or in appraising contributions to the discussion group, the tutor's authority can be seen by the students as all-pervading because of the typically unilateral nature of assessment.

It is a fact (an unfortunate one perhaps) of academic life that both tutors and students frequently collude in a sort of protocol or game, the rules of which may be expressed by: 'You may be too mature or free to be controlled by my asserted authority but I know you know I'm your assessor, even if I pretend that I'm not.'

The anxieties surrounding assessment affect many seminar groups:

> The seminar, ideally, is a place where people can take risks with ideas. Risk-taking is more likely to occur in a secure structure and the security of the seminar is sometimes threatened for students by uncertainty about assessment. Are they being assessed? And, if so, on what? The obvious conclusion, in the absence of any explanation of the assessment pro-

cedure, is that they are being assessed on their spoken contributions (frequency? length? or the elusive concept of quality?]. (Rudduck, 1978)

The tendency of some seminar tutors to maintain power by preserving the ambiguity of their assessment role can therefore create a group atmosphere which is both counter-educational and uncomfortable. As Rudduck explains:

> The shadow of assessment is likely to make the enquiry more teacher-oriented than it might if there were no assessment or if the rules of assessment were made clear to the students.

There is, of course, an essential tension between the two roles of mentor/ facilitator and that of assessor. This is particularly so where continuous assessment takes place or where students' seminar performance is appraised. In such cases as Richardson (1967) describes, the

> responsibility for assessment has to be recognised by teacher and student alike as part of the fabric of the personal relationship between them; there is no longer any way of externalising it.

Richardson's approach to the problem when working with student teachers was to bring the subject of assessment out into the open and work through the anxieties which the duality of her role implied. It was apparent to her that student behaviour changed both when essay titles were given and when essays were due to be handed in. The complex of behaviours, developed in school, to handle the student-teacher's hopes and fears about assessment in classroom revealed itself in an uncharacteristic rivalry for the tutor's approval and a mutual sense of embarrassment and secretiveness about what they were learning in preparing their essays. After the problems of assessment had been openly discussed within the group, the atmosphere changed dramatically to one of cheerfulness and buoyancy, and the group acquired a 'personal commitment and intellectual enjoyment not previously evident except in one-to-one sessions'. Yet again the value of self-disclosure (see page 55) as a trigger to have a more open climate of communication seems to have worked.

At the University of East Anglia, the 'assessment problem' has been tackled in one subject area (moral philosophy) by the drawing up of a learning contract in which the assessment function of the tutor is openly described. For example:

> It is important to make explicit that *nothing you do (or fail to do) in the small group meetings will be assessed for grading purposes.* Grades for the course will be determined by two essays . . .
> Although grades will be determined by the above essays *no grade will be given unless you keep a record of the work done for and in the small group meetings.* This record will consist of a loose-leaf folder containing:
> – Accounts of your work in the sub-group;
> – Accounts of the themes and arguments raised each week in the small group meetings;

- Three summaries of your own, developing views, to be written at the end of weeks 3, 6, and 9. (Rudduck, 1978)

In this way, what happens in the groups becomes a necessary part of the assessment procedure yet is not itself assessed. How effective this procedure was at UEA is not reported.

This section would not be complete without some reflection on the pervasive influence of a more traditional assessment procedure, the three-hour unseen examination. The mounting anxiety which increasingly afflicts the group discussion as the 'exam season' approaches is familiar to most tutors, and there is often little they can do to offset it, except to recognize it and perhaps take 'time out' to discuss its nature and possible remedies. Like most anxieties, its effect is to cause regression among the student population to the point where many of the higher-level aims cannot be realized. Students become increasingly concerned with picking up bits of knowledge to tuck away under their belts and are unwilling to engage in the more open-ended and creative kind of discussion which may have prevailed before.

Where the tutor is also the examiner or, as is even more likely, has sight of the exam papers, students may take up various stratagems to reduce their anxiety. Millar and Parlett (1974) discerned three groups of students in their study of the effects of examinations at Edinburgh University: the *cue seekers*, who actively sought to pick up hints about exam questions and tried to make a good impression on tutors; the *cue-conscious* who were equally aware but not active in their approach; and the *cue deaf* who believed that only hard work achieved success and that any impression they made on tutors would have no effect on their marks. (How these practices affect the quality of interaction in group discussion is not reported; one could make an inspired guess without much difficulty.) However, there was a clear indication that tutors became involved in an equivalent set of behaviours – hinters, tantalizers and non-hinters, depending on whether they are anxious about students not doing well in their subject, want to relieve unproductive student anxiety, or like to play a one-sided power game. As in most interactions involving anxiety, a collusive pattern of behaviour between students and tutor can easily develop. All this activity can be seen as part of what Snyder (1971) calls the 'Hidden Curriculum' – strategies which students resort to in order to survive.

GROUPS AS PART OF THE CURRICULUM

Let us now look again at the legitimate framework of learning in which tutors and groups are engaged. As we have already noted, the amount of time and physical space available for discussion groups can have a profound effect on the kind of learning which takes place. There is the world of difference, for instance, between the small group of eight students working intensively with a tutor for three hours, with a 20-minute coffee break included, and a science 'tutorial' in which 20 students assemble for one hour in a room with fixed benches or large tables arranged in rows.

Small group teaching must not be seen in isolation from the rest of the curriculum or its associated culture. In physical sciences, as indicated in Chapter 5, there has traditionally been a tendency to view small group work as an added extra, a means of improving students' understanding of lecture material for instance, rather than as a coherent mode of learning in its own right. Part of the problem is the enormous load of information in the syllabus which science and engineering lecturers believe must be transmitted (though how much is actually learned is a different matter). Yet whatever view we may take of the students' role in learning it is evident that knowledge, to be learned effectively, must be processed, its meaning incorporated into the students' patterns of thinking, and ultimately communicated by the student in a coherent and acceptable form. If the syllabus is taught as an accumulating sequence where each stage of learning is dependent on the previous one, then it is essential that the students learn progressively and not terminally: they must integrate their understanding as they go along rather than through a 'flash in the pan' revision at examination time. Group discussion is an invaluable aid to this kind of continuous learning. If it is to be used, the course must be tailored to accommodate it as an integral feature.

Timetabling group discussion

Several frameworks are possible for the inclusion of group work in the formal timetable. Some of the groups are planned to occur within lecture periods, some between; yet others are linked to practical classes. Whether or not several groups can operate concurrently will depend upon the number of students, tutors and available facilities. For example, within a large hall with moveable furniture, any number of small groups could be formed before, during or after a lecture. In a terraced lecture theatre, however, any sustained small group discussion would probably have to be left till after the lecture.

Some possible arrangements for the integration of group discussion are shown in Figures 8.1, 8.2 and 8.3.

In Figure 8.1 we can see how in teaching a large group we can introduce the kind of practices described in previous chapters while maintaining a sense of continuity and momentum. The session begins with the lecturer displaying on the OHP, while the students are still assembling, a set of headings which review the previous lecture(s), thus making effective use of what is normally 'dead' time.

The lecturer then goes on to address the outline on the OHP thus pulling together ideas and topics dealt with in prior reading, seminars and lectures. No new material is added at this stage. Note that this is the longest formal input in the session – only nine minutes!

For Stage 3, a new transparency poses a question which directs students to work in twos or threes in making an application of their previous work. The lecturer moves round the class listening, helping and clarifying where necessary.

Stage 4 comprises a further short lecture with explicitly new material: students

Time

10.00 am

Stage 1   Revision OHP displayed   10.05 am

Stage 2   Revision talk on last lectures   10.14 am

Stage 3   Task: discuss in pairs   10.19 am

Stage 4   Talk   10.26 am

Stage 5   Task: Discuss in pairs   10.30 am

Stage 6   Lecturer summarizes student answers.
          10.33 starts lecturing again.   10.36 am

Stage 7   Task: specific questions on a map: 10.42 am
          discuss in pairs

Stage 8   Lecturer answers first two questions 10.43 am

Stage 9   Continued discussion in pairs   10.45 am

Stage 10 Talk: Lecturer gives answers & lectures) 10.48 am
          (using OHPs)

Stage 11 30-second task: in pairs   10.48 am

Stage 12 Lecturer refers to handout not covered 10.54 am
          in lecture

Stage 13 Students summarize lecture for themselves 10.56 am

                                                End

Total lecturer talk   :   31 mins_____

Total student work   :   25 mins_____

Longest lecturer talk   :   9 mins

Longest student task   :   6 mins

Number of 'segments' of lecture: 13

*Source:*Alan Jenkins, Oxford Polytechnic

Figure 8.1 *Integrating group discussion into the lecture*

add new points to their handouts. This is followed by students discussing these new points in pairs while the lecturer moves round to check for understanding. A review of the students' responses is given by the lecturer in Stage 6. In Stage 7 the lecturer poses more difficult questions to the pairs concerning interpretation; this stimulates a buzz of activity at a point when one would typically expect a trough in the level of attention.

The lecturer then answers part of the question in Stage 8 and leads students to more advanced issues. The pattern of lecturer–student interaction continues till the last few minutes when students are asked to write a brief summary of the lecture.

This style of presentation requires not merely a considerable amount of assertiveness on the part of the lecturer in making sure that events move on crisply, but also a sensibility of the time needed to carry out each activity. However, a central ingredient for success in this approach is a very clear and explicit statement to the students on why one is lecturing in this way.

This sort of structure suggested in Figure 8.1 for a lecture session requires both careful planning and firm but sensitive direction by the tutor, particularly in making decisions about when to change the learning activity. A more extended version of the above scheme is shown in Figure 8.2.

Figure 8.3 demonstrates a combination of group and individual work for practicals which carries over the distilled learning from one session to the next.

This arrangement primes students for a collective encounter with the lecturer. It makes a clear contrast to the kind of lecture that ends in a throwaway comment like:'Oh, next week we shall be looking at the application of complex numbers to

Figure 8.2 *Sequencing lectures and group discussion*

2nd part of lst practical		Study time	1st part of 2nd practical
90 minutes	45 minutes		45 minutes
Groups do experiments	Paired groups share findings and discuss critically	Individuals write up reports	Paired groups appraise reports in dyads and discuss as a whole

Figure 8.3 *Combining group and individual work in practicals*

space frames', a type of ending not unknown in physical science, or a lengthy and unannotated booklist in social science.

The permutations of these arrangements are considerable and each tutor would have to work out a plan according to the aims and logistics of the course. In some cases, alternation and linking of lecture and discussion can be tightly organized as a total strategy for the whole course. In others, given some leeway, it can be incorporated within an otherwise standard timetable.

In looking at ways in which sequences of group work may be organized within a fairly traditional curriculum we should not forget that there are many courses or parts of courses where there may be much more freedom to experiment and to provide for varying degrees of self-direction in the groups. Some approaches of this kind are described in the second part of this chapter but for the sake of contrast it is worth mentioning here three other approaches.

One is the kind of group project, already discussed on pages 96–101, which is scheduled so as to allow students to learn, as the project evolves, the knowledge and skills required for its successful completion. This they do by using the staff as individual consultants on certain topics, having lectures arranged in response to emerging interests, and attending training sessions in teamwork, creative thinking and report writing.

Another approach is described by Fransson (1976) as 'group-centred instruction'. In this, though there is a curriculum to be followed, the organization of learning lies with the group who may determine how, within certain guidelines, they wish to use their tutors. The tutors in turn make certain demands of the groups, instances being the writing of diaries, assessment discussions and questions which demand co-operative work.

The third approach is the scheme in operation in the medical faculty at McMaster University where the students learn clinical work in groups, frequently with simulated patients. Their formal assimilation of knowledge mostly takes the form of library study in response to the practical problems presented to the group. Group work is considered sufficiently important for each student to be presented with learning resources on group work – eg 'The Small Group Tutorial', obtainable from the faculty of Medicine (see also Neufeld and Barrows, 1974).

Schemes like these make special demands of the students and tutors in overcoming the various constraints, habits and norms of the educational institution of which they are part. Any evaluation of success must therefore take into account the influences of the total learning milieu which may include implacable opposition by colleagues and by some of the students for whom the dispersal of authority may be extremely unsettling. Nevertheless, more traditional schemes of teaching, it seems, are often followed purely because they fulfil mutual expectations – college is, after all, the place where eminent people are supposed to give lectures and demonstrate their expertise, and where students congregate to gain benefit from them. The problem is that teaching on the one hand, and learning on the other, are likely to follow two different rhythms. When one is active, the other is frequently passive, whether we take a short or a long-term view. Accordingly, if we want to establish a curriculum which balances democratic learning principles with academic expertise we will need to take firm and continuing checks and measures to ensure balance and synchronicity.

Within any curriculum, some aims may have priority over others at different times, and an important but often neglected job of the course tutor is to organize and monitor the teaching and learning so that some sort of coherent experience may emerge. Sensitive group tutors can plan their own unfolding patterns with the group but there may be wider considerations to be dealt with. One of these occurs on the modular or unit system of course design, where students can often experience a sense of 'bitterness' in their studies (Nuffield Group, 1977). Some institutions have attempted to achieve a degree of integration across the modules by scheduling a 'synoptic study' session into the timetable. In the synoptic study students might discuss relationships between the elements, apply the separate knowledge to a particular focus (eg science and society) or solve integrative problems. A somewhat less conventional but nevertheless valuable task would be to discuss the experience of learning in each module and to explore ways of enhancing it – though this might be politically risky without the full agreement of all the tutors teaching the modules.

Nevertheless, some sort of small group experience would seem vital in the unit or modular system to give students the possibility of developing a sense of social identity and a feeling of belonging and commitment to the intellectual life of the institution. Parlett and King (1971) report an attempt to overcome many of the fragmenting effects of an orthodox timetable in which students of physics worked on 'concentrated study' – the full-time study of a single subject for a month with no competing academic demands. This curricular innovation provided enormous scope and freedom for varied and spontaneous group work. At Worcester Polytechnic Institute in the USA (ASEE, 1976), students take part in a project-based unit of seven weeks' duration in which they work exclusively on their project.

One aspect of student experience of higher education which does not appear to have received much attention is that of multiple group membership, often coupled with a complex of tasks. What looks on paper a well-coordinated and reasonably demanding course can be experienced by the individual in a very different way. Unfortunately, the day-to-day experience (not to speak of the hour-to-hour experience) of the student is not often studied by course designers. The constant need in a traditional course programme for students to switch attention across specialisms, and align themselves to different groups of people, can be either an inspiring stimulus or a muddling burden, depending on the individual student's capacity to cope with a variety of demands or, in less fortunate cases, to defend against increasing bewilderment and anxiety by opting out and possibly failing.

Whatever kinds of group activity are formally organized, informal peer grouping will inevitably, and quite properly, occur. There are, as Newcomb (1967) says, diverse motivations for students in aligning themselves with peer groups: some, for example, have strong tendencies toward conformity, while some others seem to be compulsively deviant. Both can find support from like-minded groups. Some need to be dependent on authority whereas independence is essential to others. Although the latter may seem to be immune to peer-group influence, the fact seems to be that they need it as much as the others but tend to find it in smaller and more selective circles. For some, membership in high-prestige groups is the crucial thing. Positions of 'leadership' or dominance, or perhaps just prominence, are required by still others. Some students become group members because of the interests and attitudes for which the group seems to stand, while others appear quite willing to adopt the norms of any group that becomes important to them for other reasons. Many of these and other motives can be combined in the same person as he or she finds different kinds of satisfactions in multiple and doubtless partially overlapping groups. The effects of peer-group membership will vary with such motives and with the degree to which they find satisfaction through affiliation.

It is clearly not the task of tutors to become involved in maximizing or otherwise determining peer-group affiliation and influence; to do so would be intrusive and could deprive students of essential opportunities for change and development not available to them in the organized curriculum. It can however be enormously helpful for tutors to understand something of the nature of students' extra-curricular concerns and their motives for such involvement. Information of this kind could be quite valuable in forming judgements about what the course may be failing to offer any student, particularly where most of his or her energies appear to be diverted from the educational programme. What is more, there is always the possibility, if there is no overlap between the values of peer groups and the learning group, that peer group norms entirely divorced from intellectual concerns will develop. For some students this may represent a necessary and welcome relief from the considerable demands of the legitimate educational culture. For others it could represent a disturbing influence, a constant doubting of the values of the learning group. It is probable that, as Newcomb suggests, this sort of isolation will occur where there is a feeling of anonymity within the learning groups either because of large numbers or a lack of concern for the students at a personal level. If this is so, it serves to underline the worth of aims in learning groups directed to personal development, self-esteem and a sense of belonging.

SOME CASE STUDIES IN GROUP TEACHING

In this section we shall see how various academic teachers in institutions both in the UK and abroad incorporated principles of group learning into 'real-life' teaching schemes.

The vast majority of these case studies are selected from the contents of the six Nuffield *Newsletters*, published from 1973 to 1976. The Nuffield Group for Research and Innovation in Higher Education visited several universities in the United Kingdom and compiled their reports on the basis of interviews, concentrating on larger departments with a substantial undergraduate intake. Their survey was by no means comprehensive or representative and it included a wide range of approaches and issues apart from small group teaching. The Nuffield Group based their original selection on criteria such as the applicability of the descriptions in other contexts, that they are less familiar, sometimes ingenious, and likely to cater for the interest of teachers looking for ideas as solutions to some of the problems. They were also concerned about the potential for transfer to other institutions.

The Nuffield Group also drew attention to the fact that most of the contributions were drawn from science and technology. They put this down to the possibility that these faculties were at the time of their study beset with more obvious problems:

the swing away from the popularity of their subjects among university applicants, the marked decrease in graduate employment opportunities, the logistical problems of integrating practical and theoretical work and so on.

The following selection from the Nuffield work is limited to those descriptions of small group teaching which address themselves to some of the problems and issues already highlighted in this book. They are grouped, as far as the variety of approaches allows, according to the aims and purposes they serve. However, within each is a wealth of information to do with tasks, techniques, sequencing, links with other learning, context and assessment. There are no appraisals save those provided by the contributors. The events occurred between fourteen and nineteen years ago. In some cases the schemes did not prove viable and were discontinued.

Developing particular skills

There has lately been a recognition that higher education is not just about knowing, understanding and analysing (see Bloom's categories) but also about communicating, applying, interpreting, evaluating – and even 'softer' categories of behaviour. These skills do not develop merely by talking about them or recognizing them, but by practising and incorporating them into one's behavioural repertoire.

Small groups can offer the safety to take risks in trying and testing new behaviour; they also give the tutor a greater certainty that everyone is participating. They therefore aid learning in more than a superficial sense.

Language teaching and communication studies: The Department of European Studies at Brighton Polytechnic provided courses on 'communication skills' for science, engineering and building students, who spend two or three hours a week for one year studying this subject. The first part of this course was devoted to basic aspects of communication such as identifying an audience, choosing media, and defining content, combined with learning some practical skills such as operating closed-circuit television cameras and using recorders. In consultation with their tutors the students then chose a topic related to their own degree course: the tides, cosmetics, x-rays and radio astronomy are some examples. Students worked in groups of three, preparing a script and making a 15-minute television documentary. This was criticised and improvements were suggested. The final part of the course was devoted to making a television presentation on a different topic; this second presentation was included in work to be assessed for the degree.

The purpose and content of practicals: The purpose and content of laboratory work has become a major area of concern for many science departments. The work is not only time-consuming and expensive but to many students the repetition of experiments and re-verification of established theories appear tedious and irrelevant. Greater weight, it is agreed, should be given to the imparting of skills and techniques. The first-year practical course in the Department of Organic Chemistry at Leeds was reorganised with this aim. Experiments were grouped together and planned to illustrate either a technique or an underlying principle. Students worked in groups of five to six under the supervision of a laboratory demonstrator; they were provided with detailed written instructions of the experiment they were to carry out and with a statement of the aim of the particular exercise. Each student in the group performed a different experiment but they later came together with the demonstrator to discuss their results and determine the general principle or practical implications involved. Each student was required to write his report in the context of the broader area of experimentation covered by the group.

Simulations, case studies and games: A course in the Department of Mechanical Engineering at Nottingham entitled 'The Engineer in Society' made extensive use of discussion, role-playing in industrial and other situations, and specially designed games. Some of the role-playing sessions were videotaped to facilitate an analysis of communications problems (eg in lectures, interviews and committees). The objectives of the course were to broaden the interests and outlook of the undergraduates; to interest them in the social history of engineering; to consider the responsibilities and communications problems of engineers; and to give them an introduction to management techniques useful to engineers in industry.

The study of environmental planning and pollution: The School of Environmental Sciences at the University of East Anglia had a course option on 'Environmental Planning and Pollution' (EPP) for final-year students. The course lasted three terms and involved eight hours' teaching a week. The first three weeks mainly comprised lectures and seminars in welfare economics. The remainder of the course was in two parts. For two terms the student elected to do five out of 18 options in areas in which staff have special competence. These varied from year to year, but the 1971 programme included such themes as the principles of conservation; coastal erosion and protection; water resource development; atmosphere pollution; recreation pressures; and the national parks. The remaining four weeks were devoted to case studies to which students could apply the skills and knowledge acquired in the earlier part of the course. Examples of case study areas might have included: analyses of the documentation for the Tennessee Valley Development Project; the development of Foulness; or the problems of North Sea exploration and development.

Teaching methods varied over the course: in addition to seminars and case studies there were field studies and role-playing exercises which were found particularly successful in areas of controversy (such as the problems of flooding in the study of water resources). Fifty per cent of the assessment was by examination and the remainder by course work. There was latitude for negotiation between tutor and student on the type of course work assessment preferred.

Group studies and texts in language learning: Language courses are often defined largely in terms of the final examination papers, in which students are required to translate from and into the foreign language, to write prose, and to take an oral examination. A typical approach to teaching language in preparation for these examinations is through the weekly production and correction of translations and prose exercises. Final results and examiners' reports have indicated some deficiencies in this approach, and in particular the failure of a number of students to acquire either the necessary language skills or the ability to read and study literature critically.

To meet these shortcomings the Language Centre and the Department of French at Birkbeck College, London adopted a less conventional approach involving students actively in the learning process and concentrating on the development of an understanding of what language is and how it may be used. Each week, for three hours in the first year and one hour in the second year, students learnt to understand and use the language by a direct and intensive study of spoken and written texts in French. The sessions were reinforced by small group discussions of fundamental questions related to the aims, objectives, methods and techniques of language learning. These small group studies and discussions, in which students shared experience and understanding, were sometimes tape-recorded, transcribed and used as a basis for further discussion and course development. There were plans to make video recordings of small groups at work. Two teachers were usually present at each group session.

Since the introduction of this alternative approach, the students' standards of performance in the language improved significantly in relation both to previous year groups at Birkbeck and to examination performance in London University as a whole.

There have been several attempts to base learning processes on a more careful consideration of what a physicist, or an engineer or whatever, actually does – the professional processes (qv Parker and Rubin, page 77) – or indeed what a student has to do in order to succeed. Traditionally, it has been assumed that these skills and qualities are automatically acquired through contact with the education process – learning by contagion. These few examples serve to illustrate that not everyone believes this and that students can benefit from a special focus on what they need to be able to do – their competency skills.

Training students in specialised skills: The Department of Physics at Birmingham introduced a new component in the first-year course. Once a fortnight students met for one hour in groups of about 15 with one member of staff, to engage in group activity designed to help them acquire specific professional skills. Even during the experimental stage, these sessions created considerable interest within the department. Starting with the question 'What skills are required by a physicist?' a series of problems were prepared which related to such areas as: the communication of results; the ability to translate (for example from graphs to words); the ability to formulate problems in mathematical terms; the design and explanation of experiments. Students tackled these in groups of four while the staff member circulated to give advice as required. Each session normally ended with a review during which each sub-group reported to the group of 15. Student participation was lively, partly because any one group was left alone for much of the time with a specific task to perform.

Small group work in biological sciences: During the first two terms of their first year, students of biochemistry and microbiology at Kent University attended 20 sessions, at which small groups of students carried out, with staff supervision, work designed to develop basic skills. They dealt with topics such as the working out of pH values, radiochemical activities and the handling of bacterial growth equations. This type of session was interspersed with a second kind in which attempts were made to develop awareness of general scientific methodology in biochemical studies and closely related areas. The group would be told, for example, that dead fish had been found floating on a local river; they were asked to devise a strategy for investigating the episode. Experience gained at this stage was thought to be of value in helping students to make more use of tutorial periods and of work in group projects in later years of the course. As part of their studies in bio-chemistry, second-year students were required to work on three published research papers in, eg the field of nucleic acids. They read the papers and worked over a period of three weeks on a number of questions which arose from the date in the papers and the overall philosophy of the research described. They worked in small groups during this exercise but presented their results individually. The method was found to stimulate interest and also served as a good discriminator of student ability.

Syndicate studies for engineers: The stimulation of creative talent within a group of engineering students formed an important aspect of the final-year course for the four-year sandwich honours degree in electrical and electronic engineering at City University. Students learned, through studying in syndicate groups, how to collect, evaluate and communicate information. Major features of the syndicate method of study are that it encourages active participation in critical appraisal and creative design or specification, and offers students the opportunity to undertake direct responsibility for decision-making.

The syndicate approach, which was first introduced into the course about five years ago, involves groups of from six to ten students in studying a subject of common interest in some detail: each member's activity was expected to contributed to the knowledge and understanding of the group as a whole. The subjects chosen for syndicate study, although specialist in nature, often had wider implications – they included, for example, such topics as surface transport systems and medical electronics. One staff member acted as guide, consultant and assessor to each syndicate, but did not deliver formal lectures. The study period ended with a conference at which students read papers and the work of each group was subject to general discussion.

The syndicate weighting in marks was the equivalent of one written paper: staff members who did not participate in the syndicate acted as additional assessors.

Role-playing and simulation in politics: First-year students at Lancaster University who chose, as one of their options, a part-1 course in politics, could participate in a 'cabinet decision-making game' and an international crisis simulation. The rules for these exercises and the briefs for those taking part were developed by academic staff in the department. Normally about ten students (members of a seminar group) took part in the cabinet game, and a group of up to 60 took part in the international crisis game; they were allotted roles which they were expected to play in accordance with the brief provided. There is room here for a great deal of initiative and the various outcomes would be largely determined by the way in which the parts were played and by the members' reactions to each other. The cabinet game was a regular part of the main course, and the international crisis simulation has been voluntarily undertaken over a weekend.

Platform discussions in first-year English: First-year undergraduates in the English Department at Manchester University were introduced to literary criticism and analysis by means of platform discussions between members of staff in the department. Following a lecture on a given topic the students were asked to read a relevant text. Aspects of the text were then discussed by members of staff before a student audience. Students were encouraged to interrupt this discussion and to participate in it. The idea was to demonstrate the approaches to analysis and criticism which students would be called upon to use in their studies of literature. The technique also had a socialising function, since first-year students were able to meet with and listen to several members of staff at each session. Platform discussions were seen as a useful introduction to seminar work because, with these discussions, students could see the range of opinion possible on literary topics and learn something of the art of deploying knowledge in argument.

A variant of the skills-development theme is that of encouraging the questioning of basic assumptions particularly in respect of the subject(s) students are studying.

Debating controversial issues in physics: In the third and fourth year of the physics sandwich course at Brunel University, an attempt was made to create a greater awareness of controversial issues in physical science. When this approach was originally tried in the first and second years, it was found that the critical questioning of certain basic concepts and assumptions proved disturbing to many students: the decision was therefore taken to delay the process until students had been able to acquire a greater background of knowledge and experience. Given active encouragement by the staff, many issues for discussion were then raised by the third- and fourth-year students. In particularly interesting cases, a debate was arranged involving two or more lecturers as well as the students themselves. On occasions, basic differences of approach towards a problem were highlighted by lectures involved with separate parts of the course. The conflict often resolved itself into a question of integrating separate areas of knowledge or gaining a perspective by contrasting one set of assumptions with another. For instance, in atomic or nuclear physics, the relationship of micro (or localised) systems to the main (macro) system with which they are intrinsically associated can provide conceptual difficulties for many students: it was found that such difficulties could often be resolved by exposing them to open discussion.

This scheme was not without its problems. After a few years it was evident that the genuine spontaneity demanded of the lecturers in a public encounter where professional integrity could be at risk, meant that few were willing to participate, with a consequent loss of spontaneity. After a year of experiment, the scheme became somewhat artificial and was discontinued.

Videotapes and group discussion: One of the courses offered to students in the School of Environmental Studies at University College, London dealt with perception and communication. It was voluntary, non-assessed and primarily for first-year students. One and a half hours a week were timetabled for a series of programmes dealing with basic aspects of perception and communication. Six twenty-minute video-tapes – designed to show the importance of an individual's assumptions, expectations and attitudes in communication, the effect of context, and the essentially egocentric nature of perception – were prepared by Dr M L J Abercrombie. These were intended to stimulate students to question previously held assumptions and attitudes and thereby come to a clearer understanding and command of their own processes of seeing and learning.

In the first term the videotapes were used as a prelude to group discussion. In the second term discussions on the main themes were continued but were linked where possible to the projects on which the students were working. Films were shown where relevant to the specific topic under discussion; and some lectures were given on more specialised problems of communication (for example, communication on building sites).

Evaluation indicated that some students welcomed a course which, though academically relevant, was voluntary and earned no examination credit. It was also found that students welcomed the opportunity the course provided to get to know one another and members of staff, and the way in which it helped them to express themselves.

Getting the most from lab work

Laboratory work typically occupies a lot of student time and institutional resources, yet is often a source of incipient boredom to both staff and students. Why this should be, in an area replete with openings for discovery learning, scientific purpose and the application of theoretical knowledge, is a matter worthy of research in its own right.* Suffice to say that several academics have seen the potential of making the laboratory experience more stimulating and have found ways of linking it to the rest of the curriculum in a congruent way where previously it existed as a misunderstood extra. One of the more popular features seems to be the conducting of experiments in groups followed by comparison and mutual criticism between groups. Within this format there is potential for students to develop experimental skills, a co-operative approach to study and the ability to communicate what they have found out.

New approaches to chemistry teaching: The Chemistry Department at City University instituted a number of different approaches to the teaching of inorganic chemistry to meet the changing attitudes of students and changing employment prospects for chemis-

---

*Perry (1971) recounts a 'brilliant freshman scientist who was so disgusted with "cook book" laboratory exercises that he took to playing variations on themes and finally provoked his instructor into blurting: "See here, there'll be no more experimenting in this laboratory." '

try graduates. The overall aim was to promote self-motivated, intellectually independent people through a study of chemistry.

There was, for example, a team approach to practicals. Divided into groups of four or five under a member of staff, each student was given a different but related experiment. On the completion of the experiment each student wrote it up and spoke about it in a seminar at which the group discussed and criticised the work done. Discussion with, and criticism by, their peers was found to generate a great deal of initiative and energy among the students.

[This scheme was later discontinued because it was difficult to transfer the sense of commitment to other staff.]

Laboratory seminars in physics: In the first-year programme at Brunel the customary three-hour sessions of experimental laboratory work were augmented by small group 'laboratory seminars'. Each group of six students worked with a tutor on a particular theme (for instance, insulation) and considered possible applications of various physical concepts, principles and techniques. Students were encouraged to discuss any aspect of the theme which they considered relevant; the discussion was as far as possible kept open-ended. Experimental work was introduced or developed in whatever way appeared important. All members of the group were expected to work on the design and construction of the experimental equipment and were expected to keep an up-to-date log book and to write reports. The main aims of the laboratory seminars were to encourage a co-operative approach towards the solution of problems and to give students greater confidence in their ability to communicate.

Learning about experimentation: A new approach to laboratory work was adopted in the Engineering Department at Brunel University. All first-year students attended a self-contained course in experimentation which ran over two terms. The aim was to provide an intellectual challenge through experimental work. The experiments served not only to illustrate or amplify physical laws but also provided student experience in the clear formulation of experimental objectives, the planning of an experimental programme and the unravelling of laws from data.

The laboratory periods were of three hours' duration and two such periods, one week apart, were devoted to each experiment. Students worked in two and threes: members of staff (there was one tutor to every ten students for the experimentation course) discussed progress and problems with each group during each session. The course was supported by a series of six lectures (subsequently videotaped) covering such areas as the approach to experimentation; dimensional analysis; curve fitting and technical report-writing. Students were provided in advance with a full explanation of the course, together with detailed suggestions for keeping their notebooks. The notebooks and each report were carefully scrutinised, the marks forming part of the overall assessment.

Rather than allowing students random progression through their practical work, some departments organized a clear sequence in which the evolution of skills was closely linked with a series of group tasks.

Linking seminars to laboratory work: The Physiology Department of the Nottingham School of Medicine devised a system of laboratory work and related seminars which allowed students to participate in a number of experiments without increasing the total time spent in the laboratory. For the experiments, students were divided into, say, six groups of eight. These groups carried out related but not identical experiments, and each member of the group wrote up the work in a form that was easily communicable to colleagues. For the seminars, the students were divided into another six groups, so that each new group contained at least two members of an original group. Thus each student in the seminar not only presented, or helped to present, the report of his experiment, but also heard reports of about two other experiments. [For further information see Short & Tomlinson (1979).]

Reorganisation of laboratory work: In the Department of Physics at Birmingham, the old laboratory 'circus' system, where all the equipment was set up in several laboratories through which everyone passed, was abandoned and replaced by a more structured 'unit laboratory' system. For instance, in the second year there were three 'unit laboratories concerned with transistor electronics, electrical measurement methods, and optical physics; students spent three successive periods of five weeks in each laboratory, followed by a further seven to eight weeks on a substantial project.

In each of the laboratories a member of staff set up a linked sequence of laboratory and seminar work with a group of 12 to 14 students. Staff developed the work in their own way: for example, one unit might start with very simple problem experiments, leading on to a group discussion of the lessons learned and perhaps the introduction of certain principles concerning the techniques used. These ideas were further developed by assigning more complicated problems to individual students who might report back to the group in subsequent seminars. The sequence possibly ended with short open projects involving use of the ideas developed.

There were certain advantages noted. An individual staff member had a more definite and personal responsibility for the progress of a group. Students also had the benefit of working in small groups on a connected set of ideas linking experiments with the development of theoretical understanding. It was found that student effort and attendance improved.

The following innovation was the direct result of an evaluation of the traditional style of laboratory work.

Systematic course revision in electrical engineering: Until 1973 the first-year electronics laboratory course in electrical Engineering at the University of Salford was organised on mainly traditional lines. Students followed a set pattern of structured experiments, guided by detailed instruction sheets. However, it seemed to some of their teachers that, since many students were clearly unhappy with this approach, the problem should be investigated.

First, a research fellow in the department undertook a preliminary survey of staff and student views of the course; this was followed by a detailed questionnaire aimed at discovering their perception of the aims of the course and the relative importance of the aims perceived. At the same time, a sample survey was made of 20 university departments of electrical engineering in order to find out about significant recent changes in first-year laboratory work patterns elsewhere.

The information obtained in this way led to a restructuring of the course with the aims of reinforcing lecture material; creating greater interest in the subject; and providing the opportunity for students to become familiar with sophisticated equipment. Students worked in pairs through a series of experimental problems of increasing difficulty. No direction sheets were provided, but lecturers spent more time in the laboratory and were available to help where necessary. The experiments gradually became more open-ended as the course proceeded; by the end of year they were, in effect, small projects involving problems of design and the construction of equipment.

The power of assessment can be used to advantage, too.

A lecture course with discussion groups in biology: One of the courses available for second- and third-year students in the School of Biological Sciences at Leicester University was concerned with development and differentiation. It was run jointly by two lecturers, one from genetics and one from biochemistry, and 20 to 30 students took it each year. Like all other courses in the school, it consisted of 33 lectures and 50 hours allocated for practical work. However, no practical classes were run and the time was used instead for a series of group discussions and for free time during which the students were asked to prepare for those by reading prescribed material.

Groups for discussion consisted of eight to ten students and each group met about nine times for a period of two to three hours. Topics were announced a few weeks before and were closely related to the lecture course. Extensive reading lists were issued. Each discussion was supervised by one of the lecturers, who took a fairly active role in questioning the students and encouraging them to talk freely, to question one another and to be clear and precise. Much of the prescribed reading consisted of published papers and the emphasis in discussion was often on the interpretation of experimental date, on techniques available for testing ideas, and on the nature of the experimental evidence for material prescribed in lectures. In other discussions, the object was to clear up confusion resulting from the vague use of terms such as differentiation and to discuss the general principles and aims of the course. In these discussions also, the students were encouraged to think in terms of what can be tested.

The discussions were popular and although the students initially felt that the amount of prescribed reading was too great, most of them learnt to extract information more quickly and precisely and many of them claimed to have read far more during this course than in any other. There is evidence that many became more critical and questioning in their reading, learnt to think in terms of testing ideas experimentally, became more careful in their use of words and developed confidence in their ability to cope with complex material.

In the School of Biological Sciences, part of the final mark for each course was based on an assessment of course work. In this course, the students were assessed on their performance in discussions, but were asked to write a 2,000-word review of a group of papers relevant to some aspect of the course, and in this it was hoped they would use the skills learnt in discussion. A wide choice of topics was provided about six weeks before the article was to be handed in. The reviews were assessed for breadth, thoroughness, clarity, understanding of the published papers, and critical comment.

SIMIG (not part of Nuffield Study): A flexible and versatile system in teaching biology which was developed at the University of Sydney mixed self-instructional materials with group interaction. The course known as SIMIG (self-instruction by modules with interaction among groups) combined self-paced individual work (with study guides, self-quizzes, audio tapes, tape-slides and microscope slides for working on in study carrels and group work involving peer learning, peer assessment and free discussion based on written answers to questions. The creator of the scheme (Brewer, 1985) emphasizes the centrality of group work in achieving aims that would otherwise be neglected were this a purely self-instructional course:

> The groups fulfil several purposes: they reinforce the discipline of observation learnt in independent study in the carrels; they help to bridge the gap between inert knowledge and genuine comprehension; they provoke students to apply their knowledge to the interpretation of hitherto unseen material; they provide practice in those higher-order skills used in solving anatomical problems – and they provide an essential feedback to students for monitoring their own progress.

There is a possibility that laboratory work may be seen as an end in itself or as an educational enclave. At least one attempt has been made to link it with the rest of the curriculum, however.

> *Integrating laboratory and lecture courses:* The Chemistry Departments at Cardiff and Chelsea were collaborating in an experimental project in which the section of the first-year physical chemistry course dealing with reaction kinetics was being run as an integrated activity. Some students in each university were taking this 20-hour course which was largely self-paced and had a workshop focus. Time previously used in carrying out experimental exercises was used for a wide diversity of activities with particular emphasis on the handling of data. Students would, for example, measure a rate constant as part of a group experiment on activation energy, work out their results and bring them to a group meeting for discussion and evaluation. Each student would then use the group's collective findings in his final calculation of activation energy. The lecturer's function was to develop the conceptual framework of the subject (with the help of notes issued in advance), to promote discussion and to supervise the performance of experiments and calculations. The course was assessed in both departments by a three-hour paper which included a question on data handling. This common course provided an opportunity to examine the effectiveness, in two institutions with similar course aims, of carrying out and discussing an experiment on a group basis, linked with the issuing of data for calculation, notes and questions, as against requiring every student to carry out the given experiment himself. The implications for both staff and students, of such redistribution of time and effort in practical work were then studied. [See also Magin (1982).]

Making learning 'real'

Science and engineering teachers are lucky. They have in the laboratory a ready-made, self-contained formula for students to try out their academic learning in practical tasks. The equivalents to the laboratory in the social sciences are case studies, games, simulations, role plays and so on, where students can experiment by applying their own skill to problems within a controlled environment.

> *Case studies, business games and field work in business studies:* Case studies, feasibility studies and games may be used as an end in themselves or as a focal point for illustrating and bringing together various parts of a course otherwise studied separately. This latter

approach was used at North East London Polytechnic in a four-year sandwich degree course in business studies. The selection and use of case studies was carefully planned beforehand and the activities formed an integral part of the teaching programme. For instance, a course on marketing used several case studies both in industrial and consumer marketing at the end of each series of lectures, to illustrate and consolidate the theoretical areas dealt with and to highlight the practical problems involved. The behavioural science part of the course used similar exercises to demonstrate, for example, decision-making or group dynamics.

An integrated deterministic model of the game (non-computerised) designed specifically for business studies undergraduates was used to highlight the decision-making aspects of business under imperfect information. This game also formed the basis for a study of group dynamics.

In the final year, students paid an intensive study visit to another EC country. They analysed in detail beforehand the structure and operations of four or five firms in an industrial area and, from this work, they prepared questionnaires which were sent to the firms several weeks before the visits. They spend one day at each organisation and interviewed a wide range of personnel. Evenings were used for discussing their findings. A report was eventually submitted to each of the firms visited for its comments. Visits were made to the industrial complexes of Rotterdam, the Ruhr, Zurich-Baden-Winterhur, Turin-Ivrea and Lille-Roubaix-Tourcoing.

Simulation of historical events: The word 'seminar', in the context of the University of East Anglia, was used to denote both a total course and a one-and-a-half-hour meeting between one or two teachers and eight to 15 students. In the seminar course on 'Religion, Science and Philosophy in Post-Restoration England', the class was asked in three or four of its individual meetings to simulate a relevant historical event: a parliamentary debate or the trial of a Quaker would be two examples. An outline of the exercise was given to the class in advance, and a video was usually made of at least one of the simulations. Although Professor J R Jones, who took this seminar, commented that the performance primarily suits the more extrovert student, he found that the experience of collective presentation, interlinking the imaginative and the factual, helped the majority of students better to understand the salient historical issues involved.

Providing a variety of experiences

The expanding body of research evidence (Entwistle and Ramsden, 1983; Richardson et al, 1987) which shows that students vary in the ways they learn makes it apparent that a variety of learning experiences can help meet the day-to-day needs of individual students and can cater for the differing needs of students across the board. It can also serve to create different and unexpected understandings of subject matter.

Varieties of small group teaching: A number of alternative ways of using classes (the major small group teaching unit at the London School of Economics) were explored by M J Reddin in the Department of Social Administration. He was concerned to see how the method and organisation of teaching should vary according to the needs and interests of individual students and teachers, the aims of any particular course, and the kind of material to be presented. The possibilities investigated ranged from the traditional formal paper read by a student, to sessions where the introductory presentation of a topic was split between two to four people while others in the group, having undertaken specified reading assignments, acted as 'resource consultants'. In a contrasting session students would be provided with an 'unseen' case study and with no more than a few minutes' preparation (and with no source materials), would be asked to argue the case for applying a particular policy.

Problem-solving exercises constitute a third small group strategy; two major forms have been used. The first was deliberately open-ended (eg 'You have been asked to design and introduce a system of child allowances in the UK . . .'). The students were positively encouraged to build an 'ideal' system; in fact, rules could be imposed on the exercise prohibiting consideration of presumed budgetary or cultural constraints. Other exercises (following this example) then imposed a series of closely defined constraints which could have demanded modification or compromise in relation to the 'ideal' starting-point proposals. An alternative approach, more conspicuously practical in its initial focus, was the presentation of specific human 'dilemmas' which required individual professional decisions to be made for immediate action. The aims here were to make the participants articulate the criteria for their chosen course of action and try to identify the degree to which such criteria were 'subjective' or 'objective'; to try to get the students to assess how far their criteria changed over time, particularly whether their formal education at the university affected their views; and to get them to discuss the implications of the specific policy choices.

A course on scientific communication: An optional course in the general studies programme at Surrey University, 'Science Teaching and Communication', included a component designed to stimulate a more critical attitude towards the way in which forms of scientific communication (usually dealing with aspects of the social responsibility of scientists) are presented. Students were provided with copies of newspapers or journal articles to be read before they attended the weekly discussion class with the course tutor. Each session began with an introductory talk or film appropriate to the content of the article; the class then either had a discussion as a whole or broke up into groups of four or five to discuss and criticise the style, content and implicit values of the communication. In the latter case, each group later presented the main points of its discussion to the whole class and important aspects of the exercise were drawn together by the tutor. Students were, in addition, required to write their own critical appraisal of a selection of the materials studied in this way.

Autonomous learning

Group discussion, while potentially more democratic than lectures, does not of itself guarantee student participation in the choice, pacing and direction of study. That, in a sense, is a separate 'deal', and its negotiation is one which requires of the tutor careful and judicious handling.

Student participation in course planning: A second-year option in the sociology of industrial societies was available to all students at Lancaster University with a basic knowledge of sociology. On this course, the tutor did not lay down the units or topics to be covered. Instead, students were asked to put forward their own ideas for areas of study relevant to the general theme as it appeared in the course outline. These were discussed in the first seminar; the group then agreed on a structure for the course. Based on a series of themes drawn from the list of those suggested, individuals or small groups of students undertook to study, in depth, two of the topics which were chosen, as far as possible in accordance with their particular interests, and, after a number of individual consultations with the course tutor, presented two project reports for assessment.

No lectures were given, but most students attended the group seminars, which only in the early part of the course were led by the tutor. As the course continued, students organised their own project work and presented their own papers. Each led at least one discussion related to his own special interest(s).

At these sessions students were encouraged to criticise each other's work, and to make suggestions for the improvement and furtherance of the projects underreview. Project work counted for 50% of the assessment on the course, the other 50% being awarded on a written examination. Alternatively, a student may normally have developed one of his projects into a full-scale dissertation to replace all other forms of assessment on the course.

Student planning in a Dip HE: The two-year Diploma at the Polytechnic of East London aimed to share responsibility with students for planning their own programmes. The course began with a six-week planning period during which the students worked with their objectives for the course and negotiated with tutors the form which study would take over the two years. Negotiations were formalised in a contract which was available, if necessary, to the validating board for the programme.

The programme for all students comprised work centred on regular sessions in which they aimed to develop co-operatively the skills necessary for the fulfilment of their objectives. In addition, students carried out special interest studies under the guidance of a tutor who could have been in any subject group in the polytechnic.

Assessment was entirely based upon course work. Profiles of strength and weakness, agreed by the student, were drawn up at the end of each term and certified copies of these documents were made available to the students on completion of the programme, whether or not they were awarded a diploma. To qualify, students must have done satisfactory work in special interest studies and in a group 'set situation'.

The course clearly appealed to the mature student; about half were over 25 years of age. A recent study has shown that about 80 per cent of the students in the second year of the course would like to complete an extra year in order to obtain a degree. They also expressed a strong preference for continuing to study in the same way as at present.

Though the PEL course has been changed considerably since the early 1970s it has maintained its essential elements of self-directed study via learning contracts. Nevertheless it leads us into the whole philosophy and practice of project work and raises at least three crucial issues for partners in the learning process: what is worth learning, what sort of guidance can you provide, and how do you assess? Nowhere do these issues come to light more than in group projects. Should the group take collective responsibility for everything or should there be a division of labour? How does that question affect decisions about whether to assess relative contributions or the team as a whole.

Planning, conducting and assessing group projects: Many university departments may hesitate to include group (as opposed to individual) projects because of the obvious potential difficulties of assessment. However, students in the Department of Building Science at Liverpool have for some years undertaken this kind of work. A major topic area is chosen towards the end of the second year; an example is the building of the new arts library. The full brief, as given to the architect for the actual building, is given to each student. On this basis, rough sketch plans are prepared by individual students. One of these plans is selected for further development and students then collectively decide the main feature of the proposed building (for example, heavy concrete building or frame with curtain walling). At this point they break up into small groups of two or three to study one or more of such detailed sub-areas as project management, foundations, structure, heating and ventilation, cost planning and design and contract documents.

Tutors work closely with students. There are regular committee meetings of the whole group, run by the students, and reports are written both jointly and individually. The project mark accounts for about 25 per cent of the overall assessment, and course tutors have experienced no major problems in assessing the contributions of individual students to the work of their groups.

The Nuffield Group summarizes some of the approaches to assessment in group project work:

The most serious difficulty in assessing project work is, however, assessing the individual students whose work has been done in a group. The decision in favour of group projects is taken, in spite of this, for what seem to be two main reasons: lack of apparatus or space to enable each student (or at most a pair) to work alone; or because there are positive learning advantages to be gained by group work. In the latter case, syndicate type working is common. For example, a group of chemical engineering students will work jointly on designing a continuous flow reactor, but within the project each student will have a specific task to perform; in effect, individual students carry out projects within the group project. Where syndicate working is not possible, a total mark may be awarded to a project and students may be allowed to distribute this between them. Even when no such total responsibility is given to students it is helpful to consult them at an early stage before decisions about the sharing out of marks are reached. In group project work, very close supervision is essential if the supervisor is to gain as detailed a picture as possible both about the specific contribution of each student and about the working of the group as a whole.

In seminar work, the relative contributions of students are more visible and there are schemes for assessing these which at the same time underline some of the purposes or preferred activities in group discussion.

Stimulating student participation in seminars: A method of involving students more actively in seminar work was developed in the Department of Building Science at Liverpool. One topic was chosen each week and allocated to a student who was to write a paper and distribute it to the group two days before the seminar. Another student read the same source materials and chaired the seminar. The writer opened the discussion by elaborating on his paper; the chairman's task was to draw attention to relevant issues omitted in the paper to stimulate group discussion. The course tutor played as far as possible a non-interventionist role but would attempt to correct misconceptions and to sum up at the end. Seminar performance was assessed as follows: writing of paper, 40 per cent; presentation of paper, 20 per cent; 20 per cent to contributions as chairman, and 20 per cent to participation in the discussion in other seminars.

Perhaps there is a case, which the above report points to, for ensuring that group project work is more visible to the tutor, at least for review meetings. An example of how this can be achieved with such meeting and a positive spur from the assessment procedure is described below.

*Cross-referencing in group projects:** With project work there is always a residual worry that what students gain in depth of knowledge, they lose in breadth. At Technion University, Tel Aviv, Israel, in mechanical engineering the students do project work in pairs. Every fortnight five pairs meet to review progress. One student in each pair takes the role of presenter and the other of scribe and critic. Presenter A would describe progress while his partner jotted down notes as critics B2, B3, B4 and B5 questioned him. Presenters A2, A3, A4 and A5 would then take their turns. At the next meeting the roles would be rotated.

Students do all this in the knowledge that 50 per cent of their project assessment will be based on their understanding of one of the other projects at a viva voce examination. The rub is that they are not told which project it will be until they walk into the viva!

Peer Tutoring in Engineering: † There is traditionally a heavy emphasis, in first-year engineering and science courses, on learning basic information through lectures. In addition, the students can feel very isolated in their first experience of higher education. At Imperial College, an attempt was made to tackle both issues for the fluid mechanics element of the first year civil engineering course. Lectures were replaced with Open University texts and supplementary notes; the focus of learning was the laboratory experiment done in groups of six to eight students, instructed in experimental procedure by a prepared video film. Following the laboratory work, the groups moved to a classroom where they compared their results and conclusions one group with another. When not involved in lab work the group tackled problems, some of them more conceptual than numerical. Here the procedure was to split each group into sub-groups with slightly different phenomena in the same conceptual area. Their task was then in turn to work out their answer or explanation and teach it in whatever way they chose to their companion sub-group. Two tutors circulated offering guidance where necessary. The idea was for the students to extend this 'peer-tutoring' approach to their out-of-class learning and more particularly to their examinations preparation.

Sessions on numerical problems were conducted with two of the larger groups in a different room with another tutor as chairman. Each group was given two problems; one to solve and the other to discuss. Following this, one group, each member taking turns, explained their solution to their problem while the other group checked for understanding. The tutor took opportunities to draw out general principles and clarify problem-solving strategies.

At the end of the course, though three months before the sessional exams, a one-hour mock exam was set. Students then each marked and commented on a partner's script with the aid of a set of model answers. Some students found the lack of authority and structure in this course stimulating. Others found it unsettling, especially because it took place at the beginning of their college career.

---

*Based on a discussion between the author and Ferdinand Zawistowski of Technion University. This item was not part of the Nuffield Study.

† This item was not part of the Nuffield Study, but part of an evaluation study I conducted from 1978–80.

The idea of replacing lectures with other sources of information brings to mind the possibilities of structured or step-by-step discussion and the use of video and handouts, and in many ways this could be seen as a firm step in the direction of more student-centred learning.

Background notes and course booklets for students: The Department of Veterinary Anatomy at Liverpool has given considerable attention to the provision of background notes for undergraduate courses. A complete bound set of course notes and diagrams was prepared and these were available to students for the cost of the materials used. Each student also received a detailed syllabus showing how the course developed week by week and when and how tests would be administered and marked. Formal lectures for 'covering the course' and giving out factual information were thus largely obviated, and replaced by informal lectures which were combined with spontaneous questioning and discussion. These lecture-discussions were used mainly to analyse difficult topics with the aid of overhead projector transparencies and films.

A similar approach was adopted in one of the lecture courses in the Department of Chemistry at Liverpool. The objectives of this course were analysed in some detail, and summary sheets, specifying the ground to be covered at each stage, were provided for students in booklet form at the beginning of term. Supplementary lecture material and question sheets related to the objectives were also made available: tutorials were based on the question sheets and thus directly linked to the other elements of the course.

New teaching methods and approaches in chemistry: For several years Professor Kettle of the University of East Anglia experimented in lectures with ways in which to teach 'group theory' to chemistry undergraduates in the early part of the course. An opportunity to try out a seminar approach indicated that seminars were more effective in isolating students' conceptual difficulties and in enabling students to move at their own pace towards an understanding of the subject.

A seminar course was designed which circumvented mathematical difficulties and which concentrated on helping students to understand the concepts of symmetry at their own pace. A series of about 20 ten-minute video tapes was prepared. Videos were to be shown at appropriate points in each seminar, to be interleaved with structured discussion periods. The next video would then only be shown when a pre-defined goal was achieved in the discussion (the goal to be known only to the seminar leaders). On each tape there would be a discussion of the points covered in the previous discussion period illustrated with models. The video would then raise questions aimed to take the seminar to the next conceptual stage. It was planned to use post-doctoral workers as seminar leaders. The teaching of the whole course would be discussed with them and detailed course notes indicating the logistic path of the course would be prepared and issued to them in advance. Notes would also be given to the undergraduate students.

For the first term of the first year of this course an introductory laboratory programme was designed which introduced students to the handling of models and to carrying out problem exercises. The course was first taught in this way in 1972 to 1973. It was later developed to use peer-teaching procedures.

[Part of one of the seminars on symmetry theory can be seen on the video of group discussion 'Short Extracts', one of a series available from the University of East Anglia.]

Two other aspects of group projects demand attention: the specification (where such direction is relevant) of stimulating tasks and the possibilities for interdisciplinary learning. Often the most exciting experiences for the student are to get outside the four walls of the institution and get involved in the real world.

The inhibitions of the learning milieu are not to be underestimated: the prevailing culture of academic learning and its assessment within the institution can be very constraining and a sense of both freedom and social purpose can soon be experienced when students encounter unfiltered problems.

Social responsibility and the curriculum: A number of university departments are experimenting with curricula embodying some 'social action' component. An example is provided by the Electrical Engineering Department at Imperial College, where third-year students were given opportunities to integrate their technical and non-technical studies through a choice of projects on such themes as medical electronics, safety for shipping in the Channel, and electric cars – past, present and future. Students worked in teams of five or six with a staff supervisor who acted as observer and consultant: each team had a small allocation of money for incidental expenses. Each group tended to develop a division of labour as students began to explore their relative skills in terms of making outside contacts, contributing to 'brainstorming' about the plan and scope of the work, drafting the report and so on. Much help was given by the library staff to students needing access to non-technical literature and information. The scheme in general succeeded in arousing the active involvement and interest of both students and staff. The group project represented just over 8 per cent of the final-year degree work.

Although the programme was originally limited to electrical engineering students, the plan was gradually to extend it across department, faculty (and even institutional) boundaries and hence build up a central bank of suitable project themes exploring social issues related to a number of different academic disciplines.

Law in its social context: A number of law schools responded in the early 1970s to a growing concern of students in the social aspects of the subject. The Department of Law at the London School of Economics experimented with a variety of possible approaches. One of the most successful was the organisation of a one-week group project after the first-year examination. The project (which usually attracted the participation of more than half the annual intake of 70 or so undergraduates) was planned to involve field surveys on various aspects of the functioning of the legal system: examples included a study of the awareness of tenants of their rights under the rent acts; an enquiry into the incidence of legal representation in magistrates' courts, county courts, rent tribunals and rent assessment committees in London; a review of the extent of compliance with the laws of consumer protection of window advertisements in retailers' shops. The tutor collated and published the results of the students' field-work in appropriate journals. The main benefits to the students were in terms of their participation in a published study early in their legal training, their experience in taking part in a substantial piece of research, and their opportunity to see for themselves the law in action.

Other activities included a free legal advice service for anyone at LSE (where some 12 law students, assisted by a faculty member, regularly staffed an advice session twice a week), and the planning, as a third-year option, of a 'clinical programme' involving a practical experience of professional work assessed for credit on a pass/fail basis and based on the experience of similar programmes in the USA.

To some extent the following scheme served not only to realize interdisciplinary aims but also took students out of the immediate influences of their own departments.

Collaboration between specialist engineering students: An experimental final-year group project, involving students from each of the main engineering departments at Queen's University, Belfast, was organised. Engineering students at Queen's took a common first year, after which they chose a specialisation in aeronautical, civil electrical or mechanical engineering. This project was devised to see whether students, having specialised, could fruitfully work together again on a common area, in this case, personal rapid transport. The students, who were supervised by a member of staff from each of the departments involved, met and reported on their work weekly, and more general planning meetings were held every month. Each student was responsible for a specific part of the project, and, with the help of the staff, an overall timetable and flow chart were devised at the outset. At the end of the year, each student submits to his department an individual report, on which he was assessed. A general report on the scheme also went forward to the faculty board.

A special combined studies programme: The Science Faculty at Leeds has made considerable effort to provide for students in combined or joint undergraduate courses a sense of identity and manageable workloads. The planning, co-ordination and day-to-day administration of the now numerous joint courses (some of which cross faculty boundaries) were the responsibility of the Combined Studies Department, with a full-time director, an assistant director, seven lecturers from different departments (each working one day a week for the combined studies programme) and its own ancillary staff. All were housed in the Combined Studies Centre which comprised offices, a common room, seminar rooms and the students' study room. A Combined Studies Society provided social activities and also organised the election of students to staff–student committees. These served three groups of students: those concerned mainly with biological subjects; those concerned with mathematical subjects; and those involved in other science subjects. Although the committees, on which students are in the majority, had no executive power, they were recognised as having an important advisory function. They met regularly under the chairmanship of the director; the meetings were called and the agenda drawn up by an elected student secretary.

Designing courses

The idea of the teachers themselves using group techniques in the design of courses may sound strange to those brought up to accept a culture of individual and separate responsibility for the content and process of courses. Yet the aims of course design teams are very similar to those of an interdisciplinary seminar. Similar processes might therefore be beneficial.

A syndicate approach to curriculum development: At Sussex, a first-year core curriculum in molecular science chemistry and some courses for those specialising in chemistry were developed by a number of working-groups. These groups were called syndicates, and consisted of three members of faculty drawn from differing areas of the subject. There were seven syndicates at work at one time. Since 1972, the syndicates have worked on the formulation of course objectives, and produced detailed lists of objectives for each part of the course. The syndicates selected and produced relevant materials, and devised appropriate forms of assessment. When the courses were in operation, the syndicates continued to review and evaluate them.

Group planning of Courses: The Department of Chemistry at University College, London, adopted a team approach to the development of their new first-year chemistry course. This course, on 'The Molecular Basis of Chemistry', aimed to show how the chemist relates experimental observations on matter in bulk to models at the atomic and molecular level, and how the interplay of the chemist's observations with conceptual models allowed the latter to be refined and developed.

The course, a compulsory precursor of all further main chemistry courses, consisted of approximately 70 lectures and 70 hours of laboratory, seminar and library work. It was divided into five main sections. In planning the content and teaching materials, the group of five lecturers responsible for teaching the course for the first time divided into pairs: one pair was made responsible for each of the five sections. Where possible, as a matter of deliberate policy, no lecturer worked on a topic with which he was especially familiar.

In collaboration with the London University Audio-Visual Centre, the group prepared a number of slides and filmstrips with accompanying notes and audio-tape discussions, so as to provide the students with a wide range of learning materials. Since no suitable textbook embodying this approach existed, specific and general reading notes were made available together with outline notes on each lecture. In the first year all five members of the team attended every lecture. In the two years that it ran it was a great success, especially where the class divided into small units, each with a group leader for programmed seminar, practical calculation and problem classes.

Evaluating group work

Although we shall be looking at evaluation in greater detail in Chapter 9, the following description could serve as a reminder that the best laid plans of staff and students for group learning may come to nought without a built-in means of reflection and self-appraisal.

Analysis of video-taped tutorials: A number of physics and mathematics tutorials in the School of Mathematical and Physical Sciences at the University of Sussex were video-recorded and subsequently discussed by a small group of faculty (12). Each tutorial contained one member of faculty and about five students, and by using a wide-angle lens the sessions were usually recorded in the normal surroundings of the tutor's room. The group started meeting for about one and a half hours on a weekly basis during the spring term (until the end of the summer term) and was concerned with attempting to find a more adequate language to discuss learning and teaching within the tutorial situation. Interaction analysis and discussion of the tapes led to more general discussions on the nature and purpose of tutorial and small group teaching within the Sussex pattern and an attempt to agree on some basic objectives. It appears to those concerned that the recording and subsequent analysis of tutorials may be useful not only for faculty but also for students.

Handling change

The foregoing case studies include a cross-section of several different but interrelated elements: subject area, tasks, techniques, organization, planning and evaluation – all within the context of various aims and purposes. There should be sufficient reference points for readers to recognize or identify with similar concerns in their own institution. The case studies are in the main not so much a description of problems but of their solutions. If any of them seem to fit your own concerns and inspire some sort of action, that is all to the good, but beware! colleagues might not share your analysis of the problem any more than your proposed solution. Your understanding and handling of a wider group process may be well and truly tested in your attempts to introduce even small changes to the system. Further reading might be a good idea. See for instance Huberman (1973), Havelock (1973) and Bennis, Benne and Chin (1985). But don't let opposition to change undermine your enthusiasm!

Postscript

Two excellent source books on how to improve lectures, seminars and tutorials are now available. See Gibbs, Habeshaw and Habeshaw (1989) in the Bibliography and a title on labs and practicals by Gibbs and Jaques due in 1992.

DISCUSSION POINTS

- What external influences are there on the work of groups you belong to? In what ways do they affect what happens?
- Discuss the differences between the ways members of your group relate to each other inside as opposed to outside the seminar/meeting. What seems to determine these differences?
- To what extent does the physical location and timing of various groups you belong to affect the liveliness and the level of participation in them?
- What principles of learning in groups seem to be evident in the various case studies? Draw up a classification chart.

9 Evaluating Groups

Whenever two or more people interact they are in some sense evaluating one another. Teachers do it of students, students of teachers, each of their own colleagues. As teachers it is our job to make judgements about students; we may not feel so happy about students openly reciprocating the process. Something much more precious and sensitive seems to be at stake: our self-esteem. There are, too, understandable doubts among teachers about any evaluation which attempts to judge complex phenomena in simplistic terms. Teachers, as Miller (1975) remarks, are

> sceptical that the intricate network of their experience, which contributes to their concept of themselves as a teacher, can be encompassed in some kind of measurement which is either meaningful or helpful.

Yet even if a suitable kind of measurement were available, the probability is that most teachers would find 20 good academic reasons why their self-image should not come under scrutiny.

The major part of this problem is possibly that a sense of being judged is likely to create a defensive reaction. In the view of Gibb (1961), a defensive climate results from the sort of communication which displays evaluation, control, strategy, neutrality, superiority, or certainty. Supportive or co-operative climates, on the other hand, have the following qualities: description, problem orientation, spontaneity, empathy, equality and provisionalism. Each of these corresponds to its equivalent defensive quality taken in the same area. Thus it is more supportive to say, 'Just then, it seemed as if you were having difficulty with students who wanted to go their own way in the discussion.' (provisionalism) rather than, 'You can't control discussions!' (certainty).

The way in which evaluation is handled is clearly of great importance if the results are to be accepted and acted on positively. A lot of the threat can be taken out of evaluation if as much initiative and responsibility as possible rests with the person being evaluated as in the approach for a tutor with a group shown in Figure 9.1. This process need not be just for the tutor. It could be used for any student or to the whole group.

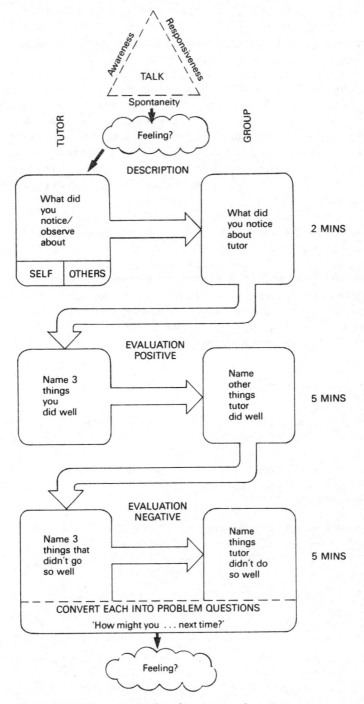

Figure 9.1 *Evaluation procedure for a tutor with a group*

The value of this approach is that, in first requiring a *description* of events, it is less threatening to the person being evaluated and should develop a greater awareness among all concerned of process as it occurs. Then, in commenting *first*, that person can anticipate the potentially hurtful things others might say or might feel inhibited about saying. Last, in having negative points converted into problems, a constructive future-orientated view is encouraged.

The timing of evaluation is important too. We do not like to hear something critical of ourselves, either when we feel vulnerable (eg when something has just gone wrong and there is an audience watching) or when it is too late to do much about it (eg at the end of a course). A 'formative' evaluation – that is, one done in order to achieve useful changes for those involved – is generally less threatening and of greater learning value than a 'summative' one, completed at the very end of a course.

Who initiates the evaluation? Who conducts it? Who processes the results and how? Where is it done? Who else is doing it in parallel? All these questions may also be of consequence in determining how efficiently an evaluation is carried out and, more importantly, how conscientiously its results are implemented. More significantly where evaluation is seen as more of a regular process in which all group members view themselves as contributors and take responsibility for outcomes, there is more chance of change through co-operation. Five minutes set aside at the end of each meeting to review how things went, are therefore likely to be of greater benefit to all concerned than any formal, externally applied, procedure.

EVALUATION AS LEARNING

It will be apparent to anyone using evaluation techniques that they are not merely a way of evaluating group work but also give individuals the chance to reflect on their own behaviour in groups. In this sense they comprise a creative source of learning, one that informs both individuals and the group as a whole about their part in its work and suggests ways of improving the group performance. As Cox writes in UTMU (1978):

> Significant developments in the evaluation of teaching will not come from staff thinking about their own courses, or from students as consumers expressing their judgements about the courses which are provided for them, but by an integration of evaluation into the learning process so that an important part of the students' learning is in fact coming to understand their own strengths, weaknesses, inhibitions, and styles of thinking and working in relation to the varieties of constraints and opportunities presented by the course.

Evaluation, whether it be of individual students, the group, the tutor or all of these, is likely to improve the prospects of training and improvement:

- if it enhances the experience of teaching by creating a climate of openness and honesty where there might otherwise be a sense of secretiveness and mistrust;

- if it is organized as a co-operative act in which both teacher and students articulate their experience and learn from it;
- when there is no question of its being used for promotion or other public purposes, except where this has been clearly opted for;
- where it is organized at stages in the life of a group rather than at its conclusion, and all concerned can have the opportunity to develop and change for mutual benefit.

As Miles (1981) comments, group members feel better about evaluation when they see the specific methods as clear and sensible, and that it is an integral part of a training programme and feeds directly into improvements.

SOME EVALUATION METHODS FOR SMALL GROUP TEACHING

The method or technique that one chooses to evaluate group work must, of course, be established and agreed within the context of the group and the overall climate of the learning situation. The consequences of unacceptable evaluation can be disastrous. Before evaluating, questions like 'Who is it for?' 'How is it to be used?' and 'How honest can we be?' have to be faced and answered.

Observation

Though the observations of an evaluator external to the group may to a certain extent be invalid and superficial, a collection of such views, provided they are to do with the group as a whole and do not refer to the behaviour of individuals, can form a useful basis for appraisal of the groups' success. The fishbowl technique can therefore be a useful device. In this, one group arranges itself concentrically round the other and the outer group acts as observer, and evaluates. This relationship is reversed to allow the second group to be observed.

Diaries

Whenever the life of a group extends over a period of time, members can derive great benefit from keeping diaries in which they can record:

- what ideas, concepts, principles and information they learned;
- what they learned about their own ability to discuss, agree and express ideas, as well as their own contribution to the group process;
- how they saw the group as a whole.

Rainer (1980) offers a host of ideas on diary writing. If these diary comments can be shared in the group even on a selective basis, many helpful insights can be gained by students and tutors alike.

Reporting back

At the beginning of each group meeting, five to 10 minutes may be allocated to one or two members who report back on what happened in, and what they gained from, the previous meeting. For this to work the reporters for the following week must be selected at the beginning of each session so that they are alerted to the task in good time. As with most forms of open evaluation there is an incidental spin-off: a sense of continuity between one meeting and the next.

Checklists

Any group is, of course, free to determine its own criteria and marking system for evaluation of its performance. On pages 177–81 are five schedules for use in study groups and workshops. They are valuable as triggers for discussion as much as for a thorough evaluation. They may be used by the group itself or by another group in a 'fish-bowl' arrangement (see above).

'Do-it-yourself' checklist

Using the 'snowball' technique (see pages 85 and 86), individuals are asked to write down a maximum of three statements worth making about the group/class/ course, and these are successively pooled and refined in sharing them with a progressively larger number of colleagues. Finally the whole group is asked to draw up a list of statements (which must be shorter than the aggregate number produced if any real discussion is to occur). These are written on a board or newsprint on public view. Each statement is then given a three-or five-point scale from 'strongly agree' to 'strongly disagree' and everyone marks their rating for each statement with a blob to make the weighting or preferences more visually apparent (see Figure 9.2).

The great virtue of this technique is that everyone contributes and the results are immediately visible. The group can thus quickly discuss some of the salient features of the ratings, particularly those where close agreement is apparent and those where there appears to be a fairly equal balance between opposing views.

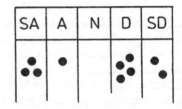

Eg: I think this group has wasted all but the last half hour.

SA	A	N	D	SD

Figure 9.2 *Statement ratings for group evaluation*

Interviews

While one-to-one interviews for all students are hard to justify in terms of time and energy spent they can be of unpredictable benefit, both in what they can reveal of the less-than-conscious experience of students and tutors, and in the way they help students to integrate their learning; interviews require participants to reflect intensively and comprehensively. One-to-two interviews are more economical but not so confidential, while one-to-group interactions can reveal to the interviewer a lot about how effectively the group operates. Who conducts the interviews is of course a problem; given an open and trusting relationship between tutors, however, there is no reason why one should not interview members of another's group. It is not our purpose here to learn interview techniques but it might be helpful to indicate to budding interviewers some of the sorts of questions which might stimulate revealing answers (though they may not all be suitable for every situation):

- How did the group go for you?
- What did you like best about it?
- What did you like least about it?
- What sort of things, apart from content, do you believe you learned from it?
- How would you describe the climate of the group?
- How would you describe this group, as distinct from any other you've experienced?
- Any suggestions on how the tutor might improve the handling/the work of the group next time round?
- Anything you would like to have said to the tutor at the time but preferred not to?
- What else stood out for you?

Questions of this kind are usually sufficient to provoke a wealth of comment on group experience. With the additional use of 'eliciting' questions, (see pages 133–5) there should be little problem in getting a comprehensive picture of what went on.

Pass-round questionnaire

Each student is asked to divide a sheet of paper into three areas to cover:

- 'Things you found most valuable, and why';
- 'Things you found least valuable, and why';
- 'Ideas for improvements';

and to write responses to each. Once completed, each sheet is passed round the group and read quietly in succession by the other students. When the sheets have circulated to the last person before returning to their author, students are invited to read out or recall any comments they agreed or disagreed with or which stood out in any other respect. Finally, the authors receive their sheets back and add any further comments to their sheet before it is collected for processing.

Self-made evaluation

More sophisticated groups may be asked to split into two or more sub-groups, each of which has to devise a technique of evaluation which it will use on the other sub-group(s), and then to administer it. It could choose from one of the above techniques or create an original one. Whether the self-made evaluation is set up as a regular monitoring task throughout the life of the group or is organized only at the end is a matter of choice, but it does have the enormous virtue of being good fun and thus raising spirits at the end of a course when they are typically at a low ebb.

Video playback

Provided the group can be recorded in its natural setting, video recording and play-back can serve to alert everyone in the group to behaviours and events which they may have failed to notice at the time they were recorded. A consultant from outside the group can be brought into start and stop the play-back at the behest of the group and to ask facilitating questions about the interaction:

- 'What was going on there?'
- 'What were you thinking/feeling at the time?'
- 'What effect did that have?'
- 'What did you fear might happen?'
- 'What was your strategy?'
- What do you think he expected of you?'

and so on.

Alternatively, the playback could be sprinkled with questions such as on the checklist on pages 177–8.

MANAGING THE EVALUATION

It is easy for an evaluation of group work to resolve itself into a critique of the tutor rather than of the whole group. Certainly, the tutor will in most cases feel responsible if things go 'wrong' but, recognizing the mutual nature of human interaction for being what it is, we must avoid the temptation of judging the success of a group in terms of the tutor's skills alone. This notion becomes more compelling when we understand the value of the students themselves learning about their own group skills through the process of evaluation.

Evaluation works best if it is seen as a continuous process engaged in by all those who contribute to the setting up and participating in the group. Many of the evaluation methods or instruments included in this chapter can be used equally well for training purposes. The choice of which one to use may depend on the preferences of the group, the style of its operation or the kind of problem that seems to beset it. The group may choose to develop new instruments and methods more responsive to their immediate situation. Whichever approach we use, we must be aware of the sorts of bias to which evaluation may be subjected, particularly the wish to please (or displease). For this to be revealed for what it is, the 'results' of the evaluation must be processed through discussion in an open climate where a balance of support and challenge can create the possibility of change (see Smith, 1980). The way in which results are presented is therefore of the utmost importance; this may be another matter to be determined by consensus in the group.

There follows a series of checklists for use in evaluating groups.

CHECKLISTS

Observation of discussion (from UTMU, 1978)

Objectives
- What was the purpose of the discussion? Was it clear to the participants? Did they accept it?
- Is the teaching method appropriate for these objectives?

Setting
- The room itself – what associations does it have? Does it encourage intimacy and relaxation?
- Seating – are the chairs comfortable? All the same? Draw a plan of their arrangement. Note empty chairs, distances between participants, prominence of any one group member, including the teacher.

Role of the tutor
- What role was dominant – facilitator, chairman, instructor, etc? (see pages 124–5 on the role of the tutor.)
- Was it clear, accepted, appropriate?
- What kind of questions were asked – open, factual, personal reactions, critical, appropriate to the level of the students, loaded. . .?
- What proportion of the time did the teacher talk?
- What techniques were used to involve group members? What use was made of praise and encouragement?
- Were students discouraged from participating? How and why was this done?

Roles of individual students
- What interpretations (if any) can be made about individual students' characteristic behaviour? What observable effects do they have on relations within the group (including the tutor)?
- What role does each student have (eg leader, playboy, passive observer, clarifier, consensus-taker, reconciler, etc)? Are these roles temporary, changing or permanent? Are they sought, accepted or thrust upon them?

Dynamics
- Length and frequency of each member's contributions.

- What status does each group member have? (nb – the teacher is a group member.)
- Is the group harmonious or competitive? How were conflicts dealt with? Denial, avoidance, repression or made explicit and worked through?
- What emotions or motives are aroused? (eg Do questions produce fear, curiosity, laughter. . .?) What are the goals of group members? Do they coincide with the teacher's objectives? How much commitment?
- Did the group stay formally as one or did it split up for different phases? What effects were produced by the changes or lack of change?
- What rules appeared to prevail? What behaviour is appropriate in the group? (eg order of speaking, not disagreeing with tutor, avoiding specifics?)

Teaching small groups – checklist for self-evaluation

Read the following list of statements and tick the box which described your own teaching best. Add four statements of your own.

1.	I find it easy to learn students' names	☐ ☐ ☐ ☐ ☐				I find it hard to learn students' names
2.	My sessions start working slowly	☐ ☐ ☐ ☐ ☐				My sessions start working quickly
3.	It is easy to get students to contribute	☐ ☐ ☐ ☐ ☐				It is hard to get students to contribute
4.	Most students prepare well	☐ ☐ ☐ ☐ ☐				Most students prepare poorly
5.	It is easy to keep discussion to the point	☐ ☐ ☐ ☐ ☐				It is hard to keep discussion to the point
6.	It is easy to keep discussion going	☐ ☐ ☐ ☐ ☐				It is hard to keep discussion going
7.	I speak more than I would like	☐ ☐ ☐ ☐ ☐				I speak less than I would like
8.	I find myself talking to one or two students	☐ ☐ ☐ ☐ ☐				I find myself talking to the whole group
9.	Sessions lack structure	☐ ☐ ☐ ☐ ☐				Sessions are well structured
10.	My students seldom express their own views	☐ ☐ ☐ ☐ ☐				My students freely express their own views

11. ....

12. ....

13. ....

14. ....

Figure 9.2 *Evaluating your own teaching*

Statements for evaluation of group function

Always   Never

	Statement	Always					Never
1.	Members of the group have agreed upon and understand the specific goals for the group						
2.	Members of the group have agreed upon and understand the ground rules for the group activity						
3.	The group has responded to the feelings or moods expressed by its members						
4.	The group has listened to and responded to members' ideas and comments and expressed recognition of contributions						
5.	All members of the group are involved and have participated in the discussion						
6.	The atmosphere of the group has been friendly and open, encouraging members to express criticisms or ask questions which expose themselves						
7.	The group leader encouraged discussion by group members before presenting ideas to the group						
8.	The group leader has synthesized related ideas and summarized concepts that the group has been discussing						
9.	The group leader has determined if all group members have reached agreement about a particular point or are ready to move on to something else						
10.	The group has confronted a member who was hindering the group in achieving its task such as undue arguing, going off topic, etc						
11.	The group has been able to discuss areas of differences between members such that it does not avoid conflict or allow the discussion to become destructive						
12.	The group leader did not dominate nor did the group defer unduly to the leader's recognition of contributions						
13.	The group has evaluated its progress toward its goals during and at the close of the session						
14.	At the end of the session the group has decided on its specific task and work required to be done for the next session						

COMMENTS

Figure 9.3 *Evaluation of the group function*
Source: 'The Small Group Tutorial', McMaster University Educ. Monograph 3, 1972

Analysing group activity

Please rate each aspect in terms of the description at each end of the scale by circling the most appropriate number.

1 *Degree of mutual trust*
High suspicion   3 2 1 0 1 2 3   High trust

2 *Degree of mutual support*
Genuine support for   Everyone for
each other   3 2 1 0 1 2 3   themselves

3 *Communications*
Guarded, cautious   3 2 1 0 1 2 3   Open, authentic

4 *Group objectives*
Not understood by group   3 2 1 0 1 2 3   Clearly understood by
                                               group
Group is committed to   3 2 1 0 1 2 3   Group is negative
objectives   toward objectives
Low attainment of   3 2 1 0 1 2 3   High attainment of
objectives   objectives

5 *Handling conflicts within group*
We deny, avoid or   We bring out conflicts
suppress conflicts   3 2 1 0 1 2 3   and work through them

6 *Utilization of member resources*
My ideas, abilities,   My ideas, abilities,
knowledge and experience   knowledge and experience
were properly drawn out   were *not* properly drawn
and properly used   3 2 1 0 1 2 3   out and *not* properly used

7 *Suitability of group method*
Group method suitable   Group methods
for the objectives   3 2 1 0 1 2 3   unsuitable for the
                                               objectives

GENERAL COMMENT

Figure 9.4 *Rating the group activity*

Group behaviour

Behaviour									
Initiating									
Clarifying									
Seeking information									
Giving information									
Integrating									
Consensus testing									
Encouraging/supporting									
Mediating									
Standard-setting									
Compromising									
Gatekeeping									
Releasing tension									
Expressing group feelings									
Being open									
Dominating									
Manipulating									
Blocking									
Belittling									
Distracting									
Splitting									
Excluding									

Task — Maintenance — Positive

Negative

Figure 9.5 *Group behaviour – observer's sheet*
These terms are explained more fully on page 182.

Group behaviours

Initiating Proposing tasks or goals; defining group problem; suggesting a procedure for solving a problem, suggesting other ideas for consideration.	*Clarifying* Clearing up confusion; indicating alternatives and issues before the group; giving examples.
Seeking information /opinion Requesting facts about a problem; seeking relevant information; asking for clarification, sources of interest etc; asking for suggestions and ideas.	*Giving information/opinion* Offering facts, providing relevant information; stating a belief; giving suggestions or ideas.
Integrating Putting related ideas together; building on others' contributions; summarizing ideas at end of period of discussion.	*Consensus testing* Sending up 'trial' balloons to see if group is nearing a conclusion; checking to see how much agreement has been reached.
Encouraging/Supporting Being friendly, warm and responsive to others; listening attentively; accepting and respecting others and their contributions.	*Mediating* Attempting to reconcile disagreements; getting people to explore their differences.
Standard-setting Expressing standards that will help group achieve worthwhile goals; applying standards in evaluating progress of group.	*Compromising* Offering to compromise own position, ideas, status; admitting error; disciplining self to help maintain group.
Gatekeeping Seeing that others have a chance to speak; bringing in and shutting out; keeping discussion open to whole group.	*Releasing tension* Draining of negative feelings by making a witty intervention; diverting attention from personally embarrassing matters; triggering laughter.
Expressing group feelings Sensing mood of group, relationships within group, feelings of others and expressing them.	*Being open* Revealing feelings/inner thoughts; expressing disquiet, frustration, satisfaction etc.

Figure 9.6 *Delineating group behaviours*

DISCUSSION POINTS

- What are the principal risks in evaluation for (a) the evaluator and (b) the person(s) being evaluated? What happens to the risks when these two are the same?
- Choose one or more of the evaluation measures to review the work of your group(s). What makes the one(s) you choose more useful or valid than any other? How might you administer it? How did it work out?
- In what ways could (or did) evaluation serve to integrate learning in your group?

(The group behaviours opposite explain the terms included in the group behaviour – observer's sheet on page 181. They may also be used as behaviour cards in a group discussion.)

10 Training Methods and Activities

The natural offspring of evaluation is learning and change. Without these consequences the task of evaluation would be sterile. The primary concern of this chapter is to consider ways in which improvement in group behaviour can be effected. There are three possible approaches:

- The *training* group: in which a small number of people (tutors and possibly students) come together to study group process either in a workshop or a regular series of meetings within a risk-free environment whose boundaries are sacrosanct.
- The *teaching* group: seminars, tutorials, etc in which the focus for learning about group process is the tutor/student group itself.
- The *task* group: for example, a staff working party or conference planning team who may, apart from their primary task, wish t · learn how to work more effectively as a team.

Each of these has its own special features. Each could complement the others as part of an integrated programme; and starting with one might well lead to the development of others.

TRAINING GROUPS

Readers of this book will by now be well aware that group processes embody a complex web of attitudes, understandings and behaviours. Some learn to function effectively within this web quite early in life but, for most of us, it appears there is a great deal of *unlearning* to do: shedding some of the expectations and stock responses we have developed over years of parenting and schooling, and acquiring new ways of listening, perceiving and acting in groups. Changes of this kind involve considerable personal adjustment and many might argue that this is too much to expect of adults, especially those in a teaching role. Yet, as Miles (1981) has pointed out, if the group itself is used as the learning medium, more change is possible than many of us are inclined to think. The various exercises included in this chapter are all based on small group activity. They assume that the small cohesive group is the most effective medium for personal understanding and growth in group skills, whether it results from a regular meeting of committed tutors or as one of several sub-groups in a large-scale workshop.

The exercises are based on one further assumption: that participants are committed to improving learning in the groups of which they are part. This does not mean there is no value in one or two antipathetic members taking part. Far from it: one or two cynics may contribute hugely to the creation of a realistic group process and may also cause their colleagues to take less for granted. Yet if, for whatever reason, their purpose is persistently negative, their presence can destroy the fabric of the group and, more importantly, the spontaneity to learn.

Whereas academic discussion in seminars often deals with content divorced in time and space from what is occurring within them, training groups have to focus much more on the 'here and now' experience of their members. Just as there is no way in which one can comprehend group dynamics without seeing it in action, so it is virtually impossible to become aware of one's own effect on a group, or to develop new skills, without participating in the dynamics of a group committed to these tasks. In order to develop more effective group behaviours, the learner must have the chance to learn from doing, exploring, trying out and getting feedback on what he or she does.

For this to happen, the group must operate in a climate where there is a degree of mutual trust and tolerance and where participants feel free to take risks in admitting failings and anxieties and in experimenting with newly learned behaviours. As feelings of safety and trust grow in a training group, it becomes increasingly possible for members to reveal their own observations about themselves and each other. Though this trust may grow quite naturally in a well-run group, there are helpful exercises in developing it, one of the most powerful of which is the Johari window (page 56). Nevertheless, an atmosphere of trust does not develop easily and it is often safer at first to employ *distancing mechanisms* (for instance video tape or role play), in which people can talk about their image or enactment. It is less threatening to learn about one's own group behaviour by watching and identifying with others in an enactment whether those others are:

(a) the group members themselves detached in time through the playback of interaction on video recorded shortly before;

or

(b) involved in a role play in which members may (semi-legitimately) claim they were not being themselves.

Such activities, though always to be valued, become less and less necessary as the degree of trust develops, excepting always that a particular problem may generally or individually pose too great a threat for live confrontation, or that it is the only way of bringing an external scenario like a laboratory within the scope of the training group's immediate experience.

Finally, it is important to stress that the central concern in training groups is to examine social rather than personal behaviour. The interpersonal has precedence over the intrapersonal (though the latter is of definite consequence). The training group is 'usually less concerned with the inner reasons for *why* someone does something and is more concerned with *how* they do it, what the impact is on others and how they can improve what they do to become more skilful' (Miles, 1981). A person may, in the course of such a group, gain vivid insights into some inner problems, especially in the way they may hinder her or his effectiveness in relating to others, but this is incidental to the primary concern of the group.

Planning

Once a training group has been launched – or even before – someone will have the responsibility of preparing and planning, whether that person is a designated or a self-appointed leader. There are various concerns he or she will have to address, each of which may affect the quality of learning in the training group. Among these are:

- assessing own motives;
- making judgements about the institutional context:
  - what attitudes and interests in group learning exist
  - what priority participants are likely to give it;
- deciding:
  - who should plan
  - who should participate
  - timing and physical arrangements
  - roles of leader(s)
  - evaluation strategy;
- organizing the content (a sequence based on psychological rather than logical criteria is usually more effective);
- choosing ways of maintaining continuity between activities or separate meetings.

Above all, the programme for a training group should be amenable to change in response to members' developing needs and interests. Ideally, it should be planned and monitored by them in the way described as a 'peer learning community' (Heron, 1974).

Leading

The role of leader in a training group (if of course it is relevant at all) need not be unlike that of the facilitator described in Chapter 7, but with a ready repertoire of techniques and skills to demonstrate, in response to issues that arise in the group. As leaders we must also be prepared to face considerably more challenge to our position than academic tutors, with their legitimated authority, might expect. We should not be put off our stroke by this, but rather see it as an opportunity for further 'here and now' discussion of the way a tutor might handle critical incidents.

For instance, if an incident arose in a training group the leader might ask 'How would you handle this if you were in my position?'

As training group leaders we may expect to be confronted with the following sorts of problems:

- initial attack or challenge to our authority, or worse still: withdrawal;
- being 'trapped' by anxiously dependent members – 'Tell us what the tricks of the trade are; how would you do it?';
- conflict over expectations and aims, especially where there are involuntary members;
- resistance to change – 'This is irrelevant, it doesn't apply to us', 'What's the theoretical justification of all this?' or long abstract discussions;
- frustration – people feel they are not getting what they want from the group;
- revolt, where a group wants to go its own separate way (fight);
- cosiness – 'Aren't we a lovely group?' – which probably means that the conflict and pain necessary to learning and change are being avoided (flight);
- low points – where spirits are flagging – can occur at any time but almost always at the end when members are likely to be somewhat depressed that the life of the group is at an end.

In tackling these problems the leader will have to draw on a range of skills, techniques and strategies, be *alive* to the need to maintain continuity and momentum, and be flexible in allowing reasonable changes of direction and alternative courses of action. Wyn Bramley's book *Group Tutoring* (1979) is full of practical hints on this sort of problem and merits close reading.

TEACHING GROUPS

The opportunity for risk-free experimentation is of course much less in a normal tutorial or seminar group. It is not easy to stand aside from the tutoring task (though opportunities for role play of a different kind might arise) and we might risk undermining our credibility if we were to expose our failings (and feelings) to general scrutiny. Nevertheless, if evaluation can be viewed as a learning as opposed to a judgemental procedure, then the possibilities are boundless. Any of the evaluation techniques described in the previous chapter could be used, provided always that it is used as a basis for developing more effective behaviours and processes in the group, and that it is conducted as a whole-group task rather than as one polarized between tutor and students.

Whether this work is done on a planned basis, or activated by critical incidents and crises as they arise, will depend on the kind of course being followed and the relationship between the tutor and the students.

TASK GROUPS

Both tutors and students are frequently called upon to work on specific tasks with a view to developing some kind of end-product. Staff working parties and student project groups are examples of these and there are close parallels between them. Yet rarely do either tutors or students reflect on their teamwork skills in their work together, or seek substantial improvement in their skills as the work progresses. This is understandable when we consider how unusual the demand for co-operative behaviour in a general climate of rivalry and competition must appear to members of a task group.

Increasingly, however, the need for improvements in this basic management skill is being appreciated in negotiating problems in teamwork. Two successful approaches to learning teamwork studies 'in the saddle' are:

- Give team members a short induction in which they practise various training exercises (those on pages 198–205 for instance), in anticipation of problems to come. This could be followed by a shorter session in the middle of the project or task as a checking and topping-up exercise.
- Encourage the group to use simple evaluative measures, checklists, or diaries, and to meet at prescribed times to discuss teamwork problems and make explicit what they are learning from their handling of them.

Student projects comprise another form of task group. In this case assessment has an important place, and there is a danger that the competition for marks will inhibit open discussion of co-operative strategies. It may therefore be a good idea to require in addition to the project report, a commentary on process issues in the project and what students learned from them. This commentary would be a necessary part of the final submission but would not be assessed. The checklist on pages 204–5 is of especial value with small groups of this kind.

But more importantly, the assessment itself could require the interlocking of group and individual marks in the light of criteria focused on contributions to the group. Gibbs, Habeshaw and Habeshaw (1989) describe such a method.

TRAINING ACTIVITIES

The following examples of training activities are not in any sense a cookbook for improving group skills. Leaders or tutors will need to adapt them to meet the immediate requirement in the light of their own abilities and the situation in hand. It would probably not be wise therefore to use the activities without reference to the rest of this book. Readers will no doubt develop their own variations and create new exercises which make more sense in their particular setting.

The activities are designed for work with groups or sub-groups of no more than eight members, possibly in a workshop format. The aggregate number of sub-groups should not exceed four or five.

In selecting any particular activity a tutor or leader might check that:

- it is appropriate to the interests and mood of members at the given time;
- it has relevance to their teaching/task needs;
- learning occurs at different levels;
- learning can readily be transferred or carried beyond the confines of the learning environment;
- the skills required for running them lie within the tutor's competence.

What may be acceptable, relevant and feasible by the end of a series of activities may be less so at the beginning. The beginning in fact requires special attention and it is usually sensible to start with some warm-up or introductory activities. The first two exercises described below are of this kind.

Paired introductions

Commonly in groups, individuals are invited to introduce themselves as a way of getting started. It is hoped thus that everyone will become more open and friendly towards each other and that defences will be somewhat lowered. Yet frequently people are either reluctant to say much about themselves or ramble on at an inconsiderate length about their own background and interests. Interpersonal boundaries often remain untouched. A procedure that appears to be much more successful in breaking the ice socially is as follows:

1. Individuals interview their immediate neighbour in the group for two or three minutes about their background, interests and what they hope to get from the group or workshop, with a view to introducing them in such a way that the rest of the group can get to know them as a person. They are in turn interviewed by the same neighbour.
2. Each person then introduces their partner to the group (in no particular sequence) preferably 'as the spirit takes them'. A time limit of two minutes or so is imposed on each contribution.
3. Any person who feel that something important about them was left out by their partner may repair the omission at the end.
4. Everyone may be asked to reflect on the experience and to consider whether they might use it with their own teaching groups.

This complete procedure should be explained to everyone before they embark on it.

Walking interviews

With a larger group it is often desirable to encourage a level of mixing which seated positions do not allow. Walking interviews encourage people to mill and ask questions of each other that they might not otherwise consider. The procedure is:

1 Members are invited to write down one (or two) questions which they would like to ask every other member of the group.

2   They then mill around, locate a partner to put their question to and themselves answer questions from. (There is an explicit proviso that anyone may refuse to answer any particular question without any consequence.)
3   When a reasonable degree of mixing has been achieved, the group may be reassembled and asked:
    - whether any general patterns of information emerged;
    - what specific items of interest people picked up.

Several other 'ice-breakers' may be found in Pfeiffer & Jones (1973 to 1990), Davison and Gordon (1978), Brandes (1979) and Jones (1991). See also Card Exchange (pages 208–9).

Prepared video

The tape or films of an unfamiliar learning group is ideal for this activity. One such tape is 'Short Extracts', made at the University of East Anglia. This shows edited excerpts of groups in different subject areas at various stages in the development of discussion. One procedure for using this tape is to play it with the leader in control of the stop/start switch but with everyone permitted to signal when they want it stopped. In the ensuing step-by-step discussion (see page 84) the leader asks questions about the group on the screen such as:

- What sort of atmosphere has been created – and how?
- What expectations does the tutor appear to have? What expectations do the students appear to have?
- How would you describe the manner of the tutor? What effect do you think it has?
- Have you any comments on the physical layout, numbers, apparent statuses? How do these affect interaction?
- How would you describe the tutor's relationship with the group?

The most suitable points to ask these questions, and others which will certainly arise, will be evident in the screened action as it evolves. The timing is a matter of judgement, bearing in mind what is to come. The workshop leader must therefore view the tape beforehand.

At certain critical points on the tape, such as when the tutor asks the group a question or a student aims one at the tutor, more specific questions may be asked – 'What do you anticipate to happen?' 'How would you respond if you were the tutor/a student?' – at which point participants could be asked to role play in pairs what they might do. Then, after the tape has been played forward to reveal what eventually did happen:

- What did you think of that?
- What other ways could the tutor have gone about it?
- What would be going on in your mind if *you* were the tutor?
- How do you see the discussion developing now?

And so on.

At other times it may feel right to ask questions which search for the emotional underlay of the discussion: 'How do you think the students/tutor feel?' 'What is going on?' or, for the intellectual life of the group: 'What do you think the students are learning?' And, whatever answers are forthcoming: 'Anything else?' in order to press for less obvious issues.

The University of East Anglia Small Group Teaching Project produced six other videos:

- 'Boxes';
- 'Inorganic Reaction Mechanisms';
- 'The Waste Land';
- 'Why be Moral?';
- 'Kyd's Spanish Tragedy';
- 'Art and Popular Imagery'.

A contract for small group discussion (Rudduck, 1978)

The following document was designed to clarify the relationships and responsibilities in seminar groups in moral philosophy at the University of East Anglia. It may be given as prior reading to the group as a stimulus to general discussion, as a step-by-step or other structured activity, or indeed as a prelude to a discussion on ground rules and contracts with a student group. It is almost guaranteed to unearth all sorts of assumptions and values in small group teaching.

The Evidence

1. A contract designed by a seminar leader to contain the effects of his authority. Moral Philosophy (please read twice and note any obscurities.)

During this term we shall be doing more than Moral Philosophy; we shall be conducting an exploratory in small group learning.

(i) Hypotheses: most small group work, as at present conducted in this school* (perhaps in the university as a whole), obstructs the intellectual independence of students and leads them to depend on the faculty leader. The faculty leader, in turn, finds intellectual and emotional security in using his authority and expertise to dominate the small group situation. Minor frustrations apart, this set-up satisfies both students and faculty; but it may be educationally disastrous.

(ii) Phenomena consistent with this Hypothesis:

1. The Faculty leader introduces, imposes and forces discussion back to his own agenda:

* ie department of the university

191

(a) he takes note and pursues only those student remarks which can be used for or bent towards his ends;

(b) his questions often have, as their only point, the eliciting of an already anticipated answer (for instance, they seldom express genuine puzzlement);

(c) tensions arise when the expressed purpose of the small group (free discussion) clashes with the faculty leader's hidden agenda.

2. In the shadows of the leader's agenda (either explicit or hidden), the students:

(a) spend much energy in trying to guess at the leader's agenda (the guessing game);

(b) try to get the leader to produce his agenda in a series of mini-lectures;

(c) are reticent in producing remarks which cannot clearly be seen to fit the supposed agenda;

(d) direct all or most of their attention to the leader's remarks and little to those of each other (particularly true of the brighter student);

(e) get many of their psychological rewards anticipating or fitting their remarks to what they take to be the leader's goal. Punishments accrue insofar as they fail in this task.

3. Many students do not feel the intellectual or social need to prepare for small group work. They can be assured that the faculty leader will take the burdens of keeping things going:

(a) watch for the use, by students, of the weapon of silence; and for the faculty leader's response;

(b) notice how preparation for small group meetings tails off when students realize that the leader will ensure that the relevant arguments, the important theses, the critical appraisals are covered regardless of volume and relevance of student contributions.

(iii) Towards an Alternative Method: If the hypotheses under (i) are correct, then there should be some arrangements which help small groups to break the stranglehold of the faculty leader and generate some intellectual autonomy amongst students. The following strategies are directed to that end and they constitute the explicit conventions under which we shall work this term.

1. Coverage of material: With the institution of examinations in the background, it is inevitable that students should worry about covering the topic. If this worry is taken into small groups then it is my impression that discussion can suffer; both students and faculty regard the small group as a means of extending coverage, consolidating information, reinforcing lectures. The leader enters the room with an agenda to be forced through, and the students attend with note-pads at the ready. To combat the demon of coverage, we shall test the following moves:

(a) small group discussions will not be geared to the subject matter of preceding lectures;

(b) coverage of material will be achieved by a set of nine or ten lectures (Monday of each week), arranged to deal chronologically with moral philosophy from J S Mill up to the present time;

(c) each student will be required to take one of the following texts and study it in depth – hopefully, in co-operation with one or two other students. An essay will be written on this chosen text or on some aspect of it. [List of several introductory texts.]

2. 'Follow-up' lectures: At the end of each week, the course is timetabled for a second lecture. This is designed to allow me to follow up questions and issues raised by the small

group meetings of the week. If there is nothing worth following up, or if we decide to use the hour differently, then the lecture will not be given. This is the only lecture time explicitly associated with the small group discussion material; the first lecture of each week is not designed to provide grist for the small group meetings.

3.   Agenda for small group meetings: The agenda for each week's seminar meeting will lie in the hands of the students. Each group of 12 will divide in half and each sub-group of six will take it in turn to sort out the week's agenda. Each sub-group will need to meet together (and with me) in the week before their week of respoonsibility to warn others of the reading required for the following week's meetings. I will try to ensure that the necessary directions for the following week are duplicated for all members – and, if possible, the necessary reading. In week two, the other half of Group A will repeat the process, thereby deciding the agenda for week three.

Two things are worth stressing. Firstly, that the sub-groups really are free to choose any topic falling under the head of 'Moral Philosophy'; they may decide to extract themes, arguments and assumptions from the manifesto of the Gay Liberation Front, or they may prefer to chop up an article by A J Ayer. Secondly, by the end of about the fifth week everyone ought to be picking out patterns of, and relationships between, various problems. By that time each group ought to be in a position to string together small group discussions so that their results are cumulative and connected.

4.   Conduct of small group meetings: it would be a mistake to think that small group meetings run on a student agenda are likely to be more informal or more comfortable. It will be an explicit convention that the sub-group in charge of the week's meetings does not present a sub-group lecture to the other members; the object of the exercise is that everyone should be prepared to contribute to the topic in question. The sub-group which has decided the agenda is obviously in a better position to guide and help the discussion, but its members have no more obligation to contribute than anyone else. At all costs we must avoid the phenomenon of a passive audience sitting through a class paper.

5.   Recessive faculty: It should be clear that our small group meetings are explicitly designed for student-control; my own role will be recessive and consultative. As the groups (hopefully) gain internal solidarity it will be easier for me to enter the discussions without fouling up the pattern. Most of my time in seminars will be spent trying to identify the emerging themes and arguments of the discussions so that I can write them up for the second lecture of the week; any questions I ask should be requests for clarification.

6.   Assessment: It is important to make explicit that nothing you do (or fail to do) in the small group meetings will be assessed for grading purposes. Grades for the course will be determined by two essays.

> (a) An essay on some one text, part or aspect of a text, chosen from the list under (1) (c). Due in: Week 6.
> (b) An essay on the title 'Why Should I be Moral?' (Reading list to follow). If you wish to choose some other title then please see me first. Due in: Week 9.

Although grades will be determined by the above essays, no grade will be given unless you keep, week by week, a record of the work done for and in the small group meetings. This record will consist of a loose-leaf folder (35p at the Bookshop) containing:

Accounts of your work in the sub-group;

Accounts of the themes and arguments raised each week in the small group meetings; Three summaries of your own developing views, to be written at the end of Weeks 3, 6 and 9.

These folders must be given in at the end of the course and, in addition, I will try to collect a few each week (from Week 2 onwards) to comment on. (They will, of course, be returned the following term after the final collection).

7.   Evaluation of the course: We shall need to meet periodically to discuss what is going wrong and how we might put it right. I will try to arrange such sessions in Weeks 3, 5 and 7. If any individual student has problems, then I am available at any time to discuss them – timetable permitting.

Consultants and assessors game

A structure which can be adapted to serve many different purposes.

Preamble: The Consultants and Assessors Game provides a framework in which a variety of problems can be examined and solutions proposed. The participants, instead of talking around issues in an open-ended way, have to make proposals to a panel of assessors. The class is split into two or three teams who take the role of consultants or experts with the task of providing a solution to a relevant problem. Their solution or proposal is presented to an assessors' panel which is composed of one or two representatives elected from each group; their job, in addition to making the final adjudication, is to set up criteria for the acceptability of the proposals or solutions. The whole exercise should take between 90 and 150 minutes.

Aims: To experience working as a team on an agreed task within a limited time-span. To produce proposals or solutions on a given problem and to subject them to critical scrutiny. To study some of the interpersonal behaviour and reactions arising from inter-group competition and perceptions.

Number of participants: A minimum of ten and a maximum of 25. All should have a reasonable level of experience in the field covered in the task (see organizer's instructions, paragraphs 2 and 3).

Time required: A minimum of one hour, but preferably two and a half hours. (The smaller the total number of participants, the less is needed.)

Materials: Whatever the teams require for the presentation of their proposals. Newsprint or OHP transparencies with pens will probably suffice.

Physical setting: A room large enough to accommodate the teams and the assessors' panel without undue sound interference; otherwise, separate rooms for each team. Also, a room (may be one of the above) in which the formal presentations of the teams' proposals can be made.

Organizer's instructions

1   Explain the goals of the exercise and describe its structure by using the following diagram.

Assessors' panel

- Formulate criteria
- Supervise presentations
- Make assessment

- Formulate separate proposals
- Make presentations to assessors' panel

Consultants' teams

2   Either announce a preselected problem or task to be worked on by the teams, or invite everyone present to suggest and agree one. The task should be one which the participants are competent to work on and which allows for a variety of solutions (for example, the design of a bridge or a study skills course, the formulation of a new law or a research submission).

3   Agree with participants on sufficient background information to define the context of the problem. It is important to remember here that definition of too much detail is time consuming, can stifle a lot of creative thinking, and can detract from the central task.

For example, if the task is to design a study skills course, the teams will doubtless need to know how many students there are in the institution, what subject areas are studied and possibly how much money the team have got; but other questions such as how long the course should be, how many tutors are available, whether any members of the team are to be tutors, when the course should be held and so on, may be left to the teams to decide within the ambit of their proposals.

4   Having negotiated the task, form two or three teams (not more than eight in each) and set them up in separate working areas.

5   Distribute the consultants' team instruction sheets.

6   After about 20 minutes, remind each team to elect two members who will jointly comprise the assessor's panel. They will not *represent* the views of their original team so much as take them into account in determining criteria.

7   Once the assessors' panel is composed, find them a suitable place to meet. Give them the assessors' panel instruction sheet.

8   At this stage the teams sometimes want a clearer definition of role, eg are they lay pressure groups proposing a new law or are they are they architectural consultants competing for a tender? If it helps to sharpen their focus, this should be encouraged. It may be one team wants to imagine they are students and the other lecturers in proposing a new course. So be it, as long as it neither inhibits the production of imaginative proposals nor undermines the competitive nature of the game. Make sure that all the teams are fully informed of any such decisions.

9   Announce a timetable and make it clear to all that it will be strictly adhered to. The timetable must allow at least 30 minutes total for the presentation and discussion of all the proposals. For example, if the overall length of the session is one and a half hours the following timetable might apply for three teams:

- Introduction and negotiation   10 mins
- Teams work on proposals   45 mins
- Presentation and discussion   35 mins

For certain problems, a longer work time (and hence total time) may be needed if proposals of sufficient quality are to be achieved.

10   Act as referee to ensure that the instructions are clear and being followed. You may need to make interpretations and variations from time to time. These should be within the context of the game and, unless there is good reason for not doing so, should be announced to *all* participants.

11   Should the assessors' panel ask whether they may communicate with the teams or vice versa, advise them to decide that for themselves in the context of the whole exercise, or just ignore the question.

12   You may also act as a neutral resource person in any way appropriate to the content of the exercise.

13   The teams will invariably be oblivious to the passage of time. They will therefore need reminding of approaching deadlines and of any other responsibilities.

14   Keep a check on any other decisions implied in the two instruction sheets.

15   Review (at least 30 mins). There are several ways in which the review session can be conducted. A lot will depend on whether the game was run primarily as an exercise in group and inter-group dynamics or as a way of producing a rich variety of ideas and plans on the problem under consideration; whether the emphasis was on process or product. The main thing is to give some recognition to things that will have gone on both within and between groups and the fact that the experience will have been both an intellectual and emotional one for most participants.

Before embarking on any discussion of process or product you may find there are a few feelings floating around which may need to be defused. You might do well to ask: 'How is everyone feeling – anyone want to get anything out of their system?' or something similar. But then, as soon as the immediate response to the question has taken place, quickly pass on to the *process* discussion.

After this you might adopt the following pattern:

(a) Ask the teams separately to discuss and report back in plenary, questions about:
- leadership and the distribution of tasks;
- how conflicts were resolved and decisions made;
- the effects of time pressure;
- the criteria by which assessors were elected;
- how the assessors felt during the presentation phase;
- how the consultant teams felt about the assessors.

(b) In plenary, draw out the answers to the above questions and try to build up a more generalized picture of the events in the game and the implications with questions about:
- how easy participants would find it to join one of the other teams to implement the winning, or any other proposal and what that implies;
- what parallels there were with 'back home' experiences, structures, relationships;
- how they might use the format of the game in their own work;
- what they learned from the game generally/about themselves;
- what things they might wish to do or change as a result.

(c) Then there are questions about the product:

- what they thought of the quality of the proposals;
- how the proposals compared with equivalent ones 'back home';
- what improvements they could make to the proposals;
- how they might use the ideas in their own work.

Of course the oppoortunity to ask questions at preordained times rarely arises. You will probably have to be fairly selective and pragmatic in the sequence of the above questions.

Instruction sheet I

Consultants' team: Your main task as a team is to prepare a proposal on the agreed topic. After ten minutes you will be asked to choose a member of your team to leave and become part of an assessors' panel. You will then have an agreed period of time in which to formulate your proposal.

You will be expected to present your proposals to the panel at the agreed time. You will have five minutes (ten if time allows – check with tutor) to present your proposals. After your proposals have been heard there will be two and a half (or five) minutes for a question-and-answer session with the assessors' panel which will then evaluate the separate proposals.

The assessors' panel has three tasks:

- To determine criteria for judging the merits of the proposals submitted.
- To take full responsibility for the conduct of the presentation session.
- To make an open adjudication on the various proposals presented to them.

You should also decide how you are going to present your proposal bearing in mind the strict time limit.

Instruction sheet II

Assessors' panel: You are independent assessors and in no way represent the teams from which you were elected.

Your task while the teams are preparing their proposals is to establish criteria for their evaluation. In addition, you should agree a procedure for the adjudication.

Each of the teams will decide for themselves how they are going to present their proposal. They will each give a five-minute presentation followed by five minutes of questions and answers with you (times may be extended by the organizer). All the presentations should be completed before the question-and-answer session starts.

You should set up the room for the presentation roughly in the pattern showed by the organizer at the start, and establish a reasonably formal atmosphere.

Once the presentations and questions are complete you will naturally wish to discuss your impressions and make the necessary decisions. This discussion should last no more than five minutes and be conducted openly so that all the teams can hear.

The adjudication may take two forms. One is to announce one of the teams as the winner. The other is to discuss openly the relative merits of the proposals. In either case you should make public the reasons for your assessment and reveal the process of arriving at it.

You are responsible for the conduct of the presentation session.

Building a team – a simulation exercise

Aims: To encourage students to discover something of the talent, skills and qualities they bring to a team to help them consider their adequacies and deficiencies as a team.

Time required: Thirty minutes to one hour, depending on size of teams.

Numbers: It is better if several teams do the task simultaneously so as to provide a richer variety of understanding about group dynamics.

Procedure:
1   The tutor distributes the task and asks each team to take regard of the time limit.
2   After 20 minutes (the timing is flexible – the main point is to ensure that the teams can reach agreement in the time allowed) invite the teams:
   (a) to explain and justify their choice;
   (b) to describe how they arrived at their choice;
   (c) to talk about what the procedure described in (b) told them about their team and the different people in it;
   (d) to predict how they might best use their collective strengths and weaknesses as a team.

Variations:
1   The details of both the task and the profiles may be changed to suit.
2   Teams can be invited to exchange members to enable each to achieve a better balance.

Task: You are working as a group of final-year students in community studies on an educational project designed to examine the problems of teaching professional courses in the health care field. The project is to be marked as a group task and you will also function as a tutorial group up to and including separate exams, each of which will include a question in interdisciplinary studies.

Your team is short of one member. Various other students are interested in joining you and their profiles are given on the attached sheet. You have 20 minutes to choose by consensus the final member of your team from those described on the profiles. You will then be asked to explain your choice and how you went about making it.

Profiles

Phil: A 'mature' student, has had a lot of experience in industrial management with a special interest in committee work and actually likes writing reports and hopes to become an NHS administrator. Is married with a family of four children. In groups he tends to create a sort of safe and trusting atmosphere.

Yvonne: An attractive personality, Yvonne matches her good looks with a fine sense of humour. She is also very intelligent and full of ideas, but does need a lot of encouragement to succeed. Yvonne tends to invest energy in her work only as long as promising results are just round the corner.

Mary: An interesting woman who cares deeply about others but has an unhappy home life. She seems to cover up for her problems by working hard and success-fully. However, she does return home every weekend, and is then not contactable. She is very critical of the way most systems are managed and her views on health and care tend to be very radical. In groups she has difficulties making her inten-tions understood.

Harry: Is a great raconteur who can make the most pedestrian incident sound fascinating. He writes well too, though his academic standing is low. He has, how-ever, a lot of drive and is usually liked by all who work with him. Groups tend to depend on his presence once he has established himself.

Gill: Is an excellent organizer. She achieves this through a mixture of charm, flir-tation and sheer persistence and she would be the first to admit that she con-sciously manipulates people when it suits her. She is good at directing the attention of the group to its own process and likes to talk openly about personal behaviour.

Geoffrey: Is very conscientious and particularly good at searching out and piec-ing together detailed information. He has a stammer which seems to embarrass him in discussion and he would probably rather work on his own. His work is how-ever always completed with great diligence.

Winnie: A somewhat aloof person, she has a fine critical intellect which frightens many people away. She gathers many admirers but has few if any close friends. She is much respected by the tutors and will probably stay on to do research. She is often valued for the intellectual discipline she exerts on a group.

NASA exercise: seeking consensus

Aims: To compare the process of individual decision-making with group deci-sion-making. To develop an awareness of teamwork skills.

Class size: Any number – several groups may be directed simultaneously.

Time required: Approximately an hour and a half.

Materials: Pencils; individual task and work sheets; group instructions; and answer sheets containing rationale for scoring.

Physical setting: An open room where participants can sit in face-to-face groups, preferably in circles.

Procedure:
1   Give each participant a copy of the task sheet and tell them that they have five minutes to complete step I of the exercise.
2   Give each team a group instruction sheet and tell them:
     (a) individuals are *not* to change any answers on their individual sheets as a result of group discussion;
     (b) the teams will have 30 minutes in which to complete step II on the work sheet.
3   When the teams have completed their rankings, than either hand out or read out the NASA 'answer' sheet. Do not get drawn into arguments about the correctness of the answers. They have been made by a 'NASA expert': you are merely passing them on.
4   Ask them to complete steps IV and V and invite each team to call out
     (a) its group score;
     (b) its average individual score;
     (c) the highest and lowest individual scores in the team.
5   Draw up a chart such as the following (I have added sample numbers to illustrate)

Group	Score Average Individual	Range	Consensus
A	55	27–71	20
B	36	20–53	57
C	41	36–45	40
D	50	30–67	26

and write explanations of the differences, especially Team B: 'What went wrong' and Team C: 'Was there not enough difference of opinion?'
6   Draw comparisons between the NASA ratings (page 203) and those of the participants.

7   Invite open discussion on issues like:
(a) whether teams had any agreed procedures for making decisions and if these worked;
(b) what sort of arguments seemed most convincing;
(c) what leadership roles emerged and what function they served.
8   If time permits, hand out the 'Teamwork' checklist and ask each individual to fill it in separately with their rating of their team. Then ask them to compare ratings and discuss any discrepancies.
9   Finally, invite comments on what everyone has learned about teamwork and what they, personally, might do about it in the future.

Task sheet

Situation: You are a member of a space crew originally scheduled to rendezvous with a mother ship on the lighted surface of the moon. Because of mechanical difficulties, however, your ship was forced to land at a spot some 200 miles from the rendezvous point.

Problem: During landing, much of the equipment aboard was damaged and, since survival depends on reaching the mother ship, the most critical items available must be chosen for the 200-mile trip.

Task: On the task sheet are listed the 15 items left intact and undamaged after landing. Your task is to rank them in terms of their importance for your crew in allowing them to reach the rendezvous point. Place the number 1 by the most important item, and 2 by the second most important, and so on, through to number 15 the least important.

Step I: You have five minutes to complete this ranking exercise by yourself. Please do not confer with anyone while deciding on your rank order.
Step II: Now rank the items as a team. Once discussion begins, do not change your individual ranking. Follow the group instructions on the separate sheet.
Step III: Fill in the expert's ranking.
Step IV: Compute the difference between Step I and Step III (all differences positive).
Step V: Compute the difference between Step II and Step III (all differences positive).

Total the differences in both the above steps. Compute the average, for your team, of the total individual differences in Step IV and compare these with the team total (Step V).

Items	Step I Your individual ranking	Step II The team's ranking	Step III Expert's Ranking	Step IV Difference steps I and III	Step V Difference steps II and III
Box of matches					
Food concentrate					
50 feet of nylon rope					
Parachute silk					
Portable heating unit					
Two .45 calibre pistols					
One case dehydrated milk					
Two 100 lb tanks of oxygen					
Stellar map (of the moon's constellation)					
Life raft					
Magnetic compass					
5 gallons of water					
Signal flares					
First aid kit containing injection needles					
Solar-powered FM receiver–transmitter					
TOTALS					

Figure 10.1 *NASA work sheet*

NASA exercise: group instructions

Instructions: This is an exercise in group decision-making. Your group is to employ the method of *group consensus* in reaching its decision. This means that the prediction for each of the 15 survival items must be agreed upon by each group member before it becomes part of the group decision. Consensus is difficult to reach. Therefore, not every ranking will meet with everyone's approval. Try, as a group, to make each ranking one with which all group members can at least partially agree.

Here are some guides to use in reaching consensus:

- Avoid *arguing* for your own individual judgements. Approach the task on the basis of logic.
- Avoid changing your mind *only* in order reach agreement or to avoid conflict. Support only solutions with which you are able to agree somewhat, at least.
- Avoid 'conflict-reducing' techniques such as majority vote, averaging, or trading, in reaching your decision.
- View differences of opinion as helpful rather than as a hindrance in decision-making.

NASA exercise: NASA's answers to decision task

1 – Two hundred-pound tanks of oxygen. Oxygen was seen as the most pressing need. Because the gravitational pull of the moon is only one-sixth of what it is here on earth, these tanks would weigh only about 30 pounds.

2 – Five gallons of water. You get into 200°F temperatures on the moon's lighted surface. There would be a pressing need for water to replenish fluid loss.

3 – Stellar map. NASA saw this as the most important single means of navigation.

4 – Food concentrate. This would be very nutritious, and food would be one of your concerns.

5 – Solar-powered radio. This could be used as a distress signal transmitter and for possible communication with the mother ship.

6 – Fifty feet of nylon rope. It has a number of uses – tying people together, climbing small mountains, trying all the equipment together and pulling it.

7 – First-aid kit containing pills and injection needles. The pills or injection medicine might be valuable.

8 – Parachute silk. This would be ideal protection from the sun's rays. One thing the task requires you to figure out is that you are on the lighted side of the moon.

9 – Life raft. This has a variety of uses. Inflated it gives protection from the sun, a means of carrying injured or equipment. NASA favoured using CO_2 bottles on the raft for propulsion across chasms, etc.

10 – Signal flares. Possibly useful if you could get close enough to the ship for them to be seen.

11 – Two .45 calibre pistols. NASA says that self-propulsion devices could be made from these.

12 – One case dehydrated milk. This could be useful as food mixed with water for drinking but less so if you already have food concentrate.

13 – Portable heating unit. This would be useful only if you landed on the dark side of the moon.

14 – Magnetic compass. If there is a magnetic field on the moon, it doesn't seem to be polarized. The needle would probably spin and angle and be of little use.

15 – Box of matches. Since there is little atmosphere on the moon, the matches wouldn't burn. So they would have little or no use.

NASA ratings
> 0–20 Excellent
> 20–30 Good
> 30–40 Average
> 40–50 Fair
> Over 50 Poor

Teamwork checklist

The following faults frequently impede the progress of discussion and decision-making.

		A	B
1	Failure to listen to what other members are saying	____	____
2	Constantly reiterating arguments	____	____
3	Constantly interrupting	____	____
4	Trying to put others down	____	____
5	Failure to participate	____	____
6	Silent members not drawn in	____	____
7	Dominant members allowed to dominate	____	____
8	Everyone pushing own views, not clarifying, developing, encouraging	____	____
9	Unwillingness to make accommodations/compromises to others' views or needs	____	____
10	Raising irrelevant or unhelpful points	____	____
11	Not recognizing how members are *feeling* about the discussion	____	____
12	Concentrating on making impressions rather than getting the task completed	____	____
13	Failure to be aware of the effect of one's contributions on other members	____	____
14	Disturbing the overall process with private conversations	____	____
15	Failure to clarify the task or objective	____	____
16	Failure to follow agreed directions and procedures	____	____

17   Not checking on progress   ____ ____
18   Failure to keep an eye on time   ____ ____
19   Not being clear about what has been decided   ____ ____
20   Lack of agreement on *who* is to take action on decisions   ____ ____

Please rate each item 5, 4, 3, 2, 1, or 0 on the following scale:

5 = the error, weakness or failure is evident most of the time;
1 = the error, weakness or failure hardly occurs at all;
0 = the fault is irrelevant in this instance.

In column A give your rating of how typical, in your experience, each particular item is for teams/groups/committees.
In column B give your personal rating according to how you saw the problems in your team/group.

Styles of teaching and learning

Aim: To look at ways in which we approach a simple teaching task and the limits we set ourselves in defining the task.

Materials: Ten index cards per group with one word on each (see below) *or* a set of ten random objects (some unusual). Observer's instructions.

Time required: One and a half hours.

Class size: Any number, divided into sub-groups of six to ten.

Procedure:

1   Invite participants to form groups of six to ten members. Read the above aim and explain that they will shortly be given a teaching task. Invite two people in each group to agree to be teachers; three to six students; the remainder to observe.
     Hand the teachers the cards or objects with the following verbal instruction: 'Your task is to teach these.' Give them cards or objects. 'You have ten minutes to plan your teaching and 20 minutes to do it! The task is clearly stated and *there should be no discussion* on its interpretation.'
     Hand the observers their checklist.
2   While the teachers are planning their teaching, ask the students to consider their thoughts and feelings about their impending class.
3   After 30 minutes precisely has elapsed call a halt to the teaching and ask the observers to use the questions on their checklist as a basis for discussion with the 'teachers' and 'students'. This should take another 20 minutes.

4   At this stage the discussion may be opened across groups in order to share findings. Ten to 20 minutes should suffice.
5   Repeat the task with the roles in each group rotated. The same or different words/objects may be used.

Possible words:
METAL
GROUPS
CRICKET
POETRY
EXPERIMENT
EGREGIOUS
MACHINE
MOLECULE
RELATIONSHIP
CAVITY
One of the best sources of objects is the office stationery cupboard.

Observer's checklist
Ask teachers:
1   What did you think the task was?
2   What teaching strategy did you use?
3   In what way did you involve the students?
4   What was your impression of the students?
5   How did your perception of the task and the students influence your behaviour?
6   What limits to the task did you assume and why?
7   How did you feel about the teaching?
8   How well did you operate as a team?

Ask students:
1   What did you think or talk about in anticipation of the teaching session?
2   How was the learning task presented to you?
3   How did you perceive the task: meaningful, useless, how?
4   What was your impression of the 'teachers'?
5   How did your perception of the 'teacher' and the task influence your behaviour?
6   What limits did you assume in your learning and why?
7   How did you feel as learner?

Peer consulting: a monitoring technique

The value of a close and confidential discussion about personal problems has been well known in the health/care field for many years. Peer consulting is merely an extension of this principle. The structure is simple. Two (or three, but no more) colleagues, preferably from different subject fields agree to meet for a fixed time period, anything from 20 minutes to two hours, on a regular or an ad-hoc basis. Their dialogue is organized according to the following schedule:

1 A describes a plan she has: an idea she wants to develop, a problem interaction or just what she has done since the two last met.
2 B listens attentively and supportively, occasionally asking gently probing questions for clarification or to help A out of a circular or confused pattern of thinking.
3 This procedure lasts half the time (less five minutes) that the pair has allotted for the consulting.
4 At this point A tells B in what ways he was helpful to her in 1 and 2.
5 The above procedure is repeated with A in the listening role.

Planning a course

Below are three cases which represent problems to do with the choice and organization of teaching and learning methods. You are asked in your group to draw on your knowledge of different methods and their particular virtues in proposing a solution to each problem.

Aims: To learn how to apply group techniques and principles in the context of a curriculum and evaluations.

Class size: Any.

Time required: One hour.

Procedure: This activity is best done by dividing the group into three teams, inviting them all to read the three case studies but to focus on solving only one, different for each team. You can then hold an inter-group plenary discussion in which each team presents its solution and the others can make informed observations.

Damned lies

A class of 20 first-year students is studying statistics. There are five other separate subjects to be studied concurrently. In past years the lectures have been poorly attended – only overseas students seemed interested. An essay and a sheet of examples are set, but they are rarely done except by overseas students. Again, in the examination in the subject, most people scrape through, revealing only a bare knowledge of the subject.

You have been asked to take this course for a study entitled 'Statistical Significance and the testing of Hypotheses'. You have a three-week period with six one-hour periods allocated to this topic. What teaching/learning methods might you use and how would you sequence them?

Jumblies

In the second year of the course, the students study six separately organized course units. During the second term they also undertake integrated projects. Partly, the idea is that they should thus become better acquainted with each course unit in order to make a more informed choice of two of them as third-year options, and partly that they should have a chance to integrate their understanding of the separate elements. The theme of the project is to be 'For the Greater Benefit of Mankind'.

In previous years the number of students in the second year never exceeded 30 and projects were pursued individually with regular one-to-one supervision by teaching staff. This year there are 50 students and it is proposed to try out the idea of group projects, dividing the students into ten groups of five, each group undertaking a separate project. There are ten members of teaching staff potentially available and there is a period of three weeks during which the students are freed of all class commitments. This block of free time must occur simultaneously for all the students, but its timing has yet to be fixed.

How would you suggest the learning experiences within the project be organized?

'And what seems to be the problem?'

There are troubles in the first year of clinical training. Among a string of complaints about the style of their education the students have cited the learning of interviewing skills. In the last few years they have been taught how to conduct interviews through three lectures by a research psychologist from the College of General Practitioners and by subsequently sitting in with consultants on diagnostic interviews with real patients. The students feel this procedure is not thorough enough for what they feel will be a pivotal activity in their future profession.

How would you organize the learning activities of the students?

Card exchange: a starting exercise

Aims: To help a large group of students get to know each other; to share values about given issues; to form teams.

Class size: Ten to 40.

Time required: One hour to one and a half hours.

Materials: Five times as many index cards as the number of participants.

Physical setting: An open-plan room.

Procedure:

1   Before the class starts, prepare several index cards by writing on them com-

ments on the subject of the course of the topic under discussion. Make some positive, some negative and some neutral, eg:
- I think . . . is the deadest duck in the academic pond.
- A knowledge of . . . is essential to any well-run organization.

Prepare about twice as many cards as there are students and hold these in reserve.

2 In class, hand out *four* blank cards to each student and ask them to write comments like those above – one on each card. Encourage them to be witty, cynical, encouraging, political, philosophical or whatever. (Allow five minutes.)
3 Collect the cards from the students and shuffle them well with your prepared cards. Then hand back to each student an arbitrary selection of *five* cards. Tell them that they will find they now have cards they would or would not wish to be associated with. Their task is to walk round the room exchanging cards until they have a set they are happy with. It is important to emphasize that exchanges should be done on a one-to-one basis with cards unseen and that the wish to give or receive a card of a type should be justified, eg:
    'I want to swap a card which cocks a snook at . . . because I don't like . . . Have you got anything more positive?'

or vice versa.

Scatter the spare cards on a table with the comment that these may be freely swapped with any cards. (Allow 15 minutes and encourage everyone to circulate).
4 Having checked that everyone is reasonably happy with their hand of cards, ask them to form teams, each of whose task it is to select one of their pooled cards to represent their outlook or to devise a new statement with the same object.

There are two ways these teams may be formed and you as organizer should decide which to choose beforehand:

- Participants freely team up with any number of colleagues according to shared values as represented by the cards.
- They form pre-ordained groups of a fixed size (this is particularly useful when work is to continue in these teams thereafter).

Once they have chosen a *team statement*, ask each team quickly to choose a *name* by which it should be known.

Finally, invite the teams to announce publicly their choice of statement and title with a short justification for each.

This is adapted from 'Game Game' by Thiagarajan (1978).

A variety of group techniques

Please tick each of the group techniques listed below according to how frequently you use them *now* on your teaching scheme.

	Now	*Future*	*Comments*
Teaching methods			
1 Seminar			
2 Case discussion			
3 Group tutorial			
4 Individual tutorials			
5 Peer tutoring			
6 Buzz group			
7 Snowball groups			
8 Crossover groups			
9 Horseshoe groups			
10 Fish bowls			
11 Groups in laboratory classes			
12 Groups in field exercises			
13 Group projects			
14 Role playing			
15 Games and simulations			
16 Video playback of individual or group activity			
17 Syndicates			
18 Brainstorming			
19 Synectics			
20 Associative discussion			

Having read about and/or discussed the various techniques listed above, mark up how often you intend to use them in the future. Explain your choices to a partner and discuss how you propose evaluating them.

LEARNING THROUGH GROUPS

The activities described in this chapter represent but a sample of the many that are available to interested readers. Christopher and Smith (1991), Miles (1981), Napier and Gershenfeld (1985) and Johnson & Johnson (1987) all include further samples of well-tested training activities. Yet whatever games, exercises or methods we may use, there are certain assumptions and principles which perhaps need to be underlined.

1   The accent is on 'whole person' learning: learning that involves both thinking, feeling *and* behaviour.
2   There must be practice of behaviour and skills – practice that is informed by guided experience and constructive feedback (see page 56).
3   There should be a strong focus on the 'here and now'. The 'there and then' is a great use with a video playback (see Kagan, 1982) but while it makes discussion of behaviour safer, it may also make it less immediate. The 'here and now' approach helps in the learning and monitoring of skills.
4   There should be general acceptance that everyone has unique styles of personal behaviour, different needs and their own way of seeing the world.
5   The emphasis should be on the 'social self' rather than on the 'inner world' of participants.
6   Personal change is best achieved where there is a judicious blend of support and challenge (Smith,1981).
7   The primary orientation should be towards the development of skills, but these should be seen within a wider framework of attitudes and values (Miles, 1981).

The whole of this chapter, and indeed the book, is based on the supposition that participants, whether they be college students or practising teachers, are willing not just to learn, but to learn how to learn and to integrate this into their future development. Learning is a cyclical process and includes the taking of risks, willingness to share, acceptance of feelings and the ability to monitor one's own experience and progress.

'Experience' as someone once said, 'is not what happens to you, it's what you do with what happens to you.'

DISCUSSION POINTS

• What principles of learning seem to be incorporated in the various activities included in this chapter? What sequences are evident?
• Draw up a contract for the work of your group.
• You have been asked to design and run a one-day workshop on group teaching. What are you going to include? How will you sequence and thread together all the activities?

Bibliography

Abercrombie, M L J (1969) *The Anatomy of Judgement* Penguin, Harmondsworth.

Abercrombie, M L J (1979) *Aims and Techniques of Group Teaching* (4th edition), Society for Research into Higher Education, Guildford, Surrey.

Abercrombie, M L J and Terry, P (1978) *Talking to Learn*, Society for Research into Higher Education, Guildford, Surrey.

Allen, E A (1965) 'Group Methods of Teaching in Higher Education' *Educational Review* 18, November.

Allport, F H (1924) *Social Psychology*, Houghton Mifflin, Boston, Massachusetts.

Amaria R, Biran, L and Leith, G (1969) 'Individual versus Cooperative Learning 1: Influence of Intelligence and Sex' *Education Research* 11.2.

Argyris, C (1968) 'Some Unintended Consequences of Rigorous Research' *Psychology Bulletin* 70.

ASEE (American Society for Engineering Education) (1976) *Experiential Learning in Engineering Education*, ASEE, Washington.

Baker, F (1974) Personal communication to Abercrombie, M L J (1979).

Bales, R (1970) *Personality and Interpersonal Behaviour* Holt, Rinehart and Winston, New York.

Banet, A G Jnr and Hayden, C (1977) 'A Tavistock Primer' in Pfeiffer, W and Jones, J (Eds) *Annual Handbook for Group Facilitators* University Associates Inc, San Diego.

Barker, R (1968) *'Ecological Psychology: Concepts and Methods of Studying the Environment of Human Behaviour'* Stanford University Press.

Beard, R and Harley, J (1984) *Teaching and Learning in Higher Education* (4th edition), Harper and Row, London.

Beard, R, Bligh, D and Harding, A (1978) *Research into Teaching Methods in Higher Education* (4th Edition) Society for Research into Higher Education, Guildford, Surrey.

Bennis, W, Benne, K and Chin, R (1985) *The Planning of Change* Holt, Rinehart and Winston, New York.

Bennis, W and Shepard, H (1956) 'A Theory of Group Development', *Human Relations* IX.

Berne, E (1968) *Games People Play: The Psychology of Human Relationships* Penguin, Harmondsworth, Middx.

Bignell, V, Peters, C and Pym, C (1977) *Catastrophic Failures* Open University Press.

Bion, W (1961) *Experience in Groups* Tavistock, London.

Bligh, D, Jaques, D and Piper D W (1981) *Seven Decisions when Teaching Students* Exeter University Teaching Services.

Bligh, D, et al (1981) *Teaching Students* Exeter University Teaching Service.

Bligh, D (Ed) (1986) *Teach Thinking by Discussion* Society for Research into Higher Education and NFER Nelson.

Bloom, B S et al (1956) *Taxonomy of Educational Objectives Vol 1* Longman, London.

Bloom, B S et at (1964) *Taxonomy of Educational Objectives Vol 2* Longman, London.

Blunt, M R and Blizzard, P (1973) 'Development and Initial Assessment of a Teaching–Learning Programme in Anatomy' *British Journal of Medical Education* 7.

de Board, R (1978) *The Psychoanalysis of Organisations; a Psychoanalytic Approach to Behaviour in Groups and Organisations* Tavistock, London.

Boud, D (1981) *Developing Student Autonomy in Learning* Kogan Page, London.

Boud, D and Prosser, M (1980) 'Sharing Responsibility: Staff–Student Cooperation in Learning' *British Journal of Educational Technology* 1.11, January.

Boud, D, Keogh, R and Walker, D (1985) *Reflection: Turning Experience into Learning* Kogan Page, London.

Boud, D (ed) (1985) *Problem-Based Learning in Education for the Professions* Higher Education Society for Research and Development of Australasia.

Bradford, L, Gibb, J and Benne, K (1964) *T-Group Theory and Laboratory Method* Wiley, New York.

Bradford, L (1976) *Making Meetings Work* University Associates Inc, Mansfield, UK.

Bramley, W (1979) *Group Tutoring* Kogan Page, London.

Brewer, I (1985) *Learning More and Teaching Less*, SR.

Brown, G and Atkins, M (1988) *Effective Teaching in Higher Education* Methuen.

Burns, T and Stalker, G (1966) *The Management of Innovation* Tavistock, London.

Bronfenbrenner, U (1977) 'Toward an Experimental Ecology of Human Development' *American Psychologist* July.

Carrier, M H (1981) *Take Five* Harrap, London.

Cartwright, D and Zander, A (1968) *Group Dynamics* (third edition), Harper and Row, New York.

Chesler, M and Fox, R (1966) *Role Playing Methods in the Classroom* Science Research Associates Inc, Chicago.

Christopher, L and Smith, L (1991) *Negotiation Training through Gaming* Kogan Page, London.

Collier, K G (1968) *New Dimensions in Higher Education* Longman, London.

Collier, K G (1969) 'Syndicate Methods: Further Evidence and Comment' *Universities Quarterly* 23.4.

Collier, K G (1980) 'Peer Group Learning in Higher Education' *Studies in Higher Education* 5.1.

Collier, K G (1983) *The Management of Peer-Group Learning: Syndicate Methods in Higher Education* Society for Research into Higher Education, Guildford, Surrey.

Cooper, C (Ed) (1976) *Theories of Group Processes* Wiley, London.

Cornwall, M G (1979) *Students as Teachers: Peer Teaching in Higher Education* COWO, University of Amsterdam, Holland.

Cowan, J and Morton, J (1973) 'MOCO – Structural Game for Undergraduates' *Programmed Learning and Educational Technology* 10.4.

Cox, R (Ed) (1975) *Evaluating Teaching in Higher Education* University Teaching Methods Unit,* London.

Cryer, P (Ed) (1982) *Training Activities for Teachers in Higher Education* Society for Research into Higher Education, Guildford, Surrey.

Davey, A G (1969) 'Leadership in Relation to Group Achievement' *Educational Research* 11.3.

Davis, J (1969) *Group Performance* Addison Wesley, Cambridge, Massachusetts.

Davison, A and Gordon, P (1978) *Games and Simulations in Action* Woburn Books, London.

Deutsch, M (1949) 'Experimental Study of Effects of Cooperation and Competition on Group Process' *Human Relations* 2.3 (also in Cartwright and Zander (1968)).

Dewey, J (1916 and 1944) *Democracy and Education* Free Press, New York.

Dunphy, D (1968) 'Phases, Roles and Myths in Self-Analytical Groups' *Journal of Applied Behavioural Science* IV.

Easton, G (1982) *Learning from Case Studies* Prentice Hall, New York.

Edwards, J (1980) 'The Engineering Syndicate Study', *Proceedings of Institution of Electrical Engineers* 8, November.

Entwistle, N (ed) (1976) *Strategies for Research and Development in Higher Education* Swets and Zeitlinger, Amsterdam.

Entwistle, N (1977) 'Strategies of Learning and Studying: Recent Research Findings' *British Journal of Educational Studies* XXV.3, October.

Entwistle, N (1981) *Styles of Teaching and Learning* Wiley, London.

Erikson, E (1971) *Identity: Youth and Crisis* Faber, London.

Festinger, L, Schachter, S and Back, K (1950) *Social Pressures in Informal Groups: a Study of Human Factors in Housing* Harper and Row, New York.

Frazer, M K (1977) *Problem Solving in Chemistry*, Mimeograph, University of East Anglia.

Fransson, A (1976) 'Group Centred Instruction: Intentions and Outcomes' in Entwistle, N (ed) *Strategies for Research and Development in Higher Education* Swets and Zeitlinger, Amsterdam.

Freud, S (1972) *Group Psychology and the Analysis of the Ego* edited and translated by Strachey, J (1975), Norton, New York.

Gaff, J and Wilson, W (1971) 'Faculty Cultures and Interdisciplinary Studies' *Journal of Higher Education* 42.3.

Gibb, J (1961) 'Defensive Communication' *Journal of Communication* 11, September.

Gibbs, G (1984) 'Using Role Play in Interpersonal Skills Training: a Peer Learning Approach' in Jaques D and Tipper E *Learning for the Future* SAGSET, University of Loughborough.

Gibbs, G, Habeshaw, S and Habeshaw, T (198?) *53 Interesting Things to do in your Lectures* TES Publications, 37 Ravenswood Rd, Bristol, UK.

Gibbs, G (1987) *Learning by Doing* FEU/Longman, London.

Gibbs, G, Habeshaw, S and Habeshaw, T (1989) *53 Interesting Things to do in your Seminars and Tutorials* TES Publications, Bristol.

53 Ways to Assess your Students TES Publications, Bristol.

53 Interesting Ways to Appraise your Teaching TES Publications, Bristol.

Gibbs, G (1990) *Improving Student Learning Project – Briefing Paper*, CNAA/Oxford Centre for Staff Development.

Goldschmid, B and Goldschmid, M (1976) 'Peer Teaching in Higher Education – a Review' *Higher Education* 5.

Golembiewski, R (1962) *The Small Group* University of Chicago Press.

Goodlad, S (1978) 'Projects' in UTMU, *Improving Teaching Higher Education* University Teaching Methods Unit,* London.

Goodlad, S and Hirst, B (1989) *Peer Tutoring* Kogan Page, London.

Gordon, W (1961) *Synectics* Harper and Row, London.

Harris, D and Bell, C(1986) *Evaluating and Assessing for Learning* Kogan Page, London.

Harris, T A (1973) *I'm OK – You're OK* Pan Books, London.

Havelock, R G (1977) *The Change Agent's Guide to Innovation in Education* Educational Technology Pubs, Englewood Cliffs, New Jersey.

Hearn, G (1979) 'Small Group Behaviour and Development: a Selective Bibliography' in Pfeiffer, W and Jones, J (Eds) *Annual Handbook for Group Facilitators* University Associates Inc, San Diego.

Hedley, R and Wood, C (1978) *Group Discussion for Seminar Leaders* Mimeograph, Faculty of Education, University of Manitoba.

Heron, J (1989) *The Facilitator's Handbook* Kogan Page.

HMSO (1963) *Committee on Higher Education (Robbins Report)* Her Majesty's Stationery Office, London.

HMSO (1964) *Report of the Committee on University Teaching Methods (Hale Report)* Her Majesty's Stationery Office, London.

Heron, J (1974) *The Concept of a Peer Learning Community* Human Potential Research Project, University of Surrey.

Heron, J (1976) *Six-Category Intervention Analysis* Human Potential Research Project, University of Surrey.

Heron, J (1981) 'Assessment Revisited' in Boud, D (Ed) *Developing Student Autonomy in Learning* Kogan Page, London.

Hill, W F (1977) *Learning Thru Discussion* Sage, London.

Hoyle, E (1972) *The Role of the Teacher* Routledge and Kegan Paul, London.

Huberman, A M (1973) *Understanding Change in Education* UNESCO.

Hudson, L (1966) *Contrary Imaginations* Penguin, Harmondsworth.

Jaques, D (1980) 'Students' and Tutors' Experience of Project Work' in Oxtoby, R (Ed) *Higher Education at the Cross-Roads* Society for Research into Higher Education, Guildford, Surrey.

Jaques, D (1981) *Behind the Scenes* Report to the Nuffield Foundation.

Jaques, D (1987) *Supervisory Projects, Educational Methods* Unit, Oxford Polytechnic.

Jaques, D (1989) *Independent Learning and Project Work*, Oxford Centre for Staff Development, Oxford Polytechnic.

Jaques, D (1991) Authority and Dependency in Higher Education, in McDowell L (Ed) *Putting Students First*, SCED Paper

Johnson, D and Johnson, F (1987) *Joining Together: Group Theory and Group Skills* Prentice Hall, New Jersey.

Jones, K (1988) *Interactive Learning* Kogan Page.

Jones, K (1991) *Icebreakers* Kogan Page, London.

Jones, R M (1972) *Fantasy and Feeling in Education* Penguin, Harmondsworth.

Jordan, W J (1961) *Synectics* Harper and Row, London

Kagan, N (1982) *Interpersonal Process Recall: Basic Methods and Recent Research* Mimeograph, Department of Counselling Psychology, University of Michigan, E Lansing.

Klein, J (1965) *Working with Groups* Hutchinson, London.

Knowles, H C, Knowles, M (1972) *An Introduction to Group Dynamics* Association Press, Folletts, Chicago.

Knowles, M (1975) *Self-Directed Learning: a Guide for Learners and Teachers* Association Press, Folletts, Chicago.

Knowles, M (1979) *The Adult Learner: a Neglected Species?* Gulf, Houston.

Knowles, M (1986) *Using Learning Contracts* Jorsey-Bass

Kolb, D (1984) *Experiential Learning* Prentice Hall.

Kolb, D, Rubin, I, and McIntyre, J (1984) *Organizational Psychology: an Experiential Approach*, (4th edition) Prentice Hall, New Jersey.

Krupar, K (1973) *Communication Games* Free Press, New York.

Kuhn, T (1973) *The Structure of Scientific Revolutions* University of Chicago Press, Chicago.

Kuiper, R (1977) 'Group Project Work: A Self-Managed "Learn and Work" Process' in Cornwall, M, Schmithals, F and Jaques, D (Eds) *Project Orientation in Higher Education* Brighton Polytechnic/University Teaching Methods Unit,* London.

Lewin, K (1951) *Field Theory in Social Science* Harper and Row, New York.

Lewis, H (1979) 'The Anatomy of a Small Group' *Studies in Higher Education* 4.2.

Lewis, R and Mee, J (1981) *Using Role Play: an Introductory Guide*, National Extension College, Cambridge.

Lowe, B, Coulthurst, A, Blount, G and Elcock, D (1982) Assessment of group projects, *European Journal of Engineering Education* no. 7.

Luft, J (1970) *Group Processes: an Introduction to Group Dynamics* Mayfield, Pal Alto, California.

McKeachie, W (1969) *Teaching Tips* (6th edition) D. C. Heath and Co, Lexington, Massachusetts.

McLeish, J, Matheson, W and Park, J (1973) *The Psychology of the Learning Group* Hutchinson, London.

Magin, D J (1982) 'Collaborative Peer Learning in the Laboratory' *Studies in Higher Education* 7.2.

Mann, R et al (1967) *Interpersonal Studies and Group Development* Wiley, New York.

Marris, P (1965) *The Experience of Higher Education* Routledge and Kegan Paul, London.

Marton, F, Hounsell, D and Entwistle, N (Eds) (1984) *The Experience of Learning*, Scottish Academic Press, Edinburgh.

Marton, F and Säljö, R (1976) 'On Qualitative Differences in Learning I and II' *British Journal of Educational Psychology* 46, 1 and 2.

van Ments, M (1983) *Effective Use of Role Play* Kogan Page, London.

Miles, M (1955) 'Human Relations Training: How a Group Grows' *Teachers College Record* LV

Miles, M (1981) *Learning to Work in Groups: A Program Guide for Educational Leaders* (2nd edition) Teachers College Press, Columbia, New York.

Miller, C (1975) 'Evaluation of Teaching and the Institutional Context' in Cox, R (Ed), *Evaluating Teaching in Higher Education* University Teaching Methods Unit,* London.

Miller, C and Parlett, M (1974) *Up to the Mark – a Study of the Examination Game* Society for Research into Higher Education, Guildford, Surrey.

Mills, T (1967) *The Sociology of Small Groups* Prentice Hall, New Jersey.

Napier, R W and Gershenfeld, M K (1985) *Groups: Theory and Experience* (2nd edition) Houghton Mifflin, Boston.

Neufeld, V R and Barrows, H S (1974) 'The McMaster Philosophy: an Approach to Medical Education' *Journal of Medical Education* 49.

Newcomb, T M (1967) 'Student Peer Group Influences' in Sanford, N *The American College* Wiley, New York.

Nisbet, S (1966) 'A Method for Advanced Seminars' *Universities Quarterly* 20, summer.

Nuffield Group (for research and innovation in higher education) (1973–76) *Newsletters* 1–7 Nuffield Foundation, London.

Nuffield Group (for research and innovation in higher education) (1977) *The Container Revolution* Nuffield Foundation, London.

NUS (National Union of Students) (1969) *Report of Commission on Teaching in Higher Education* NUS, London.

Nylen, D, Mitchell, R and Stout, A (1967) *Handbook of Staff Developing in Human Relations Training* National Training Laboratories, Arlington, Virginia.

Osborn, A (1963) *Applied Imagination: Principles and Procedures of Creative Problem Solving* Scribners, New York.

OU (Open University) (1975) *PIG – Problem Indentification Game* designed by Jacques, R and Talbot, R for the Man-made Futures Course.

Parker, J C and Rubin, L J (1966) *Process as Content: Curriculum Design and the Application of Knowledge* Rand McNally, Chicago.

Parlett, M (1977) 'The Department as a Learning Milieu' *Studies in Higher Education* 2.2.

Parlett, M and King, R (1971) *Concentrated Study – a Pedagogic Innovation Observed* Society for Research into Higher Education, Guildford, Surrey.

Parlett, M, Simons, H, Simmonds, R and Hewton, E (1988) *Learning from Learners: a Study of the Student's Experience of Academic Life* SCED Publications, Birmingham.

Parlett, M, Simmons, H and Jaspan, A (1976) *Up to Expectation: a Study of the Students' first few weeks of Higher Education*, Nuffield Foundation, London.

Pask, G (1976) 'Styles and Strategies of Learning' *British Journal of Educational Psychology* 46.2.

Perry, W G (1971) *Forms of Intellectual and Ethical Development in the College Years* Holt, Rinehart and Winston, New York.

Pfeiffer, W and Jones, J (1973) *Annual Handbook for Group Facilitators* University Associates Inc, San Diego, and Mansfield UK.

Pfeiffer W and Jones, J (annuall 1973–90) *Structured Experiences in Human Relations Training*, University Associates Inc, San Diego, and Mansfield, UK.

Piper, D W and Glatter, R (1977) *The Changing University* University Teaching Methods Unit,* London.

Pirsig, R M (1974) *Zen and the Art of Motorcycle Maintenance* Corgi Books, London.

Polya, G (1957) *How to Solve it* Doubleday Anchor, New York.

Prince, G M (1970) *The Practice of Creativity* Harper and Row, New York.

Pring, R (1973) 'Objectives and Innovation: the Irrelevance of Theory' *London Educational Review* 3, autumn.

Pring, R (1978) 'Teacher as a Researcher' in Lawton, D (Ed) *Theory and Practice of the Curriculum* Routledge and Kegan Paul, London.

Rainer, T (1980) *The New Diary: How to use a Journal* Angus and Robertson, London.

Ramsden, P and Dodds, A (1988) *Improving Teaching and Courses* Centre for the Study of Higher Education, University of Melbourne.

Reason, P (ed) (1988) *Human Inquiry in Action*, Sage

Redl, F (1942) 'Group Emotion and Leadership' *Psychiatry* 5.

Rice, A K (1971) *Learning for Leadership Interpersonal and Intergroup Relations* Tavistock Publications, London.

Richardson, E (1967) *Group Study for Teachers* Routledge and Kegan Paul, London.

Ross, M and Hendry, C (1957) *New Understandings of Leadership* Association Press/ Follets, Chicago.

Rowan, J (1976) *The Power of the Group* Davis-Poynter, London.

Rowan, J and Reason, P (1981) *Human Inquiry: a Sourcebook of New Paradigm Research* Wiley, London.

Rowntree, D (1978) *Educational Technology in Curriculum Development* Harper and Row, London.

Rubin, L J (E) (1967) *Facts and Feelings in the Classroom* Ward Lock, London.

Rudduck, J (1978) *Learning Through Small Group Discussion* Society for Research into Higher Education, Guildford, Surrey.

Säljö, R (1979) *Learning in the Learners' Perspective* University of Goteborg.

Sandford, N (1967) 'Student Performance in Relation to Educational Objectives' in Sanford, N (Ed) *The American College* Wiley, New York.

Schmuck, R and Schmuck, P (1979) *Group Processes in the Classroom* Wm C Brown, Dubuque, Iowa.

Schutz, W (1958) *FIRO: A Three Dimensional Theory of Interpersonal Behaviour* Holt Rinehart and Winston, New York.

Shaffer, J and Galinsky, M (1974) *Models of Group Therapy and Activity Training* Prentice Hall.

Shaw, M E (1977) *Group Dynamics: The Psychology of Small Group Behaviour* Tata-McGraw-Hill, New Delhi.

Short, A H and Tomlinson, D R (1979) 'The Design of Laboratory Classwork' *Studies in Higher Education* 4.2. October.

Smith, P (1973) *Groups within Organisations* Harper and Row, London.

Smith, P (1980) *Small Groups and Personal Change* Methuen, London.

Snyder, B (1971) *The Hidden Curriculum* MIT Press, Cambridge, Massachusetts.

Sommer, R (1971) *Personal Space: the Behavioural Basis of Design* Prentice Hall, Englewood Cliffs, New Jersey.

SRHE (Society for Research into Higher Education) Working Party on Teaching Methods (1975) *Project Methods in Higher Education* SRHE, Guildford.

Stadsklev, R (1974) *Handbook of Simulation Gaming in Social Education* University of Alabama.

Stanford, G and Roark, A (1974) *Human Interaction in Education* Allyn and Bacon, Boston, Massachusetts.

Startup, R (1977) 'Staff Experience of Lectures and Tutorials' *Studies in Higher Education* 2.2.

Stein, M (1975) *Stimulating Creativity, Vol 2: Group Procedures* Academic Press, New York.

Stenhouse, L (1972) 'Teaching Through Small Group Discussion: Formality, Rules and Authority' *Cambridge Journal of Education* 2.

Stenhouse, L (1975) *Introduction to Curriculum Development* Heinemann, London.

Stern, G (1967) 'Environments of Learning' in Sanford, N (Ed) *The American College* Wiley, New York.

Tara, H (1962) *Curriculum Development: Theory and Practice* Harcourt, Brace and World, New York .

Taylor, W and Walford, R (1972) *Simulation in the Classroom* Penguin Books, Harmondsworth.

Thelen, H and Dickerman, W (1949) 'Stereotypes and the Growth of Groups' *Educatonal Leadership* VI.

Thelen, H (1963) *Dynamics of Groups at Work* University of Chicago Press, Phoenix Books.

Thiagarajan, S (1978) 'Thiagi's Game – Game VI Described as a Fast-Paced Introduction to Gaming' *Simulation/Gaming* May/June.

Treadaway, J (1975) 'Do Seminars Work?' *University of London, Institute of Education Reporter.*

Tuckman, B (1965) 'Developmental Sequence in Small Groups' *Psychological Bulletin* LXIII(6).

Tuckman, B W and Jensen, M A C (1977) 'Stages of Small-Group Development' *Group and Organisational Studies* 2, 4.

Tuckman, J and Lorge, I (1962) 'Individual Ability as a Determinant of Group Superiority' *Human Relations* 15.1.

UTMU (1972) *Varieties of Group Discussion in University Teaching* University Teaching Methods Unit,* London.

UTMU (1978) *Improving Teaching in Higher Education* University Teaching Methods Unit*, London.

Weil, S and McGill, I (1989) *Making Sense of Experiential Learning* Society for Research in Higher Education and OU Press.

Wheeler, D K (1967) *Curriculum Process* Unibooks, London.

Wickelgren, W (1974) *How to Solve Problems* Freeman, San Francisco.

Wilson, A (1980) 'Structuring Seminars: a Technique to allow Students to Participate in the Structuring of Small Group Discussion' *Studies in Higher Education* 5.1, March.

Woods, D R, Crowe, C, Hoffman, T, and Wright J, (1977) 'How can One Teach Problem Solving?' *Ontario Universities Program for Instructional Development Newsletter* 16, May.

Zuber-Skerritt, O (1983) *Video in Higher Education* Kogan Page, London.

* Now 'Centre for Higher Education Studies, 59 Gordon Square, London WC1H 0NU.

Index